Univer

vs.

Disn

THE *unofficial* GUIDE®

TO American Theme Parks' Greatest Rivalry

SAM GENNAWEY

keen
communications

Published by:
Keen Communications, LLC
PO Box 43673
Birmingham, AL 35243

Cover design by Scott McGrew
Text design by Vertigo Design with Annie Long

For information on our other products and services or to obtain technical support, please contact us from within the United States at 888-604-4537 or by fax at 205-326-1012.
Keen Communications, LLC, also publishes its books in a variety of electronic formats. Some content that appears in print may not be available in electronic formats.

ISBN: 978-1-62809-014-7; eISBN: 978-1-62809-015-4

Distributed by Publishers Group West

Manufactured in the United States of America

5 4 3 2 1

CONTENTS

FOREWORD

I GREW UP AMID the theme park worlds of Southern California, which included Knott's Berry Farm, SeaWorld, and, of course, Disneyland, which opened the same year I was born. These places were intoxicating to this nerdy kid, who memorized every detail, dreamed about them in his sleep, and could have quoted the Disneyland guidebook verbatim. At that early stage in my life, I imagined designing magical rides and places, but that seemed like a pipe dream far too grand (and unlikely) to hope for.

I'm not sure how I missed it, but it wasn't until my younger cousin from Chicago came to visit, one summer when I was about 16, that, in search of something to do, we took a trip to the Universal Studios Tour. Here was a very different place from the fantastic parks with which I was familiar. Promising Hollywood glamour and magic, it was at once alluring and gritty, mixing P. T. Barnum–like tourist spectacle with the fantasy of Tinseltown and the "real life" behind the scenes of making movies.

It still surprises me that a decade and a half later, through a series of events, I ended up joining the Universal Planning and Development department, when there were only a handful of us. Together, our small but mighty team dreamed up, designed, and executed new attractions for the original tour, but we also began to create the plans for what would become Universal Studios in Orlando, Florida. It was challenging, exciting, and frustrating, but during my 14-year tenure, I was lucky to be a firsthand witness to (and, I'm proud to say, a participant in) the transformation of the Universal brand from glorified industrial tour—a distant also-ran to the mighty Disney brand—to an internationally recognized portfolio of world-class parks and resorts.

As Universal has matured and grown, it has managed to develop and maintain a unique and differentiated brand character, one that's a bit edgier, always striving to put its guests in the middle of every experience and adventure. The Universal creative team and park management group has expanded exponentially and has now, on multiple occasions, challenged and exceeded Disney in popularity, imagination, and creative and technological prowess of its environments and attractions.

The birth, survival, and eventual metamorphosis of Universal is an amazing story of sheer ambition, audacity, inspiration, innovation, and a mind-boggling combination of advances and reversals, creativity and commercialism, which is full of canny business strategy occasionally leavened with just plain dumb luck, both good and bad. It's a fascinating and complex David and Goliath story, which Sam Gennawey has reconstructed here in astonishing detail. Through exhaustive research and dozens of eyewitness interviews, Sam has synthesized an epic and dramatic tale, making for a spellbinding read.

His accomplishment here is even more remarkable than in his previous book, the excellent *The Disneyland Story*, because there had been so much previously published documentation on Walt Disney and the creation of the original Anaheim park. For this book Sam has reached deep into many archives, libraries, collections, and the personal recollections of the people actually involved to uncover previously unknown facts, dates, and behind-the-scenes anecdotes, many of which have never been fully told in a public forum. If there's a bit of a Rashomon effect to some of the individual recollections presented, that's to be expected.

Sam's book paints a vivid, overarching portrait of Universal's theme parks and resorts, and it's not a stretch to say that there's no one alive today who knows more about the details of the Universal theme park story, from its inception to today, than Sam Gennawey. It's a captivating journey . . . one with new chapters and stories created every day as Universal continues to grow, innovate, and redefine the theme park experience around the world. When it comes time to tell those stories, I hope Sam is around to tell those too.

Phil Hettema has directed the design and production of numerous theme park rides and shows, cultural attractions, and museum exhibits for more than 35 years. For 14 years he served as senior vice president of attraction development for Universal Studios Theme Parks Worldwide, where he was responsible for the creative development of all attraction planning for all five Universal parks.

Led by Hettema's creative vision and extensive experience, The Hettema Group is known for crafting attractions that focus on maximizing the guest experience through innovative storytelling, compelling technology, and a commitment to emotional resonance.

Hettema's credits also include projects for Steven Spielberg, The Walt Disney Company, and DreamWorks Animation. He has been a guest lecturer at California Institute of the Arts, Carnegie Mellon University, United States Institute for Theatre Technology, International Association of Amusement Parks and Attractions, and Kellogg Innovation Network.

Hettema holds four patents for entertainment technology solutions and has been honored with numerous Thea awards from the Themed Entertainment Association.

PREFACE

This time, it's REALLY personal!
—Universal Studios advertisement
Jaws II (1987)

UNIVERSAL STUDIOS DID NOT SET OUT to challenge The Walt Disney Company in the theme park business. The men who ran the Music Corporation of America (MCA) were quite happy with the industrial tour they created in 1964 at Universal City. The Universal Studio Tour took visitors behind the scenes of the largest and busiest back lot in Hollywood to show how motion pictures and television programs were manufactured. People came from around the world with the hope of catching a glimpse of their favorite star. Unlike Disneyland, Walt Disney's fantasy theme park in nearby Anaheim, the Universal Studio Tour provided an authentic experience not found anywhere else. It was something entirely new, entertaining, and very profitable.

In 1979 MCA bought land in Orlando 10 miles north of Walt Disney World and later announced that they were going to build a motion picture and television production studio. The new studio would have also featured a tour just like the one in California. Lew Wasserman, MCA's legendary chief executive, knew better than to compete with Disney and its dominance with fantasy landscapes. He enjoyed the fact that the two Southern California tourist attractions complemented each other, and he was making money with minimal investment.

Everything changed just a few years later. In 1984 Disney hired Michael Eisner as the new chief executive officer and Frank Wells as president. Before Disney, Eisner had been president of Paramount Pictures Corp., and Wells had been a well-respected executive at Warner Bros. Within two weeks of the Disney leadership change, MCA president and Wasserman's protégé, Sidney Sheinberg, sent a letter to his old friends proposing a meeting to discuss ideas that would be in the mutual interest of both companies.

It made sense to turn to Michael Eisner. While he was at Paramount, Sheinberg had shown him MCA's Florida plans with the hopes
of forming a partnership. Eisner liked what he saw. When nothing
came of the talks, Eisner blamed the impasse on powers higher up
the corporate food chain at Paramount's parent company, Gulf and
Western. Now that Eisner was in charge of Disney, Sheinberg thought
Eisner would be excited to become MCA's partner in Florida.

During the call, a confident Sheinberg suggested to Eisner, "Let's
get together on a studio tour in Orlando. We tried with your predeces-
sors, but they were unresponsive. We think we can help you."[1] Much
to the surprise of the MCA executives, Eisner told his old friend,
"We're already working on something of our own."[2]

That was not the reaction Wasserman and Sheinberg was expecting. "Ultimately, we were informed that they might want to do one of
these tours themselves and they did not want to be accused of somehow, whatever the word was, stealing or acting improperly, if we had
a meeting and they later decided to go on their own," Sheinberg later
explained. "That signal really surprised us, to put it mildly. It was our
first indication that they were off on a plan to do this."[3]

Then, on February 7, 1985, Michael Eisner made headlines at his
first meeting with Walt Disney Productions shareholders. Before a
packed house at the Anaheim Convention Center, he announced that
Disney would soon start construction of a third theme park at Walt
Disney World. The heart of Disney's park would be a real working production studio with two sound stages and a working animation studio.
Eisner said this "was a way to make the experience more authentic, but
these decisions would also serve our production needs as they grew."
Regarding the plans, Eisner said they were "the most exciting to come
out of Walt Disney Imagineering (WDI) in a long time." He also told the
gathering, "We're definitely doing it within a year."[4]

The men at MCA were livid. After reviewing Disney's plans, Sidney
Sheinberg claimed that Michael Eisner stole the idea he heard at the
1981 pitch at Paramount. For his part, Eisner claimed the presentation occurred "many, many years" ago and added "when I arrived at
[Disney], the studio tour was already on the drawing boards and had
been for many years."[5] Eisner ordered his team to work fast. For him,
beating Sidney Sheinberg and MCA was critical. "They invaded our
home turf," he told *Business Week*. "We will not be intimidated."[6]

A bitter Sheinberg replied, "You're going to have to work awfully
hard to convince me that [Eisner] didn't know about [MCA's plans].
That's ridiculous. He was a member of the inner circle at Paramount."
He added, "Disney obviously felt they were in trouble and felt they had
to do something about it. Disney announced it would do the theme
park and would have you believe it's been in the works since 1926—if
you believe in mice, you probably believe in the Easter Bunny also."[7]

At MCA, you do not get mad. You get even. This is how the greatest rivalry in the theme park industry began.

1   Ellen Farly, "Behind the MCA-Disney War in Fla.," *The Los Angeles Times,* 23 April 1989.
2   Michael D. Eisner with Tony Schwartz, *Work In Progress: Risking Failure, Surviving Success* (New York: Hyperion, 1998).
3   Farley, "Behind the MCA-Disney War in Fla."
4   Walt Disney Productions (minutes of annual meeting, Anaheim, CA, 6 Feb. 1985), Anaheim History Room, Anaheim Public Library, Anaheim, CA.
5   Kathryn Harris, "Florida Fund may Invest in MCA Park," *The Los Angeles Times,* 20 May 1985.
6   Ron Grover, The *Disney Touch: How a Daring Management Team Revived an Entertainment Empire,* (Homewood, IL: Business One Irwin, 1991).
7   Farley, "Behind the MCA-Disney War in Fla."

ACKNOWLEDGMENTS

I WOULD LIKE TO ACKNOWLEDGE the following people for helping with this project: Peter Alexander, Don Ballard, Adam Berger, Mark Eades, Chad Emerson, Norm Gidney, Gary Goddard, Bob Gurr, Barbara Gurskey, Rebecca Hammond, Phil Hettema, Leo Holzer, Alan Jutzi, Jim Korkis, Jeff Kurtti, Ronnie Kutys, Allison Manzi, Michelle McCarty, Molly Merkle, Laila Miletic-Vejzovic, Diane Disney Miller, Ron Miller, Tom Morris, Jane Newell, Tim O'Brien, Suphi Ogreten, Liliane Opsomer, Todd Peirce, David Price, Todd Regan, Ron Schneider, Bob Sehlinger, Marty Sklar, Len Testa, Barry Upson, Werner Weiss, Terry Winnick, and David Zanolla.

CHAPTER 1

PULLING BACK THE CURTAIN

UNCLE CARL

IT MAY BE HARD TO IMAGINE TODAY, but there was a time when those interested in learning about the process of making motion pictures had few options. This was before Hollywood needed to create behind-the-scenes content for videotapes, DVDs, Blu-Ray, and digital downloads. In those days, the only way to visit a production studio was to be working on the lot, know a VIP, or bring a letter from your hometown movie theater owner.

Not at Universal City. Carl Laemmle opened the Universal Studios gates in 1915 and invited the public to pull back the curtain and witness the creative process. At the time, he was the only studio chieftain who understood that the public was willing to pay for the privilege. If that is what the public wanted, then Laemmle was happy to provide.

Carl Laemmle emigrated from the Bavarian village of Laupheim, Germany, in 1884 and joined his oldest brother, who had been living in the United States since 1872. Laemmle began working as an errand boy in a drugstore and then took on a variety of odd jobs, always making a bit more money than he did at the previous job. He earned his American citizenship in 1889. His first big break came when he moved to Oshkosh, Wisconsin, in 1894 to work for the Continental Clothing store. Based on his strength in marketing and promotions, Laemmle rose to the position of manager in 1898.

By 1905 Laemmle had become financially secure, but he was also restless. He had saved $3,000 with the thought of opening a chain of retail stores. Then he took a trip to Kansas City that year. He visited Electric Park, an amusement park modeled after the 1893 World's Columbian Exposition in Chicago. The park would become one of the early influences on Walt Disney's desire to build a theme park many decades later. It was here that Laemmle experienced motion pictures for the first time. He took a ride on *Hale's Tours and Scenes of the World*.

George C. Hale, a retired fire chief, developed an attraction set in a railway car that seated 72 guests. At one end was a screen, and projected on the screen was a 10-minute film whose point of view was that of a camera mounted on the front of a moving train—also known as a phantom ride. During the show, machines would rock the railcar from side to side, fans would blow, and painted scenery would pass by the windows. A special mechanism mounted on the undercarriage re-created the clacking sound of the tracks. Whistles, bells, and live conductors added to the illusion. The show was very popular; by 1907 more than 500 *Hale's Tours* existed worldwide.

According to historian Graeme Baker of Cineroama, "*Hale's Tours* warmed up the public to moving pictures and demonstrated to venue owners that the market was prepared to bear the cost of higher ticket prices in return for theaters with themed entertainment spaces and quality interior and exterior design."[1] Laemmle was intrigued but decided to continue looking. Good thing. *Hale's Tours* began to rapidly lose favor, and by 1911 the last one shuttered its doors.

While on a trip to Chicago in January 1906, Laemmle was walking along the street when he heard a barker at the corner of State and Polk promoting a new type of entertainment venue called a nickelodeon. The first nickelodeon opened in 1905 in Pittsburgh, Pennsylvania, and it was the first venue specifically designed to exhibit motion pictures. No longer did the movies have to share the stage with vaudeville acts. Nickelodeons were accessible to the masses, and they would go on to change the way people spent their leisure time.

Laemmle paid his admission, entered the storefront theater, and found some 200 people sitting in the dark, watching a 10-minute program of films projected on a sheet. The audience was riveted by the images on the big screen. Laemmle spent the day watching how the audience came to the theater like moths to a flame. More important, once inside Laemmle noticed that, for many, watching movies would become an all-consuming passion that they could never really completely satisfy. It was then that he learned that motion pictures could entertain, inform, and allow people a chance to escape from the day's challenges. The nickelodeon was not a novelty like the *Hale's Tours*. This was a chance for a perceptive businessman to make money, a lot of money. Laemmle was going to be that businessman.

Laemmle opened his first nickelodeon in Chicago in 1906 in a vacant building he found on Milwaukee Avenue. The 190-seat theater was in a predominately Polish neighborhood on the Northwest side and attracted primarily working-class people. To stand out and show that his theater had class, he painted the facade white and called it The White Front Theater.

At the time, there were very few theaters in Chicago, and Laemmle said, "My friends told me that I was crazy, that I would fail, that people would soon be fed up with movies and not want to see them anymore."[2] They were wrong. The demand was so strong that the theater was open 12 hours a day. Laemmle recouped his investment within one month and opened a second theater and a film distribution company almost immediately. By 1909, he was doing business in the Midwest and in Canada and grossing $10,000 a week.

The good times would not last long. Starting in 1909, the New York–based Motion Pictures Patents Company (MPPC) tried to impose a $2 license fee upon independent operators like Laemmle. The MPPC was a trust made up of the major players who held patents on the technology necessary for making and exhibiting motion pictures. The companies included Biograph, Vitagraph, Essanay, American Pathe, Kodak, and others. Inventor Thomas A. Edison was the leader of the MPPC, and he claimed the fee was necessary to protect the patents that he and the others held. By controlling the patents, the MPPC could control the infant industry.

Not one to be pushed around, Laemmle started his own movie company. He named it Independent Moving Pictures (IMP), and as a demonstration of his wry sense of humor and his true feelings about the MPPC, he adopted a playful impish demon as the logo for the studio. Laemmle opened his first movie studio in Fort Lee, New Jersey, and the first release was a one-reel adaptation of Henry Wadsworth Longfellow's *Hiawatha*. Over the next three years, IMP would release more than 250 films.

With the MPPC breathing down his neck, Laemmle decided to follow other early film pioneers, and he moved to Southern California as a way to escape. On May 20, 1912, Laemmle bought the Nestor Company studio at Sunset Boulevard and Gower Street in Los Angeles. A few weeks later, on June 8, he and five other independent producers formed the Universal Film Manufacturing Company. The inspiration for the name came when a Universal Pipe Fittings wagon passed beneath Laemmle's window.

The new Hollywood facility had two stages. The largest was 300 feet long and 70 feet wide. The second was 50 feet long and 100 feet wide.[3] As part of the deal, Laemmle also took control of Providencia Land and Water/Oak Crest Ranch in the San Fernando Valley. When he saw the ranch for the first time, his car got stuck in the mud. It took Jumbo, an elephant that was working on a film at the time, to pull him out.

Always looking for promotional opportunities, on December 3, 1912, Laemmle opened his studio to the public so that they could watch films in production. He was the first movie producer to allow the public to witness the creative process. He changed the name of the Oak Crest Ranch to Universal City on July 10, 1913, and invited 50 Chimallo Indians, along with 100 horses from the Isleta reservation near Albuquerque, New Mexico, to move in permanently that August. Almost immediately, he began to offer bus excursions to the ranch from downtown Los Angeles.

Laemmle was not alone in his fight with the MPPC. The United States Supreme Court ruled against the trust in 1912 and again in 1915. The court stated that the MPPC was in violation of the 1890 Sherman Antitrust Act. Due to this fatal blow, the MPPC would cease to exist by 1917.

It did not matter. By this time it was too late. Although the financial center of the motion picture industry remained on the East Coast, the creative center had moved to Hollywood.

The CHICKEN RANCH

TRYING TO LIVE UP TO SUCH A GRAND NAME as Universal, Carl Laemmle thought big. Instead of a movie studio, Laemmle dreamed of a city dedicated to the art of filmmaking. He wanted to create a city-state that would be superior to the other moviemaking city-state, Thomas Ince's Inceville on the Pacific Palisades.

In March 1914 he bought the 230-acre Taylor Ranch chicken farm in the Lankershim Township for $3,500 down on the purchase price of $165,000.[4] The ranch was located in the San Fernando Valley, 10 miles outside of Los Angeles along the El Camino Real. Across the street was the site of the treaty signing by Mexican General Andrés Pico and Colonel John C. Fremont of the U.S. Army, whereby California was ceded to the United States. The *Ogden* (City) *Standard* said, "[The ranch] occupies a comparatively level plateau, forming the front of a basin something over a mile in diameter, entirely surrounded by mountains. From the center of the city one obtains a view of a greater diversity of scenery than is possible in any other place in America." It was the perfect property for a movie studio because the mountains provided a beautiful backdrop.

Laemmle did not waste time. The formal groundbreaking took place in May 1914, construction began on June 18, and the first film went into production on July 14. By October 14, the studio was ready, and the first of the 500 employees took their places. The first film completed at the new Universal City was *Damon and Pythias*, starring William Worthington and Herbert Rawlinson. The factory was functioning at full speed. More than 250 films were produced at the new Universal City that first year.

Laemmle invested $5 million in building the studio facilities.[5] When the new Universal City opened, there were two outdoor stages with muslin screens strung overhead to diffuse the California sunlight. The largest stage measured 400 feet by 150 feet.[6] In one corner was a revolving stage. In another corner was a rocking stage. The floor of the stage was removable, and underneath was a collection of water tanks that combined to appear as a lake. The second stage was 200 feet wide by 50 feet long.

Nearby was everything necessary to make movies, including 80 dressing rooms, a mill, shops, a forge, greenhouses, company offices with electric lights, and running water. The costumes in the wardrobe were valued at $35,000. There were two restaurants, one capable of serving 600 people and the other capable of serving 400 people. The buildings were designed so that each of the four walls were done in a different style of architecture, allowing them to be redressed quickly to simulate any type of environment a production might require. One day a building may be a Greek temple and the next a Victorian home.[7] Seven artesian wells, a concrete reservoir, and three pumping stations served the studio. More than 6 miles of sewage pipe was installed. Two eucalyptus trees marked the entrance to the studio.

Laemmle had Universal City incorporated under California law. Like other cities, it had its own police department, a fire brigade, library, a school, and a hospital. Unlike many other towns, Universal City was home to one of the world's largest private zoos, filled with 30 lions, 10 leopards, elephants, monkeys, and horses. An omnibus system traveling on macadamized roads connected everything. Universal City also had a specially constructed spur of the Southern Pacific Railroad. The city was also dry, meaning the sale or possession of liquor was prohibited.

Always the showman, Carl Laemmle arranged for a special Santa Fe train filled with "stars and near stars" to travel from Chicago and head toward Universal City, California. The trip began on March 7, 1915, with special guests Buffalo Bill Cody and Madame Ernestine Schumann-Heink. When the train arrived on March 15 at 10 a.m., more than 20,000 people were waiting. They came to see what a studio press release proclaimed as "a whole city where everyone is engaged in the making of motion pictures, a fairyland where the craziest things in the world happen. A place to think about and talk about for the rest of your days!" Visitors would be able to "see how we blow up bridges, burn down houses, wreck automobiles . . . see how buildings have to be erected just for a few scenes of one picture and then have to be torn down to make room for something else."[8]

Laemmle wanted the public to recognize that moviemaking was an art, and a visit to Universal City meant seeing "how we have to use the brains God gave us in every conceivable way to make the people laugh, cry or sit on the edge of their chairs the world over!" He encouraged the public to visit and "to look at it from the inside." During the opening ceremonies, Miss Laura Oakley, chief of the Universal City Police, handed Laemmle a gold key valued at $285. Laemmle joked, "I hope I didn't make a mistake coming out here." Just in case, he kept the chicken ranch open and sold eggs.

Laemmle staged a fake disaster where a dam broke and cowboys and American Indians were washed away in a flood. On the second day of the grand opening ceremonies, aviator Frank Stites's plane hit an air pocket and he plunged to his death in front of a crowd of spectators.[9]

Universal City was such a smashing success that Laemmle's former rival, Thomas A. Edison, visited on October 27, 1915, and left behind a congratulatory plaque.[10] People began to call the studio Chameleon City.

Laemmle kept the Oak Crest Ranch property and renamed it the Universal Ranch. On August 4, 1918, he turned control over to Famous Players-Lasky Corp. Later, it became part of the Forest Lawn Memorial Park—Hollywood.

Just like before, Carl Laemmle encouraged the public to visit the studio. He recognized that the number of people witnessing the film-making process may be very small, but "the few who could take advantage of it acted as an incalculable kind of leaven on the whole." He was counting on visitors to write and talk to others about their experiences and stimulate interest in his films. Laemmle had grand-stands built overlooking the stages and charged visitors 25¢ to watch movies being made. Because the films were silent, the audience was encouraged to cheer and applaud. There was also a 5¢ chicken box lunch available. Average attendance was 500 people a day. The former chicken ranch was so successful that, in 1919, Universal closed its New Jersey facility and dedicated all its resources to California.

Laemmle was an innovator. He has been credited for creating the first movie star, Florence Lawrence, by calling her the "Queen of the Screen" and paying her the astronomical $1,000 a week. *Traffic in Souls* (1913) was the first screen exposé and the first film reviewed by the newspaper drama critics. He was the first movie producer to spend more than $1 million on a film (*Foolish Wives*, 1922). His studio defined the American horror film genre with *The Hunchback of Notre Dame* (1923), *Phantom of the Opera* (1925), *Dracula* (1931), *Frankenstein* (1931), and many more. To film *The Hunchback of Notre Dame*, Laemmle had an entire part of a city re-created on his back lot, the first time this was ever done. Laemmle became "Uncle" Carl to many Universal employees.

Universal City continued to grow to keep pace with the demand and the audience's increasing sophistication. Universal built Stage 28 in 1922, the first soundstage constructed on a structural steel frame-work and set in concrete foundations. In 1925 Carl Laemmle produced *The City of Stars*, a promotional film that featured a reporter touring the facility and watching Universal's biggest stars working on their latest films.

The back lot was busy and the future was looking good. Then came the Warner Bros. film *The Jazz Singer* in October 1927. The box office sensation was part-talkie with synchronized sound, vocal musical numbers, and accompaniment. The film revolutionized the business, and now talkies would become the rage. Studios had to adapt or die, which meant that controlling noise became critical and visitors were no longer welcome on the set. At Universal, the grandstands were removed and the studio painted a sign in 50-foot letters on the soundstages that read, "Universal Pictures—Quiet," to warn away planes.

Laemmle was there at the beginning of the motion picture industry, and now the industry was moving in a new direction. The studio tours ended and the zoo was closed. By 1936 Laemmle was forced out in a stockholder revolt and retired. He died in 1939 at the age of 72.

THERE'S NOTHING *to* SEE

AFTER THE GREAT DEPRESSION and World War II, a growing American middle class was getting restless and looking for things to do. Traveling to far-off exotic places, such as Los Angeles, was high on the list for many. Of course, the natural beauty of the beaches and mountains, as well as the fabulous weather, was the primary draw. Once the tourists arrived, they found attractions such as Knott's Berry Farm, the California Alligator Farm, and Forest Lawn Cemetery to entertain them.

However, surveys showed that one of the things that Southern California tourists really wanted to do was to visit a Hollywood movie studio. They wanted to catch a glimpse of their favorite movie and television stars at work and at play. Just like in the days of Carl Laemmle, many were curious to learn how the magic was created. The surveys also showed that many would pay for the privilege.

There was only one problem. The movie moguls were reluctant to pull back the curtain. Only the well connected could get past the guard gates. The closest that most tourists could get was a visit to the Corriganville Movie Ranch in Simi Valley or Jungleland in Thousand Oaks.

Then came Disneyland in 1955. Walt Disney had been considering a tour of his studio on Hyperion Avenue all the way back to the mid-1930s, but he felt the animation process would be too boring. "You know, it's a shame people come to Hollywood and find there's nothing to see," he said. "Even people who come to the [Disney] Studio. What do they see? A bunch of guys bending over drawings. Wouldn't it be nice if people should come to Hollywood and see something?"[11] He toyed with the idea for years, but nothing came of it.

Instead, Walt Disney decided to do something completely different. In 1955 Disneyland put the visitors onstage in immersive environments based on the popular movies and television genres of the day. He would keep the backstage hidden. Disney's fantasy park opened to the public on July 18, after an unprecedented live television event the day before. The park quickly became a huge hit, with more than 1 million visitors in the first 90 days. Walt Disney invented the theme park industry.

If a tourist was looking for a more authentic Hollywood experience, they really had only one other choice, the Tanner Gray Line Motor Tours Hollywood tour. Starting in 1956, Universal International Pictures allowed the Gray Line tour buses to drive through the back lot. The studio was having a hard time, and the tours brought in a little extra cash. The buses traveled down Colonial Street, Courthouse Square, the Tower of London set, and the Western streets. After visiting Universal International, the buses would continue their tour, passing the homes of movie stars, the Disney studios in nearby Burbank, and other Hollywood landmarks.

The OCTOPUS

TOURISTS WERE NOT THE ONLY ONES interested in Universal International's back lot. Dr. Jules Stein, Lew Wasserman, and Albert Dorskind from the Music Corporation of America (MCA) were also looking at the facility.

Julius Caesar Stein was a promising ophthalmologist who graduated from the University of Chicago before he was 19 and graduated from Rush Medical College a few years later. After a year of practicing at the University of Vienna, he returned to Chicago to become chief resident at Cook County Hospital. While attending medical school, he earned money as a violinist and saxophone player. Dr. Stein was so good at arranging band dates that he decided to switch careers.

He started MCA in 1924 with William R. Goodheart Jr. He named his company the Music Corporation of America because, "RCA [Radio Corporation of America] had started two years before, and I was impressed by the name. So I used MCA."[12] He invested $1,000 and began booking dance bands and singers into speakeasies and nightclubs on Chicago's South Side. The firm grossed more than $30,000 in its first year.

Like Carl Laemmle, Stein was an innovator, and MCA grew rapidly as a result. First, he changed the contractual relationship between the booking agency and the artists. At a time when traveling bands played under the booker's name, Stein allowed the leaders to get billing. In exchange, he received exclusive rights to represent the bands. Many were soon to become stars due to the arrangement. He introduced the one-night stand to the dance band business. Previously, bands settled in to venues for long engagements.

In 1930 Stein convinced Lucky Strike cigarettes to sponsor a nightly radio program featuring MCA artists. Top artists started to flock to his agency. MCA also expanded by acquiring other talent agencies. When that was not successful, they just poached the best artists and bought out their contracts. By the mid-1930s, MCA represented 65% of the major bands in the country.

"You can't run scared and succeed in show business."[13] Dr. Jules Stein lived by this motto and taught his people to follow this and two other sayings: "Watch the pennies, and the dollars will take of themselves," and "when you start a business, do whatever it takes to be second to no one."

To help him grow the company, Dr. Stein hired the brilliant Lew Wasserman in 1936. Wasserman was a 23-year-old Cleveland theater usher and former publicity director for a local nightclub. He began as the national advertising and publicity director, earning $60 a week. Within two years, he was promoted to vice president and became Stein's protégé. Stein would describe Wasserman as "the student who surpassed the teacher."[14] Over the decades, the two would help transform "show business" into the "entertainment industry."

Now that MCA dominated the music market, their next target was Hollywood. Beginning in 1937, Stein and Wasserman were able to sign such luminaries as Henry Fonda, Greta Garbo, Bette Davis, Joan Crawford, Frank Sinatra, and Jack Benny. Like Stein, Wasserman was an innovator. For example, he was the first agent to negotiate a percentage of a movie's earnings rather than a straight salary for screen stars. This contractual arrangement made many actors millionaires. It was said that MCA represented half the movie stars by the mid-1940s.

Dr. Stein and Wasserman also took an early gamble on television. They began producing television shows featuring their stars for the major networks in 1949. By 1952 they were selling reruns to local television stations. They took control of this market with the purchase of television syndicator United Television Programs in 1954.

Dr. Stein built MCA by creating a very distinct corporate culture. He believed that a talent agent was a businessman, not a cigar-chewing promoter. He tended to hire college-educated men who were willing to comply with his dicta and his clothing preferences: conservative dark suits, white shirts, and dark blue or gray ties. No flashy clothes for these agents. He encouraged his staff to maintain an overall cordiality. He would tolerate the occasional spat, feud, or a friendly rivalry; but idiotic college boy competitions or an attempt to undermine others was discouraged. "In a certain way, everyone knew their game, knew their 'place,' and knew that a pie shared is better than a pie thrown," according to entertainment historian Jeff Kurtti.[15] Over time, they evolved from committed employees into the "MCA Mafia," a family.[16]

Working at MCA was no cakewalk. Wasserman was a forbidding figure, cold and austere, and he was famous for outbursts that would "leave a grown man in a $1,500 suit hugging the toilet in fear."[17] However, to those who did their jobs, he was known to become one of the most loyal friends you could have in show business.

One of Wasserman's closest allies was his protégé, Sidney Sheinberg. Sheinberg said, "Mr. Wasserman has an integrity and a sense of responsibility that is unbelievable. This is the core of his strength. Everybody knows that when he speaks, he speaks the truth as he sees it."[18] Reporter Frank Rose said Wasserman "had always combined an aggressive business stance with a hard-nosed, bottom-line approach that ran counter to the jackpot mentality so prevalent in the industry."[19]

Early in the 1930s, Stein and Walt Disney became close friends. Whenever Disney was stuck trying to convince his brother Roy to fund a project, he would often threaten to take it to Dr. Stein and get the project financed.[20] Dr. Stein was one of the earliest investors in Disneyland; when Disney considered developing a city in Florida, he consulted with Stein due to Stein's experience running Universal City.[21] Dr. Stein was frustrated with the responsibilities of a municipality and told Disney so. Disney was so enamored with the entertainment legend that, in 1966, he personally donated the resources to have one of his favorite artists, Mary Blair, create a 220-square-foot fired clay tile mural at the Jules Stein Eye Institute at the UCLA Center for Health Sciences.

Stein's visionary empire presented a study in contrast with Walt Disney's studio. Harrison "Buzz" Price, who was a consultant for Walt and Roy Disney, worked on more than 50 projects for Universal. When asked about the two studios, he said, "[Walt] Disney invented Friday casual and moved it to Monday through Thursday. Only the brass wore ties. For the rest it was open throat, interpreted broadly. MCA by its stark style really invented the appellation 'suits' as a description of industry personnel."[22]

REVUE STUDIOS

AMONG MCA'S MANY HOLDINGS was Revue Studios. A major player in the production of shows for television, Revue produced or coproduced more series than any competitor. At one point, the studio was making money from 45% of all the network evening shows. MCA had become both the largest employer of show-business talent and the largest show-business agent. MCA also acted as the selling agent for a dozen different television shows including *Alfred Hitchcock Presents, Ford Startime,* and *Tales of Wells Fargo.* It did not take long for the television business to become bigger than the talent agency.

By 1957 Revue had outgrown its cramped production facilities in Studio City. It needed studio space. Albert Dorskind, vice president of MCA Development Corporation, was assigned to negotiate a deal to purchase the Universal International Studios lot. "Lew Wasserman was wary of the purchase," Dorskind said. "I remember him saying when I took him around the lot for the first time that real estate in the motion picture business is a liability, too much overhead. But we needed the space."[23]

MCA bought the Universal Studio lot on December 16, 1958, for $11.25 million. The deal closed in February 1959. What MCA got for their money was 420 acres of land, the studio facilities, and one of the largest back lots in Hollywood. In a clever financial arrangement, MCA planned to lease back to Universal the studio facilities for 10 years at a rental of $1 million annually to MCA. Wasserman biographer Connie Bruck said, "Universal was, in effect, paying the cost of being acquired by MCA." Jules Stein declared it was "one of the greatest deals Lew ever conceived and made for MCA."[24]

MCA continued to grow, and in 1958 purchased the television rights to Paramount's pre-1948 library for $10 million. This gave the company more than 750 feature films to sell. The Music Corporation of America went public in 1959 and became MCA Inc. Stein and Wasserman had become the biggest of the Hollywood moguls.

As a display of strength, MCA hired Skidmore, Owings & Merrill, a leading corporate architectural firm, in November 1961. The firm was to design 320,000 square feet of new facilities, including a new commissary building, an administrative tower and bank plaza group, and the Technicolor laboratories. Albert Dorskind called the project "one of the biggest real estate developments in the history of the San Fernando Valley." The 15-story black steel and glass MCA Tower opened in 1964 and become known as the Black Tower or the Monolith.

The next target was Universal Pictures, Inc. Decca Records owned the studio and sold out to MCA in 1962. This consolidation of talent and production worried the Justice Department, and it tried to force MCA to choose whether it wanted to be a film-production concern or a talent agency. To satisfy the Justice Department, MCA decided to divest itself of its talent agency, concentrate on feature-film production under the Universal Pictures name, and branch out into nonentertainment fields to compensate for the loss in agency revenue.

1 Graeme Baker, "Hales Tours and Scenes of the World," *Cineroama,* cineroama.com/2013/05/20/hales-tours-and-scenes-of-the-world (accessed 24 May 2013).

2 *Universal Weekly,* Vol. 23, No. 2, 20 Feb. 1926.

3 Bernard F. Dick, *City of Dreams: The Making and Remaking of Universal Pictures* (Lexington, KY: The University Press of Kentucky, 1997).

4 Ibid.

5 "A City Built as a Background for Pictures," *The Washington Herald,* 23 May 1915.

6 Dick, *City of Dreams.*

7 "City Built as Background."

8 Ibid.

9 Ibid.

10 "Universal Pictures Hits 100 Today," *Deadline,* 30 Apr. 2012, deadline.com/2012/04/universal-pictures-hits-100-today-264347 (accessed 24 May 2013).

11 *The Spirit of Disneyland* (Anaheim, CA: Walt Disney Productions, 1984).

12 Kathryn Harris, "MCA Takes the Cautious Road as Competitors Plunge Ahead," *The Los Angeles Times,* 22 Nov. 1981.

13 Barry Upson, *Universal Studios Tour* training manual (Universal City, CA: Universal Studios, 1965), Box 1, Folder 10, Albert A. Dorskind Papers, Rare Books, Huntington Library, San Marino, CA.

14 Frank Rose, "Twilight of the Last Mogul," *The Los Angeles Times,* 21 May 1995.

15 Jeff Kurtti, note to author, 12 Feb. 2014.

16 Connie Bruck, *When Hollywood Had a King: The Reign of Lew Wasserman, Who Leveraged Talent into Power and Influence* (New York: Random House, 2003).

17 Rose, "Twilight of Last Mogul."

18 Ibid.

19 Ibid.

20 Ron Miller, interview with author, Napa, CA, 9 Mar. 2014.

21 Bruck, *When Hollywood Had a King.*

22 Harrison "Buzz" Price, *Walt's Revolution!: By the Numbers* (Orlando, FL: Ripley's Entertainment, 2004).

23 Sam Kaplan, "MCA Universal City: Life in the moviemaking tower," *The Los Angeles Times,* 15 Apr. 1979.

24 Bruck, *When Hollywood Had a King.*

CHAPTER 2

The INDUSTRIAL TOUR

The REAL TINSEL

WHEN ALBERT DORSKIND SURVEYED the Universal Studios property in late 1958, he concluded it was in pretty rough shape. The lack of reinvestment from the previous owners was obvious. Take the studio commissary, for example. Dorskind noticed it was hemorrhaging $100,000 a year, and to him this was unacceptable.

One Saturday, Dorskind was walking around the farmers' market in Los Angeles's Fairfax area when he noticed a Gray Line tour bus letting visitors off so they could have lunch. He asked himself, why not have the buses drive through the back lot and then drop visitors off at the Universal/Revue studio commissary? He realized that if he raised the price of the food 20% and charged $1 per person for the back lot tour, he could get the commissary out of the red. Visitors could get a taste of the real Hollywood, and MCA/Universal could make a bundle of money selling food in the off-peak hours. Watch the pennies, and the dollars would take care of themselves.

Dorskind contacted Tanner Gray Line and made the deal. Along with the fees for the access and the food and beverage profits, MCA would also make money selling postcards and a Universal International Cafe souvenir menu. In 1959, the tour was named "dine with the stars" and was enhanced with film clips and a makeup show at the end of the tour. Once again, Universal was the only studio with a daily (Monday–Friday) public tour.

The Gray Line tour was a consistent sellout and only hinted at the potential. Then Dorskind became inspired after a visit to Disneyland. He noticed the train that circled the park and began to think about a train that would run through the studio back lot.[1] Dorskind suggested to Lew Wasserman that the studio should terminate Tanner's contract and take over the tour. He wanted more control, which meant using vehicles that could be routed to expose or avoid shooting companies.

The idea excited Wasserman, but Dr. Jules Stein was not enthusiastic. Stein, like others in Hollywood, did not want the general public peeking behind the curtain. He believed that Oscar Levant was right when he said, "Strip away the phony tinsel of Hollywood and you'll find real tinsel." The magic would be gone.

unofficial **TIP**

Harrison "Buzz" Price's first job with MCA was to provide the economic support for an antitrust legal defense. The case alleged that the studios paid artists a smaller percentage of videocassette revenue (a new medium at the time) than was owed. The studios won.

In 1960 Dorskind hired architect William Pereira to draft a master plan for Universal City. Part of that team was Harrison "Buzz" Price. Price was the founder of Economic Research Association (ERA), and it was his job to supply the financial analysis. Over the years, he would go on to conduct more than 50 studies for Universal.

Dorskind brought Price back in 1961 to determine whether MCA should get into the industrial tour business. The report found that tourism was Southern California's third-largest industry. "Southern California residents and tourists have always maintained an interest in visiting the studios in the area without much opportunity to do so because of restrictions and prohibitions on visitor traffic," wrote Price.[2] People were interested in movie and television production, and Universal was in a unique position to appeal to this demand. Price noted that over the years the property had "developed into the most extensive and elaborate set complex in Southern California."[3] He recognized that MCA owned "thematic settings [that] combine to form a fascinating chronology and history of the movie business." Because no other studio was providing a tour, he figured there would be very little competition. ERA was confident that the market was ripe for the type of entertainment Universal could offer.

At the time, the biggest player in the brand-new thematic outdoor show business was Disneyland, which opened in 1955. According to Price, the Anaheim park "revolutionized tourist habits, and established a new approach to showmanship." What Walt Disney and his design team created was "a radical change from the conventional amusement park, fair, tour or fun zone." It was "a living stage for a great variety of entertainment and recreation, some old things dressed up, some fantastic new ideas in recreation but all of them done with great taste and showmanship." Price would know. He was there from the beginning. His firm was responsible for finding the location for Disneyland, Walt Disney World, and more than 150 studies for the Disney brothers.

Knott's Berry Farm in Buena Park was a popular destination. Price said Knott's success was "built on the quality food products and one family's interest in the heritage of California." Located on a magnificent site on the Palos Verde peninsula along the Pacific coast was Marineland. The aquatic park opened in 1954, one year before Disneyland. ERA considered it "basically an aquarium environment but made unique and successful by the high-quality show value of trained mammals performing in a marine theater."

Other popular attractions included Hearst Castle, Griffith Observatory, the San Diego Zoo, SeaWorld, and Los Angeles's farmers' market.

unofficial **TIP**
MCA did express an interest in buying Marineland in 1969.

Price concluded that a successful Hollywood industrial tour would consist of two elements. First, it would offer an exhibition of the vast number and different types of sets used in producing movies and television shows. Second, it would showcase "a visual inspection of the actual techniques used in shooting movies and television scenes."[4] To achieve the second objective, the studio would need to build a special area set aside for tourists and live shows.

Universal City's greatest strength was location. Adjacent to the Cahuenga Pass, the studio had direct access to an extensive and growing network of freeways. The Hollywood and Ventura Freeways provided access to the site, and through connections with the Golden State, San Diego, and other freeways, the studio was reachable by all parts of the Los Angeles metropolitan area. It was within 12 minutes driving time from downtown Los Angeles and the Civic Center, 4 minutes from the Hollywood area, and 15 minutes from Beverly Hills and Wilshire Boulevard areas. More than 100,000 cars a day passed by the studio along the Hollywood Freeway.

The ERA report recommended that visitor parking be located at the corner of Lankershim Boulevard and the Hollywood Freeway. Guests would board the tour vehicles at that location. From there, they would be escorted through the back lot, and at the halfway point arrive at the Visitors Center. The recommended location for the Visitor Center was on the Hope property at the intersection of Barham Boulevard and Forest Lawn Drive. This location would not interfere with production or the local residential areas. Dorskind would disregard this recommendation.

The study looked at a variety of tour vehicles, including conventional buses, a semi-tractor and a bus trailer, and trams. Conventional buses were ruled out because of the obstructed views. A semi-tractor and a bus trailer were also ruled out for the same reason. Trams had unobstructed views, were quieter than buses, had a smaller turning radius, and would be quicker to load and unload. Both diesel and electric trams were considered, but the steep slopes on the property made the electric vehicles impracticable. Therefore, diesel trams won out and would become one of the defining features of the tour.

The report recommended spending up to $1 million for site preparation and another $2 million to build a visitor attraction center. The planning called for only one parking lot to avoid confusion on the guests' behalf. ERA assumed that the tour would start in 1965 and concluded that the demand would be large and growing. In fact, the market potential could be as many as 2.3 million visitors a year, but operational limitations within an active production studio would only allow for a maximum of 1.5 million visitors. The ERA study predicted that the tour could draw 800,000 visitors in its first year and that it would increase to 1 million to 1.2 million during the second and third years of operation, respectively. Looking back, Price said, "Actually, we were a little bullish—the tour hit 428,000 in its first [full] year, 750,000 in its second year, and 880,000 in its third year. It did hit 1.2 million 1968."[5]

To provide the appearance of the best value (and to make more money), it was suggested that a ticket include admission, shows, and parking. Done well, the tour could produce revenues of $2.26 million in the first year. In addition, ERA stated, "The principal indirect economic benefit to MCA from the tour operation consists of public relations and advertising values, which are probably very significant if the tour is well conceived and well executed."[6]

Although it may have seemed obvious that there would be a strong demand for the studio tour, Buzz Price did have some warnings. To achieve the forecasted attendance numbers, the tour needed to be offered year-round and open during weekends and holidays. He noted, "This does not mean that actual shooting of pictures is required during these times -- only that an attraction with the same measure of public interest be provided."[7] He also suggested that the studio tour would not be enough. People would get bored just looking at static sets. The tour needed to be enhanced with live shows that depict some aspect of filmmaking. Reinvesting in the shows to keep them fresh would be critically important. He cautioned the MCA team that Disneyland's attendance growth had slowed in 1958, forcing Disney to reinvest $5 million in capital spending for 1959 to bring it back.

He also warned them about competing directly with Disneyland. One of Disneyland's great strengths was the ability to attract local repeat customers. By 1960, Disneyland's repeat customers were 57% of the total attendance. At Marineland on the nearby Palos Verde peninsula, repeat business represented only 30% of the total gate. The study showed that Universal would be more like Marineland than Disneyland. It was estimated that attendance would be predominantly tourists and their Southern California friends. His advice would come in handy over the years.

Lew Wasserman remembered, "Al Dorskind brought me a photograph—it showed the old Universal commissary, which stood right where this [tower] is." Dorskind told Wasserman, "People paid a quarter, and they walked to the second floor and watched the movies being made—and they were silent! It was taken in 1919." Wasserman asked, "Do you think they would still do it?"[8] Wasserman was about to find out.

A FUNCTIONAL TEST

TO GET STARTED, Dorskind asked for $4 million to design trams and build a food court, parking lots, and restrooms. He assured his bosses that the tour would fit in with the other branches of MCA/Universal and would appeal to a worldwide audience. He suggested that the various technical crafts and studio assets could be mobilized, such as art directors, special effects experts, and the props. The studio already had all the talent they needed on hand to create something memorable.

Lew Wasserman agreed, as long as the tour was based on three basic principles. First, the tour could not interfere with studio production. Second, Wasserman wanted the guests who visited to "leave as our friends, thinking well of us and identifying in a positive manner with our products." Finally, he said, "Although we must charge, it is our policy to give top dollar value in our entertainment."[9] Dorskind got the green light, and preparation for the tour could begin.

Although almost half of Universal City was vacant land, much of that was the hillside that attracted Laemmle to buy the property in the first place. Dorskind needed to find a place to put the tour facilities that did not interfere with production. Back in 1960, he needed to create more room for new production facilities and sold 700,000 cubic yards of hilltop to the State of California at 5¢ a yard. The dirt was used as fill for the Hollywood Freeway. For the Studio Tour he did the same thing. MCA removed 50,000 cubic yards to create a 9-acre parking lot with room enough for 1,000 cars. To make room for the future tour center, an additional 450,000 cubic yards of dirt was removed.

The tour's first general manager was Barry Upson. He said, "My original task was to put [the tour] together physically, staff it, operate it, and oversee it."[10]

Upson had been working on the 1962 Century 21 Exposition in Seattle the previous five years and was looking for his next opportunity. He had met Buzz Price on a couple of occasions at the fair and Price recommended him to Albert Dorskind as the man for the job. Upson said, "Apparently, [Price] decided I was young and cheap and he could recommend me to Dorskind."[11]

Dorskind and Upson began to experiment with a single two-car tram in the spring of 1964. Movie publicist Herb Steinberg drafted the first script, along with help from Upson. Bud Dardene from

Mini-Bus, Inc., built the prototype tram. The tram was equipped with a six-cylinder engine and a manual transmission. The seats faced out toward the side instead of the current configuration of facing forward. If you wanted to see something on the other side of the tram, you would be unable to do so.

The secretaries from the MCA Tower were invited to take the inaugural tour. As the tram left the lower lot and slowly crawled up the steep Firehouse Road toward the construction site for the new tour center, it broke down. The tram could not move forward and it could not back up. As a result, 60 angry secretaries had to walk back to their offices on the front lot. The six-cylinder engines were replaced by a V-8. Further tests proved to be more successful.

On June 17, 1964, the Universal Studios Tour quietly opened to the public, followed by the official grand opening on July 15. Dorskind and Wasserman would not allow any advertising. Barry Upson called the opening in 1964 "a functional test to see whether it was a business or not. Everybody thought it was going to be a good business."[12]

The new commissary building served as the tour center for the first year, while construction for the Studio Entertainment Center took place. Those first guests purchased their tickets at a trailer parked along Lankershim Boulevard. The offices were in a Quonset hut nearby. The opening-day staff consisted of a ticket seller, two guides, two trams, and two tram drivers. Admission cost $3.50 per adult.

GOODWILL *for an* INDUSTRY *that* NEEDS IT

TOURISTS BOARDED A FUTURISTIC-LOOKING, custom-built tram designed by Disney Imagineer Harper Goff. Goff was responsible for much of the design for Main Street USA and Adventureland at Disneyland. He was also the art director for *Willy Wonka and the Chocolate Factory, Captain Blood,* and many other films. The attractive trams were called GlamorTrams and had a distinctive profile that gave the impression that they were leaning forward.

unofficial **TIP**
Universal would go on to buy Mini-Bus and manufacture trams not only for the studio tour but also for other locations, such as Washington, D.C.; New York; Los Angeles; and the Honolulu, Hawaii, airport.

Bud Dardene and Mini-Bus, Inc. built three (three-car) GlamorTrams at a cost of $30,000 each. Each tram was painted orange and white and carried 67 visitors, also known as rubber-neckers. Learning from the past, MCA stocked the trams with a more-robust drivetrain.

Dorskind joked, "The projections were that we'd be lucky to break even. We built our first three passenger trams with engines that could fit into our regular trucks if the idea didn't work."[13] Unknown to many people, MCA was hedging its bets and had feasibility studies under way to determine if Universal City would be the appropriate site for a world's fair in 1968 or 1969.[14]

The first tour guide hired in 1964 was Tommy L. Mack. He would set the standard and was named the tour's personnel director a year later. Mack was also African American. This was at a time when Disneyland restricted African American cast members to backstage or performer roles. Disneyland's policy changed in 1968.

When the tour was over, the trams returned to the commissary. Down in the basement was a makeup show and a costume exhibit. Herb Steinberg suggested the makeup demonstration. Upson hired the legendary Westmore brothers, Bud, Percival, and Wally. Twice daily, one of the brothers—who were known for their trademark white jacket, white pants, and white shoes—would select a lucky person whose name was drawn from a glass bowl to sit in a gold chair with a gold cloth around her neck and be made up as a glamorous star. Nearby was an exhibit of costumes by Academy Award–winning costume designer Edith Head.

According to Bob Rains, a publicist at Universal, on the first day of the tour, Stein told Lew Wasserman that he now believed that the tour would make the company money. "But we do have a serious problem," Stein added. He removed an admission ticket from his pocket and said, "Look at this! Nobody took my ticket after I purchased it." He complained, "If something is not done to correct the situation, people will be giving their tickets to others once they leave the tour grounds. Think of the money we will be losing." Wasserman told Stein he would take care of it right away.

One of the first visitors taking the new tour was the influential syndicated gossip columnist Hedda Hopper. After the tour, she hurried back to her office and wrote, "For years I've been howling for the [Hollywood] studios to do something for millions of tourists who come to our town expecting to see how pictures are made."[15] Their only option was "looking at a bunch of footprints in concrete" and she wondered, "It needn't have taken a great brain to know that giving a movie fan a look inside never-never land could be a money making proposition and also generate good will for an industry that needs it."[16]

Hopper scolded the Hollywood community for sitting "on their minds and hands." The only man she applauded was Walt Disney "who up and built himself a Disneyland that turned out to be one of the greatest tourist attractions in the world. It must have given Jules Stein food for thought."[17] According to Barry Upson, her column is what launched the tour in the public's mind.

Philip Scheuer of *The Los Angeles Times* was also impressed. He said, "It's about time—or, better late than never."[18] On September 28, Universal notified theater owners that they had "been experimenting with an extended tour program at Universal City Studios, designed to give all visitors to Southern California an intimate look into the production and glamour of our industry." They encouraged the exhibitors to visit as their guests and to tell their patrons about the new attraction. Attendance that first year was 39,000 visitors. The tour may have lost money the first year, but that was OK for now.

For Wasserman, the successful launch of the tour meant that the inevitable volatility of moviemaking could be mitigated. Biographer Connie Bruck said Wasserman was "a firm believer in diversification, he had started to follow Disney's amusement park lead, with the Universal City Tour. He was determined to take advantage of the real estate potential of the 420-acre Universal Studios property."[19] Buzz Price agreed, "Universal Studios is the giant that woke up some eight years after Disneyland. It effectively and aggressively leveraged some sleeping assets: a great location, a large interesting site, a great brand name, and a great library of intellectual properties."[20] Bigger things were just around the corner.

WHAT WOULD YOU DO?

WHEN THE STUDIO TOUR FIRST OPENED, the chance of catching a glimpse of a film in production was very real. Along with the various motion pictures under production, MCA was responsible for 16 hours of prime time television programming in 1964 and 1965. It was the busiest back lot in Hollywood.

Terry Winnick was studying architecture at the University of Southern California and wanted to find a part-time job unrelated to the field. He tried to be a page at *The Tonight Show* but ended up as one of the first tour guides at Universal Studios. Some of his coworkers included future super agent Michael Ovitz, future director John Badham, and Bob Finkelstein, who would later run the Sinatra Foundation.

He said the guides approached the tour as if they and the guests had just hopped the fence and had a chance to wander around a movie studio.[21] The tours were meant to last approximately 2 hours but sometimes could go on for much longer. Actor Ron Schneider was another early tour guide and recalled that they were "free to present a tour that reflects their own interests and enthusiasm. And since every location on the back lot has been used for dozens of different productions, you can tailor your spiel to the genre of your choice or the particular point you want to make."[22]

In 1965 the tram-loading area was moved from its temporary quarters on the front lot and up to the hilltop Studio Entertainment Center. After leaving the new tram-loading area, the GlamorTrams would head down Firehouse Hill Road toward the front lot. Lew Wasserman would often sit in his office on the 15th floor of the MCA Tower and count how many people were on the trams heading toward him. If the trams were not full enough, he would call down to see how many drivers and guides were on duty and send some home.[23]

At the bottom of the hill was the front lot. The front lot was home to 32 soundstages, technical and postproduction areas, and offices. To the left of the trams were the brand-new makeup and hairdressing departments. Next door were much older wooden and corrugated metal buildings that housed the wardrobe department. On the right was the fire department. The trams continued in a loop around the front lot, passing by Alfred Hitchcock's production office, the scoring stage, and the studio commissary. Other technical services that got a nod on the tour were the stills department, portrait gallery, special effects department, and the lumberyard.

When the wardrobe department was open, the trams would stop and let visitors off to walk through it. To add a personal touch, the tram drivers stopped by the dressing room of an "actual" Universal movie star, where guests could get off and walk through the room. The gray bungalow was custom-built for the tour. It had a tiny yard and a cluster of trees off to one side. Through the years, tenants included actresses Angie Dickinson, Lana Turner, and Lucille Ball.

From there, the tram drove through two prop warehouses. The huge buildings covered 1.5 acres and held more than 5 million props. Occasionally, the trams would stop for 30 seconds or so to allow the tour guide to tell a story related to the items on display.

The next stop would be one of the soundstages. The guests would once again disembark, and the tour guide would take them on a tour. Every day was different. Guides would not know which soundstage they would be visiting until they showed up that day. Until 1974 every guide got a shooting schedule to help him or her plan out his or her day. In the early days, Stage 23 was the most common.

In later days, Stage 32 would become a regular part of the tour. Inside were six specially designed sets that allowed them to demonstrate movie special effects. The guides described the soundstage as "our biggest actor" because the sets could be changed almost as quickly as an actor changes roles. For example, by flipping switches the tour guide could demonstrate environmental effects, such as changing the lighting from day to night in the living room from *Marcus Welby, M.D.* Another set allowed the guide to make it appear to rain with the use of recirculating fountains. For a short time, visitors could walk through the witch's castle from the film version of *H.R. Pufnstuf.* Another display was a demonstration of rear-screen projection using the PT 73 boat from the opening sequence of *McHale's Navy.* It was up to the guide to bring all of the drama and comedy necessary to entertain the guests.

Once guests were back on board, the trams would drive by Stage 28, which was built in 1922 for the Lon Chaney classic horror movie *Phantom of the Opera* (1925). At the time of its construction, this was the most sophisticated soundstage in the world. In tribute to Universal's founder, Carl Laemmle, the original opera boxes from the film still stand inside.

As the tour continued, the trams slipped away from the front lot and started toward the back lot. Along the way, they passed the underwater tank used to film special effects miniatures, the plaster shop, the electrical shop, a parking lot filled with portable dressing rooms, and the transportation department with famous picture cars.

unofficial **TIP**
The producers of *The Munsters* combined the word *fun* and the word *monster* to come up with the Munsters name.

In the initial studies, Buzz Price suggested that Universal's greatest asset was an intact and busy Hollywood back lot. The back lot was filled with exterior sets that could be redressed to appear as any place a screenwriter could imagine. When the tour began, there were 561 facades. Facades, or false fronts, are common on a movie back lot. Typically, moviemakers only build the part of the structure that can be seen on film.

The first destination on the back lot was Colonial Street. Along the river channel on the northern edge of the property was a typical American street with a wide variety of residential facades. The set was built in 1950. Some of the homes familiar to tourists included *The Munsters, Leave It To Beaver,* and *The House of the Seven Gables.* At the entrance to Colonial Street was the oldest structure on the back lot, the mansion used in *Uncle Tom's Cabin* (1927). Leaving the residential street, the trams passed by the transportation department and the greens department on the way to Prop Plaza.

unofficial **TIP**
In 1981 the facade of the mansion used in *Uncle Tom's Cabin,* along with many other structures, was moved to the new Colonial Street on the hill. It was demolished in 2005 as part of television's *Desperate Housewives* second season expansion.

PROP PLAZA

PROP PLAZA WAS THE HALFWAY POINT of the tour and served as a rest stop. Guests left the tram, enjoyed the services and displays, and then boarded the next available tram when they were ready to resume the tour. The facility was located just above the New York Street set and built on two levels. The lower level was used as a storage space for props used in production, such as antique cars and miniature ships. Guests could wander and peek through the fence.

On the upper level, visitors had panoramic views of the San Fernando Valley and plenty of photo opportunities, including a World War

II fighter jet, a car-size telephone, foam-rubber rocks, and a human-size meat grinder. Early exhibits included an animated stagecoach and Model T car. Guests posed in the bouncing vehicles, while a moving background and wind from fans provided the perfect home movie opportunity. There were also restrooms, film sales, and a snack bar.

For entertainment, visitors could watch a master class in Hollywood stunt work from Jim Roberts and Hank Calia, two veteran Hollywood stuntmen. In front of a facade from the TV show *Laredo,* the two men performed a bullwhip fight, a fistfight, a shoot-out, and a high fall up to 10 times a day.

unofficial **TIP**
During the first year, before the Studio Entertainment Center was completed in 1965, Prop Plaza was known as the Visitor's Village.

After leaving Prop Plaza, the trams entered the impressive New York Street set. Lining the street were the largest facades on the back lot. On one corner was a mock-up of the MCA Tower used to test weather conditions on the building materials. Around the corner was Brownstone Street, a typical residential street in any eastern city in the United States. One block was modeled from a picture taken of East 62nd Street in New York City. Leaving Brownstone Street, the trams passed through Circle Drive and entered Courthouse Square, one of the most versatile and recognized sets on the back lot.

From there was Southern Street, where the residential structures were real buildings that housed the studio's security staff. Next door was the Apartment Complex, the set for an innovative trio of situation comedies under the umbrella title *90 Bristol Court. Karen, Harris Against the World,* and *Tom, Dick, and Mary* ran as a 90-minute block on NBC for only one year, though the Apartment Complex stood until 1981. Just around the corner from the Apartment Complex was Park Jungle. The pond and exotic shoreline were featured in *The Creature from the Black Lagoon* (1954) and the *McHale's Navy* television series.

The European Street sets were placed at the eastern border of the property along the river channel. The winding, narrow streets could be dressed like any European town in any European country. One of the largest structures was the Senate building from *Spartacus* (1960). Within the European Street sets was the Court of Miracles named for *Miracle Man* (1919), starring Lon Chaney. The location would be used over and over in numerous Universal monster movies, such as *The Hunchback of Notre Dame, Phantom of the Opera, Franken-stein,* and *Dracula.*

Continuing through the back lot, the trams drove through Denver Street, a Western set with a train depot, and past a fortress built for the *Tower of London* (1936). Westerns were a very popular television and film genre at the time; as a result, the Six Points, Texas, sets were some of the most utilized on the back lot. The area was so named because six streets radiate out from a central point. The layout allowed for a film crew to shoot more than one Western town just by turning around, saving time and money. Some of the sets date back to Tom Mix and Hoot Gibson. By this time, Universal tended to rent livestock when needed. However, the studio still needed a corral, and that was built right next to Western Street. It was the only Western set building from the silent era.

Just a few feet away from Six Points, Texas, was Mexican Street. The facades were built with little or no ornamentation so that they could easily be redressed to appear as any locale necessary. Just beyond that were two structures that would be identi-

unofficial **TIP**
The house from *Psycho* remained a shell until 1983, when the structure was fully enclosed and the house moved. In 1986 the iconic structure was moved to its current location and restored.

fied with the studio tour: the house and the Bates Motel from *Psycho* (1960). The house was built out of stock units to save money. The front of the house and the tower were the same as the Harvey house on Colonial Street. A third wall was added to the two sides used in the movie. The motel would also be used in Alfred Hitchcock's *The Birds* (1963).

The trams took a quick pass through another Western set named Laramie Street and then on to Singapore Lake. The lake was a versatile body of water that has appeared as Southeast Asia, a Russian seaport, an Italian waterfront, and many other locations.

Nearby was Falls Lake, another set built for *Uncle Tom's Cabin* (1927). Lining one edge of the lake were man-made cliffs that hid the machinery for a 30-foot waterfall. Both the height and water pressure were adjustable. Fake nature gave way to real nature as the trams drove back up the hill to the Studio Entertainment Center. The guides told the guests that this portion of the property was left untouched so that film crews did not have to leave the back lot. To the left of the trams was the "hang man tree," where many a Western villain met his fate. Off in the distance were Warner Bros. Studios, the Walt Disney Studio, the NBC Studio, and the Columbia Ranch.

STUDIO ENTERTAINMENT CENTER

DURING THE INITIAL FEASIBILITY STUDIES, Buzz Price recommended building a permanent tourist facility with shops, restaurants, and demonstrations of moviemaking techniques. After surveying the 420-acre property, he determined that 270 acres would not be essential to production. Much of that land was the hilltop. He suggested the most suitable piece of land for the tour center was at the intersection of Barham Boulevard and Forest Lawn Drive. The new entrance would be very close to Warner Bros. Studio with easy access from the Ventura Freeway.

Dorskind disagreed. He wanted to reserve the gently sloped land for future studio production needs. Instead, Dorskind decided to remove more of the hilltop. True to Hollywood tradition, with a bit of imagination, knowing somebody, and enough money, anything was possible. Dorskind negotiated a deal with the California Division of Highways to give them 1.2 million cubic yards of dirt as fill for an expansion of the Hollywood Freeway. This created 12 new acres of flat land, enough for the tour center and a future hotel. They also removed an additional 300,000 cubic yards of dirt to build a new road to the hotel and tour center.

In place of the hilltop was the Studio Entertainment Center. Built at a cost of $5 million, the 10-acre facility was initially capable of handling 6,000–7,000 visitors per day. It officially opened on July 1, 1965.

Dorskind hired Harper Goff to do the first drawings of the Studio Entertainment Center.[24] Art director Randall Duell developed the concepts further and designed the new tourist facility. Duell had already crafted the site plans for Six Flags Over Texas and Freedomland in New York and would go on to design Six Flags Atlanta, AstroWorld in Houston, Paramount's Great America in Santa Clara, and Six Flags Magic Mountain in Valencia.

For the tourists, the Studio Entertainment Center would be the start and end point for their visit. It was designed to supplement the tour by revealing how some special effects and illusions were created for movie and television productions. The new facility became an enjoyable space where they could purchase food and drinks, buy film, use the restroom, and enjoy an expanded stunt show, a new trained animal show, and an updated makeup demonstration.

The stunt show moved into a new 400-seat amphitheater called the Action Arena. Displays of old-fashioned gunfights and fisticuffs were common at the numerous movie ranches surrounding Los Angeles, such as the Corriganville Movie Ranch near Simi Valley and Pioneertown in the Yucca Valley. Cowboy stuntmen could also be found at Disneyland and Knott's Berry Farm. However, at Universal the Western stunt show took on a certain level of authenticity that was missing from these other venues because they used real working Hollywood stuntmen. Visitors could watch professionals, such as Terry Wilson from *Wagon Train,* as well as Van Cooper, Eric Cord, Hank Calia, Jim Banner, and Jay Silverheels, who played Tonto on *The Lone Ranger.* The actors demonstrated how fights and falls were staged while actor Arnold Roberts emceed.

Ideas for shows could come from anywhere. One day Ray Berwick, the famous movie animal trainer, approached Barry Upson with an idea for an animal show. Berwick was best known as the animal

*un**official* **TIP**
In 2001 the animal show was rebranded as *Animal Planet Live!* Inspired by the cable/satellite channel, the show sported a new video screen and showed clips from *The Crocodile Hunter* and *Emergency Vets,* along with the animal tricks. It lasted until 2006.

trainer for Alfred Hitchcock's *The Birds* (1963). The men agreed to meet at a local doughnut shop the next day at 6 a.m. "In the original concept, [Berwick] was literally training the birds during the show," Upson said.[25] The show would alternate with the cowboys on the same stage throughout the day.

To this day, Universal features an animal show in its studio parks. The premise remains the same. Visitors are witnessing a training session. The only changes reflect current properties that could be exploited, such as Lassie's granddaughter, a Benji look-alike, and a horse that demonstrated how Mr. Ed did all the talking. In later years, other animal actors would include *Baretta*'s money-wise cockatoo Cookie, Einstein from *Back to the Future,* Sunshine the orangutan from *Cheers,* Babe the Pig, and Henry the Hound from *Emergency!*

The makeup show was moved from the Commissary to a new amphitheater called the Pavilion of Glamour. Roberta Ross put together a show in which selected members of the audience were made up as a glamorous star, a movie monster, or a child clown. If the ladies wanted to bring a little bit of Hollywood home with them, they could purchase the Cinematique makeup products used in the show. Universal claimed that the demonstration was "a feature especially popular with the ladies," where they could "learn first-hand the most glamorous makeup techniques from experts who make up the stars."

The structures' exteriors within the Studio Entertainment Center were designed to provide the illusion of a fully dressed set in the back lot that was within touch of the visitors. Scattered throughout the area were photo opportunities.

The Hong Kong Waterfront was primarily a food service area with the Flower Drum Café and Hattie's Bar. Café Madrid, a full-service restaurant, was the major draw to the Spanish area. The Commissary managed all of the eateries on the studio tour.

At the Early American Section, guests could play with "the only push-button snowstorm in the world" or enter the Fog Set, where at the push of a button, man-made fog would appear. Guests entering The Munster Laboratory could push a button and bring to "life" an animated Herman Munster. Nearby was a photo opportunity with the Creature from the *Creature from the Black Lagoon* (1954).

Another area for guests to wander was the Cecil B. DeMille Roman Court Yard. This replica of an ancient Roman courtyard contained props from other Hollywood studios, such as the chariot from MGM's *Ben Hur* (1959).

A lagoon was the site of numerous special effects demonstrations. At the beginning, there was a wave machine, wind, and rainmakers, as well as "a device which creates lightning by exploding bursts of fine aluminum power," according to a handout. A giant flagpole was placed on Water Tower Hill, the highest peak just above the Studio Entertainment Center.

Not long after the grand opening, the War Lord Tower was moved from the lower lot to the Studio Entertainment Center and became the exit for the tour. The castle turret structure was built for the 1965 Charlton Heston film *The War Lord*.

"We dragged the tower up the same grade that the first tram could not make," said Upson. "The base of the tower was wider than the road. It had to be shifted every 2 feet. It took forever and it was blocking the major road between the upper and lower lot. That did not make Mr. Wasserman very happy."[26]

In the early days, everybody did everything. One day, Terry Winnick was asked to announce the stunt show and suddenly became the announcer for the park. He went from the stunt show to the animal show to the Tony Urbano puppet show and then started all over. Later, they recorded his voice for the park announcements. The public address system was located behind the War Lord Tower.

Albert Dorskind and Buzz Price were right. If MCA built it, people would come. By any measure, the studio tour was a hit. Attendance jumped to more than 425,000 visitors in 1965. They had proven to Dr. Jules Stein and Lew Wasserman that MCA could make money and expand its brand with the tour.

The Universal Studio Tour capitalized on the pent-up demand by tourists who wanted to enjoy an authentic Hollywood experience, and Barry Upson found a way to let people take a peek behind the curtain without interfering with studio operations. At a time when most of the major studios were dismantling their back lots just for the real estate value, Dorskind and Upson found a creative way to revitalize that asset while padding the bottom line.

By 1964 the Hollywood moguls had invested more than $110 million modernizing the property, and they were rightfully proud of the Studio. In a typical Hollywood overstatement, they proclaimed Universal City as the "Entertainment Center of the World."

This success did not go unnoticed by the other Hollywood studios. The tour may have been the only one of its kind, but it was vulnerable to competition. After all, in Hollywood, imitation is the sincerest form of flattery. Starting in May 1965, Warner Bros. opened its back lot to visitors. It started with six single car trams, and the free tour passed through its back lot and included the sets for *The Great Race* (1965). A year later, MGM allowed third-party tour buses inside the gates for a 2-hour tour of its legendary, decaying back lot. Within two years, it had more than 100,000 visitors. Twentieth Century-Fox started with a lengthy walking tour consisting mostly of the sets from television's *Peyton Place*. Later on, it created a VIP tour for a pricey $50, including limos, starlet guides, and a Champagne lunch.[27] Its tour lasted until 1968.

For the 1966 season, MCA expanded the tram fleet to 18 vehicles, added Sunday tours, and even experimented with night tours during the summer. During peak periods, trams left the depot every 3 minutes. As a result, more than 800,000 additional tourists pushed through the turnstiles.

To create additional parking spaces for 1,400 more cars, MCA dug another 950,000 cubic yards of dirt from the hilltop. Albert Dorskind became one of the leading advocates of the proposed Beverly Hills Freeway slated to open in 1975. If the project moved forward, Dorskind would have been able to sell to Caltrans more than 4 million cubic yards of dirt from the Hope Avenue and Barham Boulevard area. The freeway project did not happen.

Early visitors loved the tour. One tour guide noticed, "The Midwesterners are the most naive but they have the most fun. The New Yorkers act above it all, and the Californians say they're only here to show out-of-state friends around."[28] Dorskind and Barry Upson beat the competition because they followed the MCA philosophy of being smarter and more prepared than the competition and then ruthlessly eliminating them.

The **STARS** of the **TOUR**

VISITORS WENT TO UNIVERSAL CITY to see television and motion picture stars at work. The intimacy of the tram experience suggested an opportunity to see an actual actor. Barry Upson said, "There was a lot of flexibility in moving the tour route around to take advantage of 'friendly' production teams such as *McHale's Navy* and Ernest Borgnine."[29]

Some stars took great pleasure meeting the tourists. Jimmy Stewart, Shirley MacLaine, and the crew from *McHale's Navy* frequently were seen signing autographs. John Wayne enjoyed eating hot dogs in the Studio Entertainment Center. Actor Robert Wagner was a fan favorite. As a friend of publicist Herb Steinberg, he helped out whenever he could. Telly Savalas, star of television's *Kojak,* used to hand out his trademark Tootsie Pops.[30]

On the other hand, Terry Winnick said, "A lot of actors did not like the tour." Jim Drury from *The Virginian* would walk off set when the trams came by.[31] Writer Bill Davidson recalled one visit when "Raymond Burr *did* rush past. There were squeals and 'ooh' and 'ahhs,' and every camera in the tram began clicking." But not all were impressed. A woman from West Covina said, "How can that be Raymond Burr when he's not in his wheelchair?"[32]

Columnist Jack Smith wrote about one visit. He overheard a tour guide ask a tramful of visitors, "How many came to see a movie star today?" When everyone's hand went up, he added, "Well, we're surrounded by dressing rooms here, so if you happen to see someone you recognize, feel free to *stare* at that person. Oh, and be sure to yell out his name, so everybody else can see him. But don't *attack* him."[33] Some visitors did not heed the tour guide's advice.

"MCA executives encouraged their actors to show up smiling for the fans as often as possible," according to biographer Frank Rose. "Cary Grant used to hide behind his bungalow until the trams passed before sneaking into the commissary, but wise tram drivers began doubling back whenever some sharp-eyed tourist caught a glimpse of the elusive actor." The result? "He was mobbed every time."[34]

For the first three years of the tour, there were not enough visitors to impact production, which allowed the tour guides to have great freedom. Barry Upson wanted to make sure that every guest got a good show. He explained in a training manual that the guides were the stars in "a new show in show business," the "Outdoor Thematic Show." They were trained that their role "deals with our audience in a sensitive person to person relationship. Here in our tour program, we meet our audience face to face. In truth, they are our personal guests."[35]

This mandate put a lot of pressure on the guides. Terry Winnick said, "We were watched very carefully. We were the front door to the studio, and when business started getting into the tens and twenty thousands, which happened in 1968 and 1969, we got big attention." He recalled, "We got visited regularly by not only Mr. Wasserman but a number of studio executives, 'messengers.'" Studio manager Gordon Forbes and head of security Jim Knott would come up to visit a few times a week. Working with Jay Stein was the assistant manager Bernie Fischer, who was known as Captain Numbers. Winnick said, "It was big money and it was cash."[36]

By 1968 more than 100 tour guides worked during the summer. The tour was so popular that more than 60,000 people visited during the week between Christmas and New Year's Day. Attendance had topped 1.2 million visitors for the first time and would remain at that level for the next few years.

1 Barry Upson, interview with author, Napa, CA, 10 Mar. 2014.
2 William S. Lund and Harrison A. Price, Economic Research Associates, *Planning Factors and a Financial Analysis for the Proposed Revue Studio Tour,* 26 July 1961, Series I, Box 9, Folder 196, Harrison "Buzz" Price Papers, Special Collections & University Archives Department, University of Central Florida Libraries, Orlando, FL.
3 Ibid.
4 Ibid.
5 Harrison A. Price, Harrison Price Company, "Confessions of an Itinerant Consultant," speech to Universal Creative of Universal Studios Recreation Group, 24 June 1999, Series III, Box 60, Folder 116, Harrison "Buzz" Price Papers, Special Collections & University Archives Department, University of Central Florida Libraries, Orlando, FL.
6 Lund and Price, *Planning Factors.*
7 Ibid.

8 Connie Bruck, *When Hollywood Had a King: The Reign of Lew Wasserman, Who Leveraged Talent into Power and Influence* (New York: Random House, 2003).

9 *Universal Studios Tour* training manual (Universal City, CA: Universal Studios, 1965), Box 1, Folder 10, Albert A. Dorskind Papers, Rare Books, Huntington Library, San Marino, CA.

10 Upson, interview with author, 10 Mar. 2014.

11 Ibid.

12 Upson, interview with author, 10 Mar. 2014.

13 "The Rubberneck Rush," *Newsweek,* 21 Aug. 1967.

14 "Council Expected to get Universal City Fair Plan," *The Los Angeles Times,* 24 Sept. 1964.

15 Hedda Hopper, "New Studio Tours Generate Goodwill," *The Los Angeles Times,* 11 Aug. 1964.

16 Ibid.

17 Ibid.

18 Philip K. Scheuer, "So You Want to Visit a Studio? Don't bother with VIPs," *The Los Angeles Times,* 19 July 1964.

19 Bruck, *When Hollywood Had a King.*

20 Ibid.

21 Terry Winnick, telephone interview with author, 23 Jan. 2014.

22 Ron Schneider, *From Dreamer to Dreamfinder* (Clearwater, FL: Bamboo Forest Publishing, 2012).

23 Winnick, telephone interview with author, 23 Jan. 2014.

24 Upson, interview with author, 10 Mar. 2014.

25 Ibid.

26 Ibid.

27 "The Rubberneck Rush."

28 Ibid.

29 Upson, interview with author, 10 Mar. 2014.

30 "Universal Studios Tour Now in 20th Year," *The Los Angeles Times,* 6 June 1984.

31 Terry Winnick, interview with author, Las Vegas, NV, 25 Feb. 2014.

32 "Universal Studios Tour Now in 20th Year."

33 Jack Smith, "Parting is Such Sweet Sorrow," *The Los Angeles Times* 29 Jan. 1976.

34 Frank Rose, "Twilight of the Last Mogul," *The Los Angeles Times,* 21 May 1995.

35 *Universal Studios Tour* training manual, Albert A. Dorskind Papers, Rare Books, Huntington Library, San Marino, CA.

36 Winnick, interview with author, 25 Feb. 2014.

CHAPTER 3

A **PEEK** *Behind* *the* **CURTAIN**

A **NEW BOSS**

ALBERT DORSKIND WAS ANXIOUS to meet the promised attendance projections and decided to make a change in 1967. He fired Barry Upson. Upson was responsible for making the tour a reality, but "Dorskind decided I was more of a creative and design type of guy and he wanted a hard-nosed businessman to run the tour," according to Upson.[1] He went to work for the architectural firm of Smith and Williams and would continue to work on projects at Universal Studios.

In Upson's place, Dorskind hired Ed Ettinger, the marketing director at Disneyland. He lasted six months. He found the culture at MCA to be nothing like Disney. Terry Winnick suggested that this was because a job at MCA was being part of a family and the culture was tough on outsiders. "Disney was Walt and his employees," Winnick said. "At MCA, you could screw up if you were honest. Just don't make the same mistake twice. You can make a new mistake but you better damn well admit it before anybody finds out about it."[2] John Lake took over for a short period of time, but he was put on a very short leash.

Dorskind must have figured that only an MCA veteran could survive the pressure, and he looked to his staff. Dorskind chose Jay S. Stein to run the tour. Stein started in the mail room in 1959 and worked his way up. He became responsible for scheduling the soundstages and the back lot for productions. He knew everything about the process to make movies and he knew everybody who was making the movies. Plus, he was a numbers guy.

Little did Dorskind know that he put in charge a man whose ambitions were as great as Walt Disney's.[3] Jay Stein would become a transformational figure at Universal and for the theme park industry. Over the years, he built the Studio tour into the equivalent of a box office smash every year without the risk or the reinvestment. When the time came, he began the shift from the industrial tour into the only real competitor with the Disney theme parks in North America.

Actor/writer Ron Schneider described Stein as "a thin, neat businesslike fellow with a curt demeanor and a reluctant smile. He says what he means and pulls no punches; he doesn't have to. And I always believed that the reason he liked—or at least tolerated—me, was that I always treated him with the same attitude of irreverent disrespect he showed everyone else."[4] Terry Winnick considered Stein a mentor and said, "He was the most demanding guy. As intense as Lew Wasserman."[5]

Barry Upson described Stein as a "critiquer." He said, "If we put together some kind of fairly complete concept with drawings and scripts he would critique it. He had a good sense of the marketplace and how to attract people in general. But he was absolutely no help in designing things either physically or operationally."[6]

Creative consultant Gary Goddard was a fan of Stein's and said he "had a wickedly dry and wry sense of humor, which I really appreciated."[7] He added, "The great thing with Jay was you always knew where you stood during and after each meeting. He did not pull punches, ever. He told you exactly what he thought, and that makes for an amazingly productive approach to making complicated projects happen." Goddard had worked at Walt Disney Imagineering for a time and compared the two companies. He said that Stein "was tough as nails" and "the corporate culture at Universal was very different than at Disney and the executives at Universal swore up a storm and used language that would cause outside people, at times, to burst into tears or walk out of meetings in a state of shock."[8] Welcome to Hollywood.

WASSERLAND

FOR THE FIRST FEW YEARS, the tour ran three trams a day during the winter. Terry Winnick said, "You would go where they would let you go. There were not enough visitors to impact where we went. So if you had 1,500 people a day, you opened at 10 a.m. and your last tram was at 3:30 p.m. in the wintertime. In the summer we would open earlier but the last tram would still go out at 3:30 p.m."[9]

Things were getting busy enough by 1967 to force the trained animals that shared the stage with the cowboy stunt show to move to their own venue. Universal opened a new petting zoo called the Ma and Pa Kettle Farm. The original set from the comedy film series was moved from an area known as Gausman's Gulch on the back lot and a primitive outdoor performance area built for Ray Berwick for his animal show. To handle the summer and holiday crowds, the GlamorTram fleet grew to 20 trams, and, as a result, attendance rocketed to 1.1 million.

The shows and the back lot sets were nice, but the real reason tourists wanted to visit Universal City was to see a movie or television unit at work. The creative process fascinated tourists. A glance at the postcards sold in the gift shop would suggest that on the Universal Studio Tour, guests had a golden opportunity to casually come upon a live set and witness a real production in action. That was the case for the first couple of years.

By 1968 the reality was much different, due to changes in the industry. More and more, motion picture and television production was moving indoors or on location. MCA's grip on prime time programming had diminished. New rules from the Screen Actors Guild barred visitors from the soundstages where 75% of production took place. Stein knew something had to be done to provide a consistent show.

To supplement the lack of action on the back lot, Stein started to look for and create special effect demonstrations that were not necessarily tied to a specific property. That way, no matter when visitors took the tour, they would experience a consistent show and be impressed with something unique and memorable.

The search began before Stein took charge to find existing assets on the back lot that could be turned into exciting demonstrations of moviemaking technology. The first effort from the studio's special effects staff was the snow set. A little house was set up on the back lot and the guide would push a button and fake snow made of white plastic shavings would fall.

The next gag would become the first example of the Universal stand-by of putting the tourists in fake peril. Some of the studio technicians rigged a rope and pulley system between two palm trees and hung a fake stuffed gorilla. Using a garage door opener, the tram driver could push the button and the gorilla would come swinging through the trees. Sometimes they would dress the character in polka dot shorts or have him eating a human hand. The gag rarely worked and was soon removed.

The longest-lasting of these early demonstrations was the Flash Flood set. The demonstration debuted in 1968. The special effect was used previously in an episode of *Wagon Train* and other television productions. The tram entered a Mexican village set and stopped. The tour guide would explain how movie directors could control the weather at the flick of a switch by the use of rain bars, which direct a spray of water upward, which then falls and looks like rain.

Along with the rain was lightning and thunder produced by powerful strobe lights and speakers hidden in the bushes. As the tour guide tried to bring the demonstration to an end, the sprinklers would continue to operate.

unofficial **TIP**
Later on, the Flash Flood set was updated with an additional blast of water, which would burst through the windows of a building to the left of the tram, and two cannons that fired water under pressure next to the tram. The old tree was replaced with a sign-post that was toppled by the torrent of water and a wooden cart that was pushed perilously close to the tram.

Suddenly, at the top of the hill, 20,000 gallons of water would rush 200 feet down the narrow village street and threaten to engulf the tram. The force of the water knocked down an old tree that would swerve, threatening the back car of the tram. As the tram pulled away, the water would be pumped back up the hill and stored in the two tanks for the next tram.

Early on, technicians struggled to get the water levels right. Terry Winnick called it a maintenance nightmare. "It would leak, spill, the water would overflow," he said. "You could see the tanks."[10] Reportedly, a group of dignitaries, including actor John Wayne, got an early peek and walked away soaked. The effect has been in continuous use to this day.

There was more in store for visitors in 1971. Along the backside of a facade on New York Street was the Boeing 747 set. As the tram drove past, visitors could catch a glimpse of a breakaway view of a jet airliner used for movies and television. Visitors would encounter a close call with the Torpedo Attack/Submarine set in the lagoon used for *McHale's Navy* (1962–66) and the *Creature from the Black Lagoon* (1954). Skilled craftsmen created a scale model of the pink submarine from *Operation Petticoat* (1959). As the model moved forward, it would fire and a 30-foot, air-charged geyser detonated on cue. Over the years, other miniature ships were added to the fleet.

With all of these additions, attendance hovered around 1.1 million visitors annually from 1967 until 1972. The tour became second only to Disneyland among Southern California attractions, grossing more than $6 million a year. That meant more than 12,000 people a day were visiting during the summer months. The lines were winding out into the parking lot, and sometimes the wait could be up to 3 hours just to buy a ticket. Then guests had to stand in another line that could last up to 2 hours to board a tram. Down by the soundstages, there might be seven or eight trams parked in front waiting for a new load.

What little advertising was done was local and aimed for the tourists who were already in Southern California. *Western Airlines* magazine was a popular forum. Television ads starring Alfred Hitchcock also started about this time.

Wayne Warga of *The Los Angeles Times* dubbed Universal City "Wasserland."[11] Columnist Charles Champlin quipped, "It is not quite the same as looking over Mervyn LeRoy's shoulder, but it is a very useful promotion for Universal in particular and Hollywood in general. And it will turn a pretty penny."[12] Bill Davidson wrote, "The bedraggled condition of the movie-TV industry being what it is, one could estimate, conversely, that the tour profits add up to a tidy bonanza cancelling out the combined losses of such Universal turkeys as *Matt Lincoln*, *Sweet Charity*, and *The Private War of Harry Friggs*."[13] Lew Wasserman was very happy.

Melody Sherwood worked for Mr. Wasserman and knew he kept a weekly tour count (every hour of each day, written on long graph paper) in his desk drawer. She said, "If I hadn't given it to him at 11, he'd buzz me at 11:05 and say, 'Well, what's wrong?' And I'd have to call over and find out why we didn't have it—maybe the machine had jammed."[14] Each count was accompanied by a description of the weather, including the temperature range. Sherwood added, "It was a game. He loved numbers. And I guess if it was 10% over the previous year, he liked that."[15]

This success was no surprise to Jay Stein. "At first some MCA executives were concerned that revealing the secrets of moviemaking would hurt the box office of our films," he said. "It's just the opposite. People are stimulated to see more movies."[16]

BREAKING DOWN
the PROSCENIUM

BY 1970 STEIN FELT THE TIME WAS RIGHT to put his stamp on the tour. He justified the $2 million investment to Lew Wasserman and Albert Dorskind as a risk management issue. He argued that it would be unsafe to have lines of people winding through the parking lot. He hired Smith and Williams to design a distinctive, colorful entrance plaza. The facility was flexible enough to act as the gateway to the tour during the day and then convert into a young adult nightclub for 500 people at night. The most prominent new landmark was a giant flagpole.

Stein had the makeup show retooled. The Singer Corporation sponsored the Singer Glamour Pavilion, where designers used volunteers to demonstrate how they drape fabrics to create the latest fashions. The theater could hold approximately 100 visitors. The practical demonstration was meant to inspire, with the hope that visitors would go home, buy a new Singer pattern, some fabric, and create a masterpiece using their new Singer sewing machine.

The petting zoo was enlarged, enhanced, and renamed The Ark Park. The Mt. Ararat petting zoo contained more than 200 animals and birds representing 30 species. It was complete with goat ladders and obstacle courses. Next door was Noah's Nursery and the Noah's Love Inn playhouse for children and animals. To serve the locals, the petting zoo had a separate admission of 25¢ for non-tour guests.

The new amenities were nice, but it was the *Make Believe Screen Tests* show that would prove to be the most important. Surveying the Southern California destination market, Buzz Price noticed that Universal's competition, including the Studio Tour at the time, was "basically an audience-performer relationship" and "in every case the visitor is at best a passive participant—a rider, a spectator, an audience." Those venues provided "great entertainment and mood, but little or no visitor involvement—the visitor is held at arm's length—always a spectator, rarely a participant." He recommended, "The use of the psycho-drama technique in the activities program, visitors will become a part of, not apart from, the recreational environment."[17]

He suggested that Universal Studios should avoid becoming another Disneyland or Marineland because those venues "are the economic victims of their own high program quality" and required constant reinvestment of capital and high operational costs to maintain the quality and quantity of their increasingly sophisticated shows. If they did not make those investments, their attendance and net economic return would suffer.

Price suggested, "MCA can produce a unique recreational attraction by offering an activity program that features visitor participation and involvement rather than a purely spectator environment." By breaking "down the 'proscenium' barrier between its 'show' and its visitor by involving him directly in the action that surrounds him," Universal would have something unique in the marketplace. By "playing a different game on a different field while maintaining the highest performance standards, serious regional competition would be discouraged for a long time to come."[18]

Activities would take "a real everyday event, amplify it for effect, place it in a believable frame of reference so that it doesn't become a caricature and the event becomes real again—but now is larger than life." Using all of the tools in making motion pictures, such as characters, dialogue, sets, props, lighting, and so on, the production team could "transform basic, everyday recreational forms into larger-than-life experiences for the visitors and give him a sense of heightened awareness."

When the visitor was the star of the show, his or her expectations and "performance standards become much more lenient because he is, in effect judging himself as the performer." They added, "Only recreation programs which offer a level of personal involvement and commitment can meet these needs and capture the inherent economic rewards."[19] By following Price's advice, Stein would make Universal City unique as well as save the studio a lot of money.

The *Make Believe Screen Tests* show debuted in a new outdoor amphitheater called Stage 70. The venue would become home to numerous variations on the same interactive show.

Selected audience members participated in a 30-minute show where they were placed in familiar scenes from comedy classics. The volunteers acted out on command while being taped on a closed-circuit color television system. The taped elements would be quickly reedited and played back to the audience, to their delight. "From the bank robbery through the chase scenes, right up to the pie-throwing climax, the laughs never let up," according to one press release.

To keep the show fresh, it would constantly be updated, reflecting Universal's latest hit television program. In 1972 *Adam-12* would drive the action. Then, in 1975, the newly renamed *Screen Test Theatre* featured *Emergency!* During that show, volunteers helped to put out flames bellowing out of a brick building from a full-size fire truck while the comedic results were quickly reedited and put on display on large monitors over the stage.

The show was retooled again in 1978 and renamed the *Airport '77 Screen Test Theatre*. Based on the Universal disaster film *Airport '77*, Stein felt the movie had a good chance of becoming a hit. Winnick brought in studio veteran editor Bill Parker to "edit the two-hour movie to eight minutes without losing the essence of the film." Then Winnick found spots to insert the guests. "These were the most exciting scenes that Bill cut," he said. "Let's see what we can get. We can make them jump into the water, crash the plane, they can do whatever. And I had to come up with the idea of how to fit this in the show." Before a live audience of their families and friends, volunteers would re-enact the jumbo-jet crash, the underwater escape, and the dramatic rescue scenes from the movie. When Winnick told Stein that he would have everybody jump into a water tank, Stein knew he had a great commercial and the project moved forward. The creative team re-created five of the sets used in the movie. Like before, the footage was spliced into actual footage from the film featuring Jack Lemmon, Brenda Vaccaro, and Darren McGavin.

In 1970 the very popular Western stunt show was moved into a new amphitheater. It could seat 1,500 guests with another 1,500 able to rest on concrete risers. The stage elements were placed on railroad tracks so that they could easily be moved. Stein started to think about how the stage might be repurposed as a nighttime venue. Barry Upson had tried a nighttime tour in 1966, but that was short-lived.

During the day, the tour was drawing 85% of its attendance from people visiting from outside of Southern California. At times it seemed the only reason a local would visit was to take the out-of-town relatives. In a moment of sheer inspiration, Terry Winnick came up with the World's Longest, Cheapest, Peanut, Beer, Hot Dog, Wine Outdoor Film Festival. For three nights over the Labor Day weekend, visitors were encouraged to bring a blanket and watch old films while enjoying peanuts available from horse troughs. They showed old Universal monster movies, such as *Dracula* (1931), *The Wolfman* (1941), and the Abbott and Costello films.

The festival was popular with locals and drew standing-room-only crowds. It proved to MCA executives that local residents would come to the hilltop with the right kind of programming. Universal Studios executive Ned Tanen suggested to Lew Wasserman that rock concerts and Broadway shows could work. To test the concept, the amphitheater was rebuilt during the 1972 off-season and expanded to 3,800 seats. The stunt show would continue to use the stage during the day.

The amphitheater reopened on June 28, 1972, featuring the Andrew Lloyd-Webber musical *Jesus Christ Superstar*. MCA released the concept album at the time and brought the Broadway show west for a six-week run. The show was a smashing success and extended to 11 weeks, until the weather got too cold.[20] The show was not without controversy. Throughout the run, there were noise complaints from the neighbors. The last scene of the show with Jesus Christ on the cross was especially a problem. Terry Winnick faced the problem head-on when he got a call from actor and comedian Jonathan Winters. When Winnick arrived, Winters pulled out a tape recorder and played a portion of the musical. Winnick was impressed and asked if he recorded that at the amphitheater. Winters said no. The recording was made from his backyard. MCA immediately began to fix the problem.

*un*official **TIP**
In *Parting of the Red Sea*, instead of highlighting the water trough, the special effect was used to enhance the point of view of another display. Obscuring the view of the *Sweet Charity* bridge was a "bigature" of the S.S. *Venture* from Peter Jackson's *King Kong* (2005). A *bigature* is a large-scale, highly detailed miniature, which can be filmed up close. To add to the realism of the display, 140 fog nozzles were installed, along with a weather station that gauges temperature, humidity, wind speed, and direction.

For the 1973 season, a $400,000 expansion increased seating to 5,200 and sound walls were added to muffle the sound. On June 29, the Grateful Dead kicked off a 12-week season of concerts at the Amphitheater. They were the first rock band to play on the Universal stage. Wasserman was proud of the amphitheater and took a personal interest in the facility. At one point, Schlitz was going to be a sponsor and supply the venue with beer. Wasserman killed the deal. He told his staff that Budweiser was America's beer and that is what they should serve.[21] The venue had become such a success that Wasserman had a bust of Ned Tanen made with the engraving "The Father of the Amphitheater."[22]

MAKE *a* GREAT COMMERCIAL

FOR JAY STEIN, the formula for success was becoming obvious. According to Terry Winnick, when Stein thought about additions to the studio tour, he believed, "If you couldn't make a great commercial, you shouldn't build it. Then, if you build it, you better deliver."[23] Budget approval arrived in January, and it had to be ready for summer crowds.

The first tour enhancements were designed and built by studio special effects personnel. For 1973 they put together two new demonstrations, The Parting of the Red Sea and The Burning House. What could be better than allowing guests to become Moses and part the waters? The Parting of the Red Sea would be the first in a long line of attractions that used the same gag. The tram approaches an obstacle, has two choices, picks the wrong choice, and mayhem ensues. In this case, as the tram skirts Park Lake, it comes upon the bridge used in *Sweet Charity* (1969). When the tour guide realizes that the tram is too large to cross the bridge and too large to back up, he proclaims that only a miracle can save them. The tram pulls closer to the water's edge, tripping a mechanism that drains 40,000 gallons out of a 600-foot-long, 15-foot-wide, 5-foot-deep trough in less than 3 minutes. As the tram enters the trough, the visitors' point of view is eye level to the water.

Originally the tram had a limited amount of time to make its way across the lake before the mechanism would begin to reset. After dunking numerous guests in Park Lake, two safety mechanisms were installed. Infrared sensors were placed to detect if the tram had cleared the area, and the tour guide had to manually push an all-clear button.

The Burning House was another dramatic special effects demonstration. As the tram pulled up to a facade of the white, two-story mansion, it would suddenly catch on fire. Visitors learned how the studio controlled fire effects. The structure was clad in fireproof building material with strategically placed gas jets.

Along with these two attractions, the park opened The Motion Picture and Television Museum, a new static display and the only museum dedicated to the movies in all of Hollywood. Some of the items on display included the red dress worn by Judy Garland in *Meet Me in St. Louis*, the roller skates used by Barbra Streisand in *Funny Girl*, and the first movie camera ever invented. The combination of new elements helped to propel attendance to more than 1.5 million visitors in 1973.

This was all good, but Stein was running into a growing problem. The reliability of the special effects demonstrations was very poor. Due to their training, the studio technicians were capable of making any illusion happen at least once for the cameras. That was fine for filmmaking, but that did not cut it when the gag had to be repeated dozens of times a day for the tour.

Jay Stein turned to Terry Winnick. Winnick had been an enthusiastic employee with the tour since the beginning and had studied architecture, so Stein figured he was as well qualified as anybody. Winnick would become the studio tour's first attraction designer at the age of 24. One of Winnick's first projects was to design a pedestrian bridge that would connect the hotels to the park entrance. That bridge still stands today.

Looking for the 1974 crowd generator, Stein saw that Universal was going to release an all-star disaster film called *Earthquake*.

unofficial **TIP**
The Burning House was originally located on the upper lot, next to the Action Arena, and then moved to the lower lot in 1982. It was finally removed in 1992 due to air-quality issues and expense of the natural gas.

The Los Angeles region made headlines in 1971 with a large earthquake in Sylmar, and the story was fresh in the minds of the public. What a perfect opportunity for the tour. Stein wanted to hurtle fake boulders down a hill straight toward the trams yet somehow not hit anything, and he asked Winnick to come up with something. Winnick said, "Jay wanted to scare people. It had to be threatening."[24]

Terry Winnick figured nothing could be more threatening than tossing boulders at the trams. RockSlide was placed along a rocky hillside just below the Studio Entertainment Center. The trams would stop, and suddenly Styrofoam boulders would roll down toward the trams, hit a ledge, fly up in the air, and then land in a trough just shy of the visitors. The Oliver & William Elevator Company developed an 8-inch, V-shape, tilted platform that was 100 feet long at the bottom of the hill. A metal scoop bucket would gather the boulders and then transport the boulders back up the hill to their storage place behind Hong Kong Hattie's. The scoop would then lower back to the bottom of the hill, and the entire process would repeat every 90 seconds.

At least that was the idea. RockSlide never really worked. The scoop mechanism was very slow and was not able to keep pace with the trams. If the hillside was wet, the rocks would absorb the water and spray the visitors as they slammed into the bottom of the hill. When the hillside was dry, the rocks would occasionally bounce into the trams and create havoc. If it were a windy day, the rocks would jump the tram. Plus, the rocks would only last for about 100 "earthquakes" before they started to disintegrate.

The effect lasted until 1978, when it was removed to make room for Battle of Galactica.

The other big draw in 1974 was the Collapsing Bridge. The bridge was a far more sophisticated and convincing demonstration than the fake boulders. *The Los Angeles Times* called it "one of the most exciting special effects ever created."[25] Winnick said, "It was the first independent use of the design and engineering group that was not related to the studio construction department."[26]

As the tram approached a dilapidated bridge, the tour guide would tell the visitors that it was one of the oldest structures in the complex, built around 1914. Instead of going around the hazard, the driver would shift into low gear and start across while the guide yelled out, "No, no. Remember the memo that came out yesterday warning us about it?" The driver would reply, "I wasn't here yesterday, and I think we can do this." Winnick added a car wreck at the base of the bridge to create a sense of urgency. Of course, the tram driver would not heed the guide's warning and drive over the bridge. When the tram reached the halfway point, the bridge began to creak and timbers started to fall away. Suddenly, the deck of the bridge would drop a few inches, giving the visitors a scare. When the tram pulled away, the gag was revealed, and the visitors could see the bridge reset itself.

Terry Winnick came up with the idea while he was digging a trench in front of his house in Northridge during a downpour in 1973. He quickly rushed into the house and told his wife about the gag. She liked it and told him to draw up a few sketches. He showed them to Stein, who said, "This is great. It has all the elements. It was movie-making. It was fun."[27] As usual, Winnick had just a few months to put it together.

 unofficial **TIP**
The Collapsing Bridge was retired from daily use in October 2005. It was never really meant to handle the larger Super Trams. However, it has been reopened on occasion when another major attraction along the tour has been under refurbishment.

Winnick brought in Jim Kessler to engineer the bridge, as well as Kermit Achterman, who was the general manager from a hydraulics company in Glendale. Achterman, an inventor, told Winnick that he could design the cylinders, Kessler could design the deck, and Winnick could take care of the art design and make sure the project could be completed in time for the summer season. The bridge was built with hydraulic lifts like those found in an elevator. It was controlled by a computer system with redundant safety systems. This was the first time that the gag involved the tram vehicle being physically manipulated.

The Collapsing Bridge generated a record crowd of more than 1.8 million visitors in 1974. Wasserman could see that Stein's tiny team could produce great work without having to rely on the studio's technical resources. Barry Upson said the bridge was the beginning of the "Ride the Movies" concept. He said, "The idea was ingrained into the work that we did."[28] It also brought Jay Stein a promotion. He was now a vice president of MCA, Inc.

TRAINS *and* TUNNELS *and* MONSTERS

STEIN AND WINNICK WERE ADDING NEW ATTRACTIONS at a breakneck pace in 1975. The Runaway Train promised to run over a tram every 2 minutes. While driving past Denver Street, the tram would approach a railroad crossing. For some unknown reason, the tram would stop with the center car over the tracks. Off in the distance, the loud chug of a steam train and its distinctive whistle could be heard, and the warning light next to the tram would wave frantically. Then the visitors would see it. Bearing down on the tram at 7 miles per hour would be a 9-ton locomotive. Fortunately, the train would stop inches from the tram. As the tram pulled away, the locomotive would quietly roll back to its hidden position, and visitors could see the ride reset like the Collapsing Bridge. Air motors with two braking systems powered the locomotive. The demonstration took four months to build.

Next came the Doomed Glacier Expedition. The attraction was loosely based on Clint Eastwood's *The Eiger Sanction* (1975). A pivotal part of the film was set in the Mount Rainier National Park. In the attraction, the trams would leave the back lot, drive past Falls Lake with its fake rock cliffs, and approach a set dressed with rocks, a snow-covered A-frame lodge, and avalanche warning signs scattered all over the place.

Once again, the tram driver would be presented with the option to drive around the hazard but would insist on taking the shortcut. As the tram approached the cavern, the tour guide would caution visitors that the slightest movement or sound could cause an avalanche. Of course, something would happen, and the tram would get caught up in the "avalanche" and appear to tumble.

*un*official **TIP**
The glacier tunnel was redressed to look like a mineshaft in 1997 to promote Universal's *Dante's Peak* (1997).

To achieve the tumbling effect, Winnick used reflected forced perspective, a filmmaking technique used to create a greater sense of depth. Combined with a spinning tube large enough to cover the entire tram and the use of Universal's Academy Award–winning Sensurround system, the Doomed Glacier's ice tunnel was a startling and realistic effect. The tube would rotate around the tram, creating the desired visual effect. Trams full of visitors would lean, believing that the tram was moving.

Another change was a reimagined makeup show. The show had been an integral part of the Universal experience from the very beginning. It had to absorb the large crowds descending on the tour, so a new, 1,500-seat amphitheater was built and the show had to run up to 10 times a day. Jay Stein and Terry Winnick had approached Nick Marcelino, head of makeup at the studio, and asked him to find someone who could create a new show.

Marcelino recommended makeup artist and musician Verne Langdon. Langdon had worked on *Hello Dolly!* (1969) and the five *Planet of the Apes* films. His most-recent work was running the Ringling Brothers clown college. He learned that Stein had a special affection for the Universal monsters and built the show around the studio's reputation as the birthplace of the American monster movie. The show was called the *Land of a Thousand Faces*.

An actor made up as "The Spirit of The Mirror" hosted the show. The actor lip-synched to a prerecorded narration track voiced by actor John Carradine. The Spirit would reminisce about the great screen makeup efforts of the past, including Lon Chaney in the *Phantom of the Opera* (1925); Charles Laughton's Quasimodo in *The Hunchback of Notre Dame* (1939); and the Lion, Scarecrow, and Tin Woodsman characters from MGM's *Wizard of Oz* (1939). In the background was an eerie theater organ sound track that was composed and performed by Langdon.

Prior to the show, two visitors were selected to become Frankenstein's Monster and the "New" Bride of Frankenstein. During the 20-minute show, the makeup application would be completed in front of the other visitors, using a special process created by Verne Langdon and Robert Zraick. During the show's climax, the Spirit would remove his makeup and become a "mad doctor," who would introduce the new monsters and then lock them away in an "eternal life" cabinet. He would throw an electrical switch, and the cabinet would explode. When he opened up the cabinet, only two charred skeletons would remain. The final line in the show was, "This is John Carradine. Father of Kung Fu."[29]

Another addition was the Treacherous Quicksand Pit, a new element for the Western stunt show. One unlucky cowboy would accidentally step into quicksand and rapidly sink into the muck. Another stuntman would try to rescue him with a bullwhip but with no success. The stuntman would slip under, never to be seen again. At least until the next show.

Stein and Winnick kept the crowds coming. To cram more visitors through the turnstiles, a fourth car was added to the trams. Just like before, the engines could not handle the strain of the extra weight, and there were frequent breakdowns. Universal set another record with 2.3 million visitors in 1975. That was more than a half million more than the previous year. Just when Stein thought things could not get any better, along came a shark named Bruce.

JAWS

EVERY ONCE IN A WHILE, a motion picture comes along that changes the industry. One such film was Steven Spielberg's *Jaws*. Released in the summer of 1975, the film would go on to become the biggest box office champion of all time, grossing $133.4 million.

Jaws was the first summer blockbuster. In the past, the studios released their biggest films toward the end of the year. That summer, with a demographic bulge created by the baby boom, a large population of young people with disposable money was looking for air-conditioned entertainment, and they found it at the local movie theater. The thriller was the right film at the right time. Sensing an opportunity, Jay Stein quickly added a replica shark as a photo opportunity and placed it near the Visitors Center.

Once Stein learned that there were parts left over from the production, he quickly hired special effects wizard Bob Mattey to rebuild the mechanical shark that he created for the film. Mattey was best known for building the giant squid for Disney's *20,000 Leagues Under the Sea* and the animals that inhabit Disneyland's Jungle Cruise. They removed the scary house and a wave machine demonstration at Singapore Lake and re-created part of the quaint village of Amity from the film.

According to the billboard at the entrance to the area, the town was celebrating its annual Fourth of July regatta. As the trams skirted around the edge of the quiet bay, visitors would spot George the fisherman sitting in his dinghy. Unbeknownst to George, a huge dorsal fin was heading straight toward the fisherman, and the shark would then pull both him and his boat under. The resulting blood bubbling up from the bay was a reminder that this show was something you would never find at Disneyland.

Leaving this horrible scene, the tram would pull forward and park next to a pier. The guide would point out a floatation barrel loaded with shark bait off in the distance. Suddenly, the barrel would be pulled under the water by some massive force. A fragment of the pier was then towed out to sea, collapsing the main section under the tram and leaving all aboard dangerously approaching the water level. With the audience distracted by all of the commotion, many would not notice, until it was too late, the 25-foot great white shark as it came to attack the tram. As the tram pulled away from the pier, the visitors would watch the shark reset and prepare for the next tram. The show opened on April 10, 1976.

The body of the shark was struck from the Bruce sea-sled mold used in the movie. This meant the bottom was missing so that the shark could move along a short track. This is the same body mold used today. At first, the shark was painted green with a pale blue belly. Later, it was repainted bluer on top with an off-white belly.

Mattey sculpted Bruce's head using the movie poster as the model. The shark in the poster had extra long teeth to look menacing. When Mattey finished sculpting the drawing in three dimensions, the shark looked rather comical instead of scary. This shark became known as Carrot Tooth, and he lasted until 1978.

Unfortunately, the special effect was not reliable. Once again, what works for a movie production does not hold up under the stress of the tour. The new parts were based on the old parts, and those were meant to last one or two shots before having to be rebuilt. Terry Winnick was brought in to fix the problems. He started with the shark. He toned down the shark's jowls and improved the mouth by allowing it to scoop up more water to splash the visitors. This shark jumped out of the water at a steeper angle. Jim Kessler was responsible for fabricating the new shark.

The Mark II version of the Shark made its debut in 1978, in conjunction with the release of *Jaws II*. The head was widened and his eyes were made completely black. For a time, out in the lagoon was *The Orca*, Quint's fishing boat seen in the film. When director Steven Spielberg finished *Jaws*, the studio knew it had a good movie, but it never expected the film to turn out to be the gigantic hit that it became.

Like most productions, many of the props and sets were either sold off or given away. This was the case with *The Orca*. A special effects technician purchased the boat, restored it, and used it to go sword fishing along the California coast. With the film a hit, somebody approached the technician and asked if they could buy the boat back. Seizing the opportunity, he gladly sold back the boat at a profit. *The Orca* was placed in the lagoon and left there for many years. Rumor had it that Steven Spielberg would occasionally sit on the deck and have lunch. When the wood began to rot, the boat sank into the shallow lagoon. In 1996 they tried to remove the boat, only to watch it break in half.

Another original prop brought back for the attraction was Ben Gardner's boat. Ben Gardner was the shark's victim that scares Richard Dreyfuss when he goes for a dive. The boat was placed to the right as visitors entered Amity Island. Originally painted blue for the film, the boat was repainted white in 1981. In 2005 the boat was removed.

In 2001 the Jaws experience was upgraded with fire effects and became known as Jaws on Fire. George the police boat diver replaced George the fisherman. This is the version of the shark that would remain to terrify visitors.

Keeping the tour fresh with new demonstrations proved to be a winning strategy. Attendance in 1976 jumped to 2,772,000. The first generation of practical demonstrations allowed Universal to beat back the competition from other movie studios before they could get a foothold in the market. The gags enhanced the tour and guaranteed that every visitor, no matter what day they visited, would get a consistent show. MCA publicist Herb Steinberg said, "We have developed a high degree of sophistication in being able to reveal all the secrets, what we do, how we do it, show all the tricks. And it hasn't hurt us a bit—it just piques a moviegoer's curiosity that much more."[30]

The popularity of the audience participation shows pushed Stein to add another venue. For 1977 the new show inside Stage 32 was the *Six Million Dollar Man/Bionic Woman Testing Center,* the most sophisticated interactive show to date. The demonstration was based on the hit television shows *The Six Million Dollar Man* starring Lee Majors and *The Bionic Woman* starring Lindsay Wagner. As in the other participatory shows, selected visitors demonstrated incredible feats of strength through the magic of special effects. For example, one petite or elderly woman would be pitted against a group of strong men in a game of tug of war, and she would win. Another woman could lift a 3,000-pound truck with one hand. One cast member would demonstrate another special effect by leaping over a 12-foot barrier.

At the studio tour, the bottom line was the bottom line. Barry Upson said, "The goal was not to build big but to find things that could make a good commercial and draw a crowd. We wanted to clean up what was already there."[31] Stein was always looking at the studio production schedule to find shows that he could exploit. In 1977 he noticed a new CBS television program called *The Incredible*

Hulk, based on the Marvel Comics character. He found his promotion for the summer of 1978.

When the television show debuted, it was an instant hit, and Stein was ready. He had Upson and Winnick build a special breakaway brick wall inside of the *Land of a Thousand Faces* show for $30,000. A guy in green paint would break through the wall and then run out of the theater. The first Hulk was bodybuilder Jake Steinfeld, who would go on to fame as Body by Jake. The gag was so effective that it was credited with an additional 100,000 visitors, bringing attendance up to 3.3 million.

BATTLE *of* GALACTICA

THE FIRST TOUR ATTRACTION to seriously challenge Disney's level of technical sophistication was Battle of Galactica. Opened on June 9, 1979, this was the first themed attraction to feature audio-animatronic characters outside a Disney park and the first dark ride to combine sophisticated animatronics and lasers with live actors. The budget was an astronomical $1 million.

One day, Stein and Winnick were talking about all of the things they could do with a tram. "We could fly it." Winnick said. "We could sink it. We could put it under water. We could shake it. We could drop stuff on it. What else could we do to a tram?" For every television show or movie in production, the two would look for ways they could fit a tram in there. At one point, Stein suggested we could "fly a tram full of tourists into outer space—or at least give the illusion."[32] They just needed the right intellectual property.

Stein heard about a new science fiction show called *Battlestar Galactica*. At a cost of $7 million, the 3-hour pilot was the most expensive one ever produced at the time. He asked Robert Zraick to see the pilot a week prior to its initial airing in October 2004. After the viewing, he said, "Then we knew what we wanted to do."[33] When the show aired, it was a huge hit.

Inspired by the television pilot, Terry Winnick and Robert Zraick put the visitors in peril by having them abducted and then find themselves in the middle of a laser battle before escaping. He said, "When I saw *Close Encounters*, I wished I could have gone aboard the spacecraft, and I wanted to participate in the excitement of one of the battles in *Star Wars*; not just watch it, but experience it."[34]

On a lonely road along the hillside where RockSlide's fake boulders used to plummet, the trams approached a show building disguised as a spaceship. The facade was crafted out of plastic, wood, sheet steel, and polyurethane.

In a tightly written script, the tour guide would get into an argument with two life-size robotic Cylons (warriors) sitting in an alien armored vehicle parked in front. The Cylons would tell the visitors that they were now prisoners and force the tram to enter their base by firing a cannon and blasting a rock nearby.

Inside the show building, the tour guide would get in an argument with an audio-animatronic Centurion. The spaceship would be ready to take off, and the visitors would never see Earth again. At the very last minute, a human actor portraying a Colonial Warrior would appear to rescue the humans, and an all-out laser battle would begin on all sides of the tram. When the battle ended, all that was left were three Cylons split in half, spewing smoke, and a gaping hole in the side of the ship through which the tour guide would direct a hasty escape. As the tram left the building, for the first time, the audience could not see the special effects reset. Battle of Galactica was not a demonstration of a movie special effect. Instead, visitors got to really ride the movies.

Designing the attraction was especially difficult. As before, it was one thing to create special effects for the screen, but it was much more complicated when designing special effects for a theme park attraction. "In a film you can animate the laser beams, but here we had to deal with a real-life setting," Robert Zraick said.[35] Therefore, the solution had to be safe, durable, and repeatable every 2 minutes and 45 seconds.

They first considered hidden strips of light on the walls. A Cylon Warrior would raise his gun, touch the wall, and out would come a beam of light. However, it was quickly decided that the effect did not look very convincing. It seemed the only thing that would look like lasers would be real lasers.

To see if lasers could be used safely in this application, Terry Winnick arranged for a demonstration of real lasers by Dr. Sandor Holly of InterScience Technology Corp. Dr. Holly determined that to achieve the desired effect, the argon and krypton lasers would have to be so powerful that they could blind or burn a person. He created a safety system using photoelectric devices that would shut down the lasers if they strayed from the intended target. The light beams shot from three 25-watt laser devices, installed underground, firing at 1,600 impulses per second. The beams travelled through a trench and then were split by prisms, creating a multicolored shower of powerful light rays. This was the first theme park show controlled by a computer.

*un*official **TIP**
The final Battle of Galactica came in 1992 to make way for the Starway and another groundbreaking attraction: Back to the Future—The Ride.

Originally, the show was to feature all audio-animatronics characters. Zraick joked, "Humans have played robots, and robots have played humans, but so far as I know this is the first time in the history of theatrical events that robots have played robots—unless you want to count R2-D2."[36] For the Colonial Warrior, it was decided that Universal did not have the technology to animate a credible human figure. That seemed like something only Disney could do. Instead, they decided to use a live actor.

Universal hired 10 actors with at least three available at any time. Their movements had to be safely choreographed with the movements of the robotic characters and the laser blasts. Zraick noticed, "The performers really get into it. It's really exciting for them to dress up and play hero."[37]

Along with the Colonial Warrior, the show featured 20 audio-animatronic figures. Two of the robots were outside and the remaining 18, including the Imperious Leader (voiced by actor Patrick Macnee) and some Ovions, were inside. Robot maker Alvaro Villa of AVG Inc. was hired to build the audio-animatronic figures. Villa had previously worked at Disney.

It took Universal's special effects team nine months to build the attraction. Ewing Architects was responsible for the interior design of the 15,000-square-foot show building. Along with the lasers, smoke, and robots, other special effects included the Imperious Leader's henchmen blasted away in flames made of Mylar, fans, and CO_2. The audio system source was a 16-track directional sound track and a Sensurround low-frequency generator to augment explosions and the spaceship's rumble. Universal's DiscoVision videodisc system was used for the video monitor readouts.

Universal City was firing on all cylinders. By 1979 Albert Dorskind once again needed more land to expand. In the past, it was simply a matter of scraping a bunch of dirt off the hillside and moving it somewhere else. Dorskind wanted to grade 67 acres of the back lot and build a 1,500-car parking lot and new film sets. Plans called for the removal of 1.88 million cubic yards of earth.

Dorskind did not see the buzz saw he was about to run into. California environmental laws and fierce opposition by the surrounding residents made the effort more difficult. In a bold move, Dorskind sent letters to members of the Hollywood Manor Home Owners Protective Association offering them a deal. For the 20 homes that overlooked the vacant property, MCA would pay $6,000 to install air-conditioning or soundproofing. Four of the homes would get an additional $4,000 for new landscaping. In exchange, MCA demanded "the only provision is that you do not actively oppose them [MCA] at the hearings." Many of the neighbors we offended by the offer. "What MCA is offering is a kind of bribe," homeowner Franz Morrison said. "They want to butter us up. If you take their money, you can't go down and protest. You're supposed to keep your mouth shut."[38]

After months of hearings and protests, the Los Angeles County Regional Planning Commission approved MCA's expansion plans with 29 conditions. The most important was that the Universal Amphitheater had to be enclosed. Other conditions included heavily landscaped buffers that exceeded the county's requirements, and the county planning director had approval rights on the sets to be constructed on the property. As part of the deal, the Universal

Amphitheater closed in 1980 for a $20 million rebuild. Universal spokesman Dan Lubin said, "The only thing that will be familiar will be the foundation of the original seats. To call it a facelift is not accurate; it's a total reconstruction."[39]

When it reopened on July 30, 1982, at a gala concert starring Frank Sinatra, the audience found the seating increased to 6,251 seats and the stage expanded to 70 feet. For the performers, the entire back end of the stage could be opened for easy load in. There was a new, seven-row balcony added to the rear perimeter of the auditorium. For the Hollywood elite, the venue was perfect. The farthest seat from the stage was only 150 feet.

At one point, the theater was under consideration by The Academy of Motion Picture Arts and Sciences to host the Oscars. However, the theater was rebuilt with limited fly and wing space, and the 3-hour Oscar broadcast required many set changes to sustain interest.

CASTLE DRACULA

ATTENDANCE FOR THE STUDIO TOUR set a record of 3.8 million visitors in 1980. Jay Stein and Terry Winnick were constantly looking for ways to keep all of those people busy. They started with a $2.5 million update to the *Land of a Thousand Faces* show. The old amphitheater was fitted with a roof and expanded from 1,500 seats to 2,500 seats. A new, five-level stage was built that measured 95 feet across and 38 feet high. To coordinate the five major special effects, the eight animated figures, the live actors, and the unrehearsed visitors, a state-of-the-art computer system was installed.

Late one night, Stein was watching a new television show produced by Universal called *The Curse of Dracula* starring Michael Nouri. At one point, Dracula turns to the screen and growls. This moment scared Stein. He had never seen Dracula growl. He was convinced he could scare an audience with a growling Dracula.

Winnick brought Verne Langdon back to update his own show. This time Langdon would be able to take advantage of the controls and special effects that could only be done indoors. Stein wanted the audience to feel as if they were in jeopardy, and Winnick spent a lot of time trying to re-create the growl that Stein heard. After much trial and error, they found the right sound. From the green light to the debut of the *Castle Dracula* show on June 13, 1980, the project only took seven and a half months.

Guests entered the new theater while it appeared to be in the midst of a ferocious thunderstorm. Claps of thunder shook the floor using Universal's Sensurround technology, while red-orange clouds were projected from behind onto two windows embedded with plastic prisms flanking the stage. On the stage were torture racks and a replica of a 6-foot black wolf.

During the 20-minute show, Langdon continued the tradition of transforming ordinary visitors into hideous monsters. In this case, two volunteers would be introduced at the beginning of the show and then go backstage to be made up as Frankenstein's Monster and his bride. Dracula with Renfield, his bug-swallowing valet, and a rudimentary animatronic Phantom of the Opera hosted the show.

For the climax, Stein wanted bats to fly over the audience members' heads, but that was deemed too dangerous. So Winnick hired Ray Berwick to train a flock of little green parrots who would be painted black using a special dye. After three months of training, it was time for a final run-through. At the proper moment, the cage door was lifted and all of the parrots flew toward the stage, took a hard left, and flew out of the arena, never to be seen again. Berwick started over using pigeons.

Although the show was successful in sucking up a huge number of visitors, Jay Stein was not satisfied. He felt that nothing really worked the way he wanted. It did not scare anybody. He already began searching for a replacement.

The Western stunt show also became an opportunity for change. Since 1972, the Western stuntmen shared the same stage that would be used for concerts at the Universal Amphitheater. In July 1980, with the amphitheater about to be enclosed, expanded, and purposely designed for music, the cowboys got to move into their own new 2,000-seat arena. The often-humorous new show was named *The Wild Wild Wild West Stunt Show*. It featured three stuntmen demonstrating various fighting techniques, including the use of a bullwhip, ax handles, and guns. The show ended with a three-story high fall.

The Universal Studios tour hit another all-time attendance record in 1981 with more than 3.7 million visitors. The tour became the third-most visited tourist attraction in the United States, led only by the two Disney parks. Stein's desire to build a larger empire had now begun.

1 Barry Upson, interview with author, Napa, CA, 10 Mar. 2014.
2 Terry Winnick, interview with author, Las Vegas, NV, 25 Feb. 2014.
3 Winnick, interview with author, 25 Feb. 2014, and Peter Alexander, interview with author, South Palm Beach, FL, 21 Oct. 2013.
4 Ron Schneider, *From Dreamer to Dreamfinder,* (Clearwater, FL: Bamboo Forest Publishing, 2012).
5 Winnick, interview with author, 25 Feb. 2014.
6 Upson, interview with author, 10 Mar. 2014.
7 Gary Goddard, interview with author, North Hollywood, CA, 12 Jan. 2014.
8 Ibid.
9 Winnick, interview with author, 25 Feb. 2014.
10 Ibid.

11 Wayne Warga, "Studios Invite the Outsider for Inside Look," *The Los Angeles Times,* 13 Oct. 1968.

12 Charles Champlin, "Thar's Gold in Them Fake Hills," *The Los Angeles Times,* 13 July 1966.

13 Bill Davidson, "Pop! There Goes the Grand Illusion," *The Los Angeles Times,* 11 Nov. 1971.

14 Connie Bruck, *When Hollywood Had a King: The Reign of Lew Wasserman, Who Leveraged Talent into Power and Influence* (New York: Random House, 2003).

15 Ibid.

16 Vernon Scott, "Universal Considering Central Fla. Tourist Attraction," *Tampa Tribune,* 10 June 1980.

17 William S. Lund and Harrison A. Price, Economic Research Associates, *Planning Factors and a Financial Analysis for the Proposed Revue Studio Tour,* 26 July 1961, Series I, Box 9, Folder 196, Harrison "Buzz" Price Papers, Special Collections & University Archives Department, University of Central Florida Libraries, Orlando, FL.

18 Ibid.

19 Ibid.

20 Tom Link, *Universal City–North Hollywood: A Centennial Portrait* (Chatsworth, CA: Windsor Publications, 1991).

21 Alexander, interview with author, 21 Oct. 2013.

22 Bruck, *When Hollywood Had a King.*

23 Winnick, interview with author, 25 Feb. 2014.

24 Ibid.

25 "Universal Offers Look Behind Scenes," *The Los Angeles Times,* 13 June 1975.

26 Terry Winnick, telephone interview with author, 7 Apr. 2014.

27 Winnick, interview with author, 25 Feb. 2014.

28 Upson, interview with author, 10 Mar. 2014.

29 Winnick, interview with author, 25 Feb. 2014.

30 Maynard Good Stoddard, "420 Acres of Make-believe," *The Saturday Evening Post,* 1 May 1984.

31 Upson, interview with author, 10 Mar. 2014.

32 Alan Brender, "The Battle of Galactica at Universal Studios," *Starlog #28,* Nov. 1979.

33 Ibid.

34 Ibid.

35 Ibid.

36 Ibid.

37 Ibid.

38 Claire Spiegel, "Universal Studios Offers Money to Blunt Opposition," *The Los Angeles Times,* 24 July 1979.

39 "Universal Amphitheater Undergoing Renovation Work," *The Los Angeles Times,* 8 Sept. 1981.

CHAPTER 4

DEFINING *the* UNIVERSAL EXPERIENCE

▌ WE ARE SOLDIERS *in a* WAR

THE REAGAN RECESSION OF 1982 was the most severe since the Great Depression of the 1930s. Attendance at Universal Studios Hollywood plummeted to 3.1 million, a sharp drop of 600,000 visitors. For a park dependent on out-of-towners, a slump in domestic travel, fewer foreign visitors, and the opening of Epcot Center at Walt Disney World in 1982 did not help. Things were so bad *The Wall Street Journal* suggested that MCA was going to change the name of the park to "Universal Movie World."[1]

To immediately reverse the slide, Jay Stein figured he would celebrate the tour's 20th anniversary a year early. For 1983, he wanted to retool the *Castle Dracula* show. Shortly after the show had opened in 1980, Stein realized that he had a dud on his hands. It was not scary. It was not funny. It was not successful in giving people a backstage peek. It was not working. He needed help, so he placed a want ad for a new design director. Answering that ad was Peter Alexander.

Alexander had come from WDI and was put in charge of the cost analysis for Tokyo Disneyland and Epcot during their construction. When he told Carl Bongirno, president of WDI, that the $800 million Epcot project was actually going to cost $1.1 billion, Bongirno told Alexander, "No. Don't tell anyone. You tell them that they will fire me. That is what happened on the Magic Kingdom."[2] Alexander knew sooner or later that corporate management would find out and, as the newest guy there, they would fire him.

At the age of 30, Alexander was very ambitious, and he learned that WDI was filled with lifers, so there wasn't a lot of room to advance quickly. He said that while he was at WDI he had learned from the best, such as John Hench, Claude Coats, Bob Gurr, and Wathel Rogers, and it was time to move on.[3]

Disney handled a great deal of its ride, show, and overall park development in-house through its WDI subsidiary. As a result, even the smallest additions or changes in the parks had to absorb Imagineering's inflated overhead. The design firm began to bill the park operations for its time and services. Every decision at Disney was based on the attraction's return on investment. Would the new attraction generate enough new attendance or justify an increase in admission to make it economically viable? As a result, many of the creative people were leaving the building.

In early 1982, Alexander interviewed with Barry Upson. After looking at Alexander's experience, Upson told him that he was not qualified for the designer job, but he could work at Universal as his assistant director of planning and development and work on the stuff he did not want to do. Alexander took the job. It was not long before he picked up additional responsibilities when Terry Winnick quit.

During his final days at WDI, Disney executive Dick Nunis took Alexander aside and said, "We had a really good guy, Ed [Ettinger], and he was one of our best guys. And he went to Universal. When he left here, his hair was all black. When he came back six months later his hair was all white."[4] Alexander was soon to understand why.

It started on his first day when the personnel director pulled him aside and suggested that if he wanted to succeed he had to remember, "Universal was every man for himself. We here are soldiers in war." Then, when he attended his very first staff meeting, he entered a large, imposing conference room with a very long table. He took a seat with the rest of the team, and then Jay Stein walked in. Alexander's first impression was "I swear to God the room darkened. This guy had such a cloud over his head." Things only got worse. During this first meeting, whatever Terry Winnick pitched would get a quick "What's the Disney guy have to say?" Alexander was not used to this. He said over at Disney, Card Walker might get upset and yell at somebody now and again, but at Universal, yelling at somebody was elevated to a fine art. What Alexander did not know at the time was Stein had just come back from his meeting with Wasserman where they demanded he find a partner for the Florida project.[5]

It was not long before Lew Wasserman called Alexander in to get the "Disney" guy's candid assessment of Stein's proposal. The land deal in Florida had closed back in 1979, and there were some preliminary plans and a lot of money spent but nothing to show for it. When first asked his opinion of his bosses' plans, Alexander replied that they were OK. Then Wasserman pressed. "What do you really think?"[6] Alexander suggested, "They were a little old-fashioned."

Wasserman demanded more details. "The design was strictly from the mind of Jay Stein and he was not a designer," according to Alexander. "He had a central core laid out of all these themed streets, New

York Street, Hollywood Street. The problem was there was only one side to the set facades, and any movie director will tell you there has to be both sides of the street and returns on either end so that you can shoot the street."[7]

Stein had also proposed a movie musical show. Alexander said, "Movie musicals were no longer a big thing and had not been for some time." Wasserman agreed. He said, "You know, we haven't made a good musical since I have been here. We spent a ton of money on *Best Little Whorehouse* and it barely made it back and I don't think much of musicals." Alexander mentioned that Stein was confident the attraction would be a success. He had signed up a young actor named John Travolta to star in the film. Wasserman replied, "Twenty years from now nobody is going to know who John Travolta is."[8]

Alexander also suggested that the makeup show was not edgy enough for the Universal audience. Some of the shows like King Kong were designed as walk-through attractions. Alexander said, "The first thing you learn at Disney is walk-throughs don't work. People don't like walk-throughs. They want to sit down."[9] Alexander passed the test. He later learned that if he had answered Wasserman's queries differently, he would have been replaced.

Wasserman had had enough. He shut the Florida project down. Stein could continue to look for a partner, but any new attractions would have to find a home in Hollywood or just get filed in a drawer somewhere.

HAVE YOU SEEN
the DRACULA SHOW?

ALEXANDER'S FIRST ASSIGNMENT was the *Castle Dracula* show. Sidney Sheinberg did not think an update would be enough. He was beginning to lose confidence in Stein, so he invited Peter Alexander and Stein's number two man, Bernie Fischer, to meet with him. Sheinberg told them about *Conan the Barbarian*, a movie starring his friend, body-builder Arnold Schwarzenegger. The movie was being released in 1982. Sheinberg thought the sword and sorcery genre seemed like a good fit and something that Disney would never touch. Alexander started to develop a Conan show.

To find just the right person to draft a treatment, Alexander turned to his Rolodex and called Disney Legend Rolly Crump. Crump listened attentively but declined to work on the project. It was live entertainment and he said that really was not his thing. However, he did know somebody who would be perfect for the job. He recommended Gary Goddard.[10]

Goddard had also worked at WDI. He was the youngest person ever hired at the design company. After a few years, he left Disney and became a successful consultant. He was already a big fan of the Conan stories and fully understood the mythology. When Alexander asked him to look at the current *Castle Dracula* show, Goddard came back and said, "That show was just a huge disaster."[11] He agreed with Alexander and Sheinberg that the show was unsalvageable and it was better to come up with a new concept.

Peter Alexander said, "For the first time I harnessed these people who were starting to leave Disney."[12] He was creating a development process that was very different from the way Disney did business. Alexander would rely on a lean team of consultants to implement projects fast and at a low cost.

Alexander wanted to re-create a scene from the movie and demonstrate all of the special effects seen in the film done live. Goddard disagreed. He said, "I don't think re-creating things from the movie is the way to go. You've got to create the spirit, the feeling. You can't get the scares and the thrill in a stage show that you get in a movie because you don't have close-ups or long, lingering shots that build suspense. It is a different medium."[13] A big constraint was Stein's insistence to include an audience participation component. Goddard felt that the use of audience members destroyed the suspension of disbelief necessary to create a solid stage show.

When they were ready, they went to a meeting to sell Jay Stein on the Conan idea. Stein started by looking right at Goddard and asked, "Have you seen the Dracula show? I would be willing to pay a lot of money if someone could make that work."[14] Goddard's heart sank. He realized that Stein was not interested in Conan. Stein wanted his original idea using Dracula and the other Universal monsters to work. Goddard quickly figured out that Stein loved the Universal monsters and that this pitch was going to be an uphill battle.

The men pressed on with their Conan presentation. "What we are doing is going to create the magic of the movies onstage right before your eyes and you are going to have the same visceral and emotional reaction," Goddard explained. "We are going to weave a spell and bring people into it." Stein's reaction was, "How the [expletive] are you going to do that?" Goddard argued, "Just like great theater. Go see some live theater. We're going to add pyrotechnics and the fire-breathing dragon, we are going to do things that nobody has ever seen on stage before and I think if we do this and do this well, people will respond to this and this will be a step forward."[15]

Then Stein stopped them and said, "This is the worst [expletive] idea I have ever seen. I don't care about these audience members. *Conan* is an action film. We should be doing an action play. This storyline is terrible."[16] Now Stein was the one trying to convince the two men to do a Conan-based show without a volunteer from the audience. This was something new for Universal. This would be a pure fantasy show. This would be something Disney would consider if it were not for the source material. Alexander ran with it and made up a new story line on the spot.

As they waited for a decision, Goddard interrupted the silence, "Mr. Stein, isn't it better if you are going to spend the money to have a new show and you could market a new show? Isn't that better than saying come back to a new Dracula show?"[17] That struck a chord. Now they were talking in a language that Stein really understood. They got the green light to proceed.

When Sidney Sheinberg signed off on the project, he told Alexander that he "wanted an 'E' ticket," referring to the highest-priced ticket for a Disney attraction.[18] They started with a budget of $800,000 and ended up spending $3.75 million.

HOW *about a* DRAGON?

THE ADVENTURES OF CONAN: *Sword and Sorcery Spectacular* was a first of its kind. No other live show in any venue combined laser technology, live actors, animated characters, and other special effects to this degree. Gary Goddard and Tony Christopher wrote the 18-minute show, which featured a battle that pitted Conan and Red Sonja against the evil sorcerer Taras Mordor.

Comic book artist Claudio Castellini designed a giant snake to terrorize the audience at the show's climax. Lew Wasserman stepped in and said no to the snake. Wasserman told Peter Alexander, "No snakes, Peter. People don't like snakes." Alexander said, "How about a dragon?" Wasserman replied, "Perfect."[19]

Alexander hired the team at Sequoia Creative to design and fabricate the dragon. Thomas Reidenbach, Dave Schweninger, and Bob Gurr were all Disney veterans. Reidenbach worked on Walt Disney World for eight years, Schweninger helped build It's a Small World at Disneyland, and Gurr, who started in 1954, had been responsible for the Monorail, the Autopia cars, and virtually everything else that moved on wheels at Disneyland.

Originally, the plan was to build three serpents for the climax. One would be 24 feet tall with an 8-foot tongue that shot flames. Two much simpler serpents would have joined it. Instead, cost overruns forced the team to concentrate on building one 18-foot figure. Even at that scale, it would be the largest animated figure built at the time. Reidenbach said, "Earlier in the '50s, Disney did some big dinosaurs in a diorama, but they simply moved their heads and mouths a little bit. The serpent is absolutely and completely programmed into the show to work with live actors. It was out of a whole new realm of animation, although the technology was really there already."[20]

The serpent had to rise 42 feet from the full down position. Gurr said, "As the size of an animated figure goes up things get heavy really fast. The flexible skin can be so heavy it will tear apart from gravity if the design is just to scale up of a regular-size figure."[21] Gurr saw the dragon as a tall, pivoting pole on a gimbal base with a big serpent head stuck on top. The head was 6 feet long and had two long fangs. The serpent could also project fire 8 feet. To enable the effect, an actor stabbed the serpent in the throat and then stood on a pad.

It also had to be reliable. "It's one thing to build a special effect for one take and get through the shot, but it's a whole other ball game when you start building a serpent that has to come on cue every single time," Reidenbach said. "So it did present some problems that heretofore we had not experienced."[22] Gurr recalled a time when an actor was in the wrong position, got slightly burnt, and yelled out, "Watch out, that thing will turn you to ashes." The serpent became known as Ashley. "I cried the first time I saw this happen on opening night," Gurr said. "Poor thing, she was my baby."[23]

Larry Lester was the project manager. Terry Winnick described Lester as "a pusher and a very smart technician."[24] Bob Gurr had worked for Walt Disney and the team that built Disneyland and was impressed with the way Larry Lester got things done. Gurr knew that during construction all of the crafts were trying to get their jobs done, which means they needed to occupy the same space as the other crafts. Lester acted as the space referee. Gurr said, "You better not upset him if you wanted fair access for meeting your installation dates."[25] In the morning, Lester would roll around a chalkboard and give out orders. In the Universal tradition, Gurr said there were "no committees, no coordinators, no printed forms, just Larry barking every morning from this board he pushed around in the dirt."[26]

Peter Alexander said, "[Larry] always wanted to have one thing he designed himself, so I gave him the part of the show where little Conan grabs the sword and lifts it up, and then a big explosion occurs, and then he transforms into big muscle Conan. A double switch. Larry designed that, and he loved it."[27]

In a first for a theme park, Basil Poledouris composed an original sound track that was recorded by the London Symphony. Goddard also included a tribute to his mentor at Disney, animator and Imagineering legend Marc Davis. At the end of the show was the line, "You have faced all the forces and swords and sorcery. Now you must face me and all the forces of hell!" This is the line the villain Maleficent utters as she turns into a dragon in Disney's animated classic *Sleeping Beauty* (1959). Goddard first used the line as a placeholder because he knew no theme park would allow the word *hell* to be part of a script.

He recorded the sound track with and without the word, but when nobody commented, it remained. He was surprised and shocked. Universal was certainly not Disney.

After seven months in production, including six weeks of rehearsals, the show was ready. All of the special effects were coordinated by a custom Intel computer system. An Allen Bradley computer system controlled the actors' interface with all the technical devices. Larry Lester said, "The Allen Bradley serves as the nucleus for all of the digital information that comprises the sensors for all the safety devices. It says, 'if this is true, this is true and this is true, then we can do this.' Essentially, it's the safety device." [28]

The safe use of high-power lasers was especially important. "With each specific laser effect, where there is the potential danger of the actor getting involved in an area where the laser might be, there are pressure-sensitive mats in the floor that require an actor to have a foot on each mat," Lester said. "The minute he lifts a foot, the laser is disabled. If he is not on that mat, then he's someplace else on stage, and one of those places that he could be is in the way of the laser." [29] Another layer of safety was the laser safety officer and the technical director. Both had to press a button that was flashing to enable the special effect.

Just before opening on June 18, 1983, the fire marshal inspected the theater and demanded that MCA install an air-conditioning system. Wasserman and Sheinberg said enough, cut the budget for theming the building, and applied the funds to adding a $400,000 air-conditioning system. Goddard proudly said, "All of the money for the show was spent from the proscenium arch on back." [30] He added, "No one will blame you for having an ugly building. No one will blame you for a bad preshow. If the show sucks, that is what they are going to say." [31]

Unfortunately, the show was not an immediate hit with the public. Tour attendance declined 10% to 2,941,000 in 1983. Alexander said the big crowds went to SeaWorld in San Diego to see a new penguin exhibit. Times were still tough. Sidney Sheinberg said, "We've been hitting ourselves on the head looking for new things to do." [32] He thought his team had come up with a winner.

Although the show did not bring in the crowds, it would become a defining moment for Universal. After the first week, Goddard said to Stein, "Jay, you have fallen into something. You are using real water, real fire, real smoke, real stuff, and the audience responded. I think this should be your mantra from now on. Whatever you do, you won't do the fake stuff like Disney does. You won't use a CO_2 blast. You are going to use a pyrotechnic. It is going to go bang. You will feel the heat." According to Goddard, "With Jay as the guy in charge, we decided to be what Disney could NOT be. We would create 'in your face' attractions. We would not make you a passive observer, but by the greatest degree possible, while remaining safe, we could 'put you in the middle of the action.'"[33] It was also the first time that Lew Wasserman and Sidney Sheinberg could see that the MCA Recreation Group could produce Disney-quality shows. The show became required viewing for the Disney Imagineering staff.[34]

MCA also tried to preserve a little bit of old Hollywood in 1983 and in exchange get a new, low-cost attraction. They offered to place the barn used by Cecil B. DeMille to film *The Squaw Man* (1914), the first full-length motion picture, on its back lot. Daniel Mayer Selznick, Louis B. Mayer's grandson, donated the barn to the Hollywood Heritage Committee and fought to make sure that the barn did not leave Hollywood. A frustrated Herb Steinberg said, "We are doing this as a gesture to save what is really the beginning of the motion picture industry in California." The barn never made it to Universal and ended up just across the street from the Hollywood Bowl.

In anticipation of (nonexistent) larger crowds, MCA funded and built the Universal Center Drive overpass across the Hollywood Freeway in 1983. Making history, this was the first time in California a private corporation took the initiative to build and pay for access across a freeway. The new bridge provided a second entrance to Universal City. The project was part of a much larger $120 million expansion of Universal City, including another hotel and four new office buildings.

A **THREE-CAMERA SHOOT SEVEN TIMES** *a* **DAY**

BY THE EARLY 1980s, the biggest fights at Universal City were not between the cowboys at the stunt show but between Albert Dorskind and Jay Stein. The land on top of the hill was becoming a limited, precious resource. Dorskind was focused on expanding the studio, building a shopping center, office space, and hotels, while the tour needed all the room it could get to handle the crowds. Stein knew he was alone and in trouble unless he could find a productive, profitable use for the land.

Once upon a time, Westerns were the staple of the movie and television business. The mighty cowboy standing his ground against all who might invade was a story told within the genre in a thousand ways. That was no longer the case. Westerns were no longer the go-to genre. This change in the public's taste opened up an opportunity for the theme park team. Maybe they could update the stunt-show genre with a second venue and protect a 2-acre parcel of land near the tour entrance? Stein knew the cowboys were secure in their central location, so this would make for a perfect land grab.

Peter Alexander looked at various Universal intellectual properties to find inspiration. The first concept was going to feature a battle between K.I.T.T., the talking car from televisions' *Knight Rider,* and Mr. T from *The A-Team.* What Alexander did not know at the time was the producers for each of those shows, Stephen J. Cannell and Glen Larson, were once partners and refused to work with each other again. With that idea out of the way, Alexander turned his attention toward developing an A-Team show.

The *A-Team* was a "renegade group of Vietnam veterans who help the innocent while remaining on the run from the military," according to a press release. Alexander was attracted to the *A-Team* because it was a nonviolent show that used a lot of stunts. "[Stephen J. Cannell] said there mustn't be any blood because nobody actually gets hurt on the *A-Team* and insisted that we remain true to his characters," Alexander remembered. "For instance, Cannell said that B.A. Baracus [the tough but gentle character who catapulted Mr. T to superstar status] is not on the show just for his muscles but rather because he's a genius mechanic."[35]

Now that Alexander had the right intellectual property, he needed to think of a clever way of presenting the material. Inspiration came when he was watching the television production team completing a three-camera stunt shoot. "I can do a live show that is just like this big scene with the van jumping, explosions, because they got to get it right," he said. "On a television budget, you could only run that sequence once. So I thought I will do that."[36]

Alexander gathered a creative team, including John Peale, Gary Goddard, and Richard Hoag of Landmark Entertainment Group. Larry Lester was in charge of the set design, and the stunt director was Jim Winburn. The $1.5 million show was placed in a new, 3,000-seat arena. Nothing like this 18-minute show had been done before.

The show was located in fictional San Rio Blanco. From the grandstands, the visitors could see an adobe church, a cantina, a warehouse, and, off in the distance, the parking lot and the front of the Universal Amphitheater. In front of the facades was basically all dirt with dirt hills for the stunts. Although the set was simple, the technology developed for the show would set the stage for later innovations. The show had to repeat up to seven times a day, and Alexander said, "We have developed the show from not only an imagination standpoint but from an engineering standpoint, which will enable the stunts to appear exciting but eliminate most of the risk."[37]

A five-man team of stuntmen performed controlled crashes, rollovers, artillery duels, gunfights, and motorcycle jumps, with plenty of explosions. Every so often, the action would pause and an announcer would explain how some of the stunts were performed. Alexander recalled, "We've got rocket launchers, motorcycle jumps, explosives, and all the elements of the hit television series—only it's live."[38] One of the most memorable stunts was when the Mr. T look-alike jumped a burning van across a bridge.

The show opened on June 16, 1984. At first, the pacing was very slow, and the stunts were in between a lot of dialogue. The Landmark crew was asked to pump up the show, and they did.

Goddard cut the show into two parts. The first part was a preshow that used a shill placed in the audience. Prior to the show's beginning, a show producer would look for a woman with kids in the audience and ask them to play along as if their patriarch was being pulled into the show. The "volunteer" was called up from the audience to help demonstrate some of the stunt techniques used in the *A-Team* show. The first stunt was pretty easy. The second stunt was something that gave the audience pause. The volunteer was strapped into a moving jeep and asked to fire a machine gun.

The third stunt was something no real volunteer would be subjected to, but the result was very funny. He was asked to save a blow-up doll of a woman from a tent before the dynamite could explode. The stunt coordinator told him he had 10 seconds, and the audience would provide a countdown. Goddard said, "It was just like an old Warner Brothers gag. There was a special fuse line that we had rigged that would burn slowly for the first 5 seconds and then burn very rapidly before the count reached 10."[39] Then the tent would explode with the "volunteer" inside. Just like the cartoons, the actor would exit the tent to loud cheers, makeup on his face, and his costume adjusted to appear as if he just survived the explosion.

The second half of the show was all of the special effects of the original show compacted into only 8 minutes. Years later, Disney would copy many of the gags as part of their *Indiana Jones Epic Stunt Spectacular* at the Disney-MGM Studios theme park, including the use of a "volunteer."

For Peter Alexander, the best thing about the *A-Team* show was how it got him back on Lew Wasserman's good side. Wasserman was disappointed that *Conan* ran over budget. When Alexander suggested that he needed to go overtime to finish the *A-Team,* Wasserman exploded. Wasserman picked up his letter opener, started yelling at Alexander, and kept jabbing it in Alexander's direction as he made his points. Alexander pushed back by leaning forward with his hands on the desk, getting very close to the letter opener. In the end, Alexander brought the project in on time and under budget. His reward was the honor of sitting with Wasserman at lunch in the Commissary.

In September 1984, the original stunt team walked off the job in a wage dispute. The team asked for a $5-per-performance raise, while management offered them a cut in pay from $65 a show to about $50 a show.[40] This kind of tactic was not unusual. Actor Ron Schneider said of the Universal management style, "I began to chafe at their way of handling the front-line staff. The folks who had made the place a success."[41] This action forced the park to let the team go and to hire and train new actors who worked for an outside firm. It would not be long before the entire show was replaced with something even more sophisticated and spectacular.

BANANA BREATH

KING KONG WAS A MILESTONE in early cinema when it was released in 1933. In the RKO film, special effects wizard Willis O'Brien created a lifelike giant ape using stop motion animation. The film fueled the imaginations of generations of filmgoers. So it was no surprise that other filmmakers wanted the chance to remake the classic film.

In 1974 Universal began negotiations with RKO General, who owned the rights. At the same time, movie producer Dino De Laurentiis and Paramount Pictures were also negotiating with RKO General for the rights. Hollywood being Hollywood, the two studios immediately sued each other.

The legal dispute was settled in 1976, with De Laurentiis winning the rights to release his film. Universal was forced to wait 18 months after the Paramount version was released. As a consolation prize, Universal did gain the rights to use the character in its theme parks. When the De Laurentiis film bombed at the box office, Universal put off producing its version for decades. However, Jay Stein immediately started thinking about how the character could help the tour.

Stein decided that King Kong would be the centerpiece of the Florida studio and tour. He hired the Elliott Group Architects in April 1981 to work on preliminary concepts for a Kong attraction. The original show was going to be similar to a scene in the 1976 movie in which the 45-foot ape is put on display in a New York theater, gets angry, and threatens the audience. The audience would sit passively and watch the figure go through the motions. Stein did not think the idea hit the mark. He liked shows that were in your face. There was not a "Jay Bang."

Stein then asked legendary art director Henry Bumstead to take a look. At the time, the concept for the park was a walking tour of the front lot and a tram ride through the back lot. Bumstead suggested that the Kong attack the tram as it passed over New York bridge and then reach into the vehicle. Peter Alexander expanded on the idea. To add suspense, the tram would first come upon a scene of destruction where Kong had already been. The tram would slowly go around the corner, and the visitors would hear Kong on the move. When they came to the bridge, there he would be, and he would rock the bridge. Bob Ward drew up the initial drawings.

Peter Alexander immediately contacted Bob Gurr and Gary Goddard. Gurr would be assigned to create a realistic King Kong, and Goddard would write the script. They started tossing around ideas based on Bumstead's original concept of King Kong reaching into the tram. The location became the Brooklyn Bridge, and instead of him reaching into the tram, he would grab the bridge and rock it back and forth.

Now they had to convince Stein. Gurr had his team build a 30-foot-tall painted Kong and place it on top of the workshop at Animated Show Productions in Arleta, California. Gurr wanted to show Stein and his "limo full of suits" just how big the figure would be.[42] Stein was impressed, and he authorized a test starting with the legs. Gurr suggested they start with the head, and Stein agreed.

Barry Upson said, "We told them it had to stand up to very close scrutiny with the face 6 feet from the audience. It had to have different moves like snarls, nose flares, raised eyebrows, scowls, flashing eyes, and hot, moist breath with a 'banana smell.'"[43] Gurr built the head out of fiberglass tubing like an aircraft space frame. At 37 feet, Kong would be the world's largest computerized creature. The first prototype did not work. "It was sculpted with the mouth slightly open," said Gurr. "The result was the mouth barely moved, and it had a stupid duck quack look when trying to close."[44] To fix the problem, he tried a thinner skin and a lightweight mouth with simple air cylinders.

To create the illusion of life, Kong had 29 different computer-controlled, air-driven movements, including a movable tongue and nostril flare. Ten movable plates in his face created realistic expressions of anger and ferocity. Gurr was so proud of his gorilla head that he could be occasionally found riding inside of the head as it went through its motions. In fact, at one point he had eight coworkers inside of the head enjoying the ride. He even did this while the show was open to visitors.

Gurr worked on the Mr. Lincoln figure at Disneyland and knew that audio-animatronics were best seen far away. Alexander wanted the gorilla within 3 feet of the tram. He admitted, "It defies the normal rule of animated figures."[45] Kong's 10-foot head would be so close to the guests that they had to attach his whiskers one by one by hand. It took nine experts to sew his 660 pounds of fur into place. Adding to the terror were the 32 giant teeth in his mouth.

Now that they knew they could build a believable King Kong, the next question was where to put the tour attraction? It was Lew Wasserman who suggested placing the show building near the New York Street set on the back lot. After all, the action was going to take place on the Brooklyn Bridge. A purpose-built soundstage was placed on the location where the fleet vehicles used to be stored. Inside of the 26,000-square-foot soundstage were full-scale buildings for the close-ups, forced-perspective miniatures used in the mid-ground, and "cut out" flats used in the background.

unofficial **TIP**
In tribute to MCA's latest acquisition, the television station featured in the King Kong attraction was named WWOR-TV.

The show's first act was designed to ramp up the feeling of danger. Looking through windows of New York apartment dwellers, the visitors in the tram could see a television news broadcast showing shots of a news reporter in a helicopter. Suddenly, the screens would go static and the fuselage of a Hughes 500 would fall toward the tram. Larry Lester was a helicopter pilot in Vietnam and sent Bob Ward an aircraft to use in the ride.

Stein wanted people to feel threatened, so Bill Watkins designed a sliding bridge with Teflon plates that slid the 88,000-pound tram 3 feet back and forth as Kong "rocked" the bridge. The gorilla's arms were supported from the bridge cables, thereby utilizing free (nonmechanical) animation. "Right opposite of the King Kong figure, there was absolutely nothing, just a black wall," Alexander recalled. "If the guests happened to look away from Kong as he 'attacked' the tram, they looked at a blank, black wall and the illusion of being in New York City was broken." Concerned, Alexander went to Jay Stein to see if he could free up more funds to fix the problem. Stein shook his head no and said, "If they are looking away from Kong, you have real problems."[46]

One of the most talked about gags was King Kong's banana breath. "The idea came to me while I was making one of the first presentations on the L.A. show," Peter Alexander recalled. "I just sort of tossed in the idea that as the tram passed Kong, the last thing the guests would experience was Kong's 'banana breath.' After hearing this, my boss, Jay Stein, lobbied for bad breath, but I kept mentioning 'banana breath' in each and every pitch. After awhile, it became accepted."[47]

How to implement the gag was Larry Lester's doing. They tried using a rotted wet sheepskin coat under a fan but that did not work. About a week before opening, Alexander asked his father, a veteran aerospace engineer, what might be available to blast a scent to a specific point yet not create so much that would linger through the rest of the building. His father suggested an impeller. So Alexander and Lester went shopping and found an impeller. Lester went about modifying it so that it would do the job. They bought some banana juice and installed the device into Kong's head. It worked.

Universal really ramped up the promotion machine for King Kong. MCA produced a national advertising campaign, taking ads in *USA Today, Daily Variety, The New York Times, Orlando* (Fla.) *Sentinel, Chicago Tribune,* and *The Hollywood Reporter*. Public previews began on March 18, 1986, and the official opening was on June 14. Alexander recalled, "On opening day, Jay was prepared to give the team notes. When he heard a tram full of visitors cheering as they exited, he was heard to say, 'Well, I guess they don't need these notes."[48]

King Kong cost $6.5 million to build. That was about half the cost to produce a feature film. But it was money well spent. Steve Lew said, "We're more dependent on the world economy, the price of oil and the price of airline fares than most theme parks. We are definitely excited about the rest of the year."[49] He was right to be so confident. Attendance topped 4 million people for the very first time.

Bob Ward said, "Kong was the first really significant milestone. With its powerhouse combination of immersive scenery, high-octane special effects, and the incredible animated King Kong figure, it launched an all-new era of storytelling at Universal."[50] Steve Lew told the press, "King Kong will do what Jaws did in the mid-'70s, which was to make us a major outdoor attraction."[51] In a display of confidence he added, "We have faith in the product and intend to be here many, many years. We believe in the tour and in Southern California as a destination."[52]

Sidney Sheinberg took the opportunity to get in a dig at Michael Eisner. On opening day, MCA placed a full-page ad in the *Orlando Sentinel* with Kong's face that read, "Plan on seeing us in Florida one day." Sheinberg said, "Let everyone wonder . . . Let Disney wonder."[53]

The JAY BANG

JAY STEIN SAW THE WRITING ON THE WALL and knew that the *A-Team* television show was going to be canceled. In 1987 he ramped up production for a replacement show based on Sylvester Stallone's memorable character, Rambo from the movie *First Blood* (1982).

Gary Goddard was hired to do a treatment for the live action stunt show. He had crafted an action-packed script filled with amazing special effects. The script dealt with drug trafficking, and at one point audience members would be taken hostage. The climax was going to be a Harrier jet flying over the stage set. Then Sidney Sheinberg saw the script.

Stein quickly went looking for a new show producer. Barry Upson and Peter Alexander hired Phil Hettema, who was a Disney veteran. Hettema grew up in Southern California and was a big fan of Disneyland. He suggested he got a job in the wardrobe department at the age of 18 due to his imposing height. At 6 feet, 6 inches, he could reach higher than most. While at Disney he learned everything he could about the character department. After attending the Art Center College of Design he went to work for the 1984 Los Angeles Summer Olympics and Sid and Marty Krofft.

When Hettema joined the Planning and Development group, there were only six people. Peter Alexander and Bob Ward were focused on Florida, so Hettema was put in charge of Hollywood. He was excited to get started, and at his first meeting on his first day, he turned to his new coworker Molly Rose with a big smile and said, "Glad to be here." He knew he would be working on the big new Rambo show. This was the biggest thing he had ever done. Her response was not what he was expecting. "Boy, you have your work cut out for you."

A confused Hettema replied, "Yeah, but we have a script." She said, "Oh, didn't you hear? On Friday they threw out the script, and you are starting over again." Hettema was given one week to rework the show without the hostage-taking. Plus, he had to use the special effects that were already in production. Hettema quickly learned why the rush. "It was bad juju and Sid just didn't want to do it," Hettema said.

Before the week was up, Hettema was sitting in Larry Lester's office working on the presentation of the new script when Jay Stein stopped by. This was the first time the two men had met. Hettema mentioned that he was looking forward to presenting his ideas the next day. Instead, Stein said, "No, no, just show me now." After the quick presentation, Stein told the men, "No, no. This is not good enough. This is not big enough." He was looking for the "Jay Bang."

Actor and writer Ron Schneider defined a Jay Bang as "that moment when the guest will be stunned, shocked, surprised or splashed with water."[54] Hettema learned that a Jay Bang was a 10 on an imaginary scale. Peter Alexander coined the term. The creative people who worked for Stein learned to write the "Jay Bangs" right on the front cover of their scripts. "That was really part of his business personality," said Barry Upson. "The showmanship. He wanted fear or some version of fear or a surprise to be part of every attraction."[55] Gary Goddard was impressed with Stein's intuition. He said, "Over the years, Jay had developed a sense of what best fit the Universal Studios customer, as opposed to Disneyland and Knott's Berry Farm and other such places."[56]

When Stein asked Hettema how many tens there were in the Rambo show, he suggested five or six. When Stein asked for an example of a 10, Hettema's reply was not satisfactory. "[Stein] loved to intimidate people," Hettema said. "He loved to have somebody stand up to him as long as they knew their stuff." Hettema turned the table and asked, "What is a 10 in the *A-Team* show?" Stein hesitated and then said, "Well, the exploding shack, that's a 10." Hettema replied, "Jay, that's a four." The two men got along well after that. Hettema learned, "The main comment I would get back when I would submit a written treatment to Jay was NGE. Not Good Enough."[57]

Six weeks later, Stein tells Hettema that the show is no longer based on *Rambo*, but on the popular television show *Miami Vice*. He also told him that the June opening date would not change. The ad buys had already been placed. It was now March. The massive set was redressed to look like a West Indies smugglers' hideout. The reworked script called for a speedboat to race through a simulated mine field. Since there was no lagoon, a production assistant was sent out to the site to mark off the outline for the lagoon with chalk dust for the construction crews. When asked how deep Hettema told them, "Just dig 5 feet deep and we will get back to you." Along with the speedboat, the show would feature a hovercraft.

To add to Hettema's woes, he had to deal with noise issues. The *A-Team* show featured a lot of explosions, and the surrounding residential neighborhoods were not very happy learning about a bigger show. The pressure was on to reduce noise impacts during expansion talks with the surrounding community. As a result, the technical team developed a new type of radio system to ignite the pyrotechnics.

The 15-minute *Miami Vice Action Spectacular* opened on July 4 at a cost $5.4 million. Out front, where dirt hills once stood, a concrete lagoon large enough to allow a speedboat to race through a simulated mine field was built. The show began with a raid on the hideout by Miami detectives Sonny Crockett and Ricardo Tubbs (portrayed by stuntmen look-alikes for actors Don Johnson and Philip Michael Thomas). Like before, an on-set director who explained what was going on to the audience stopped the action sequences.

The show was loaded with more than 50 high-tech special effects with plenty of pyrotechnics. To ensure the safety of the six cast members and audience, many of the special effects could only be triggered with the consent of the actor hitting a fail-safe switch and the technical director in the control booth pressing a redundant button.

Additional protection came from pressure-sensitive mats embedded into the set and positioning the grandstands at least 20 feet away from the action. Any set pieces that were meant to fly away were either restrained by short cables or made of light rubber or plastic materials. Phil Hettema said, "You don't need this advanced technology for film and television. In film you only do it once and use five cameras to make sure you get it."[58] At the theme park, they would perform the show up to eight times a day.

A new sound system was installed to enhance the sound effects. Hettema said, "Most of what people hear [on television] is not the sound of dynamite—it's enhanced electronically. We're giving the audience what they want to hear."[59] A highlight was two stuntmen bursting out of a building, guns blazing, riding a mine car along a roller coaster track, and being launched into the air after an explosion.

The climax included an aerial attack from a helicopter that rose from behind the set and was shot down by the detectives. The full-scale mock-up was mounted on a mechanical arm that gave the appearance of hovering in mid-air. For many months after the show opened, the helicopter sported rotating blades. However, during one technical rehearsal the blade ripped off and went right into where the audience would have been sitting. The special effect was rebuilt. The *Miami Vice Action Spectacular* would last for eight years.

1 Laura Landro, "High-Tech Thrills at Universal Studios," *The Wall Street Journal*, 7 Nov. 1983.
2 Peter Alexander, interview with author, South Palm Beach, FL, 21 Oct. 2013.

3   Ibid.

4   Ibid.

5   Ibid.

6   Ibid.

7   Ibid.

8   Ibid.

9   Ibid.

10 Rolly Crump, interview with author, Anaheim, CA, 3 Aug. 2013.

11 Gary Goddard, interview with author, North Hollywood, CA, 12 Jan. 2014.

12 Alexander, interview with author, 21 Oct. 2013.

13 Goddard, interview with author, 12 Jan. 2014.

14 Ibid.

15 Ibid.

16 Alexander, interview with author, 21 Oct. 2013.

17 Goddard, interview with author, 12 Jan. 2014.

18 Alexander, interview with author, 21 Oct. 2013.

19 Ibid.

20 Beth Anderson, "Universal's Adventures of Conan Bewitches Audiences with EFX & Live Action," *On Location,* Aug. 1983.

21 Bob Gurr, *Design: Just for Fun* (Bloomington, CA: Ape Pen Publishing and Gurr Design, 2012).

22 Anderson, "Universal's Adventures of Conan."

23 Gurr, *Design: Just for Fun.*

24 Terry Winnick, interview with author, Las Vegas, NV, 25 Feb. 2014.

25 Gurr, *Design: Just for Fun.*

26 Ibid.

27 Alexander, interview with author, 21 Oct. 2013.

28 Anderson, "Universal's Adventures of Conan."

29 Ibid.

30 Goddard, interview with author, 12 Jan. 2014.

31 Ibid.

32 Laura Landro, "High-Tech Thrills."

33 Gary Goddard, e-mail to author, 9 Apr. 2014.

34 Goddard, interview with author, 12 Jan. 2014.

35 Karen West, "Attraction Produced by Local Resident 'Mayhem' Erupts in Universal Studios Show," *The Simi Valley Enterprise Weekender*, 24 July 1984.

36 Alexander, interview with author, 21 Oct. 2013.

37 West, "Attraction Produced by Local Resident."

38 Ibid.

39 Goddard, interview with author, 12 Jan. 2014.

40 West, "Attraction Produced by Local Resident."

41 Ron Schneider, *From Dreamer to Dreamfinder* (Clearwater, FL: Bamboo Forest Publishing, 2012).

42 Gurr, *Design: Just for Fun.*

43 James Bates, "For Sequoia Creative, Offbeat Jobs Are Its Meat and Potatoes," *The Los Angeles Times,* 11 Nov. 1986.

44 Gurr, *Design: Just for Fun.*

45 John McMasters, "King Kong," totallyfuncompany.com/kongmedia/articles/kong1
    .htm (accessed 11 May 2013).
46 McMasters, "King Kong."
47 Ibid.
48 Alexander, interview with author, 21 Oct. 2013.
49 Linda Deckard, "King Kong Project Universal Studios Tour's Most Costly," *Amuse-
    ment Business*, Apr. 1986.
50 Adam J. Bezark, "Painting with Bulldozers," *The 15th Annual THEA Awards* (Burbank,
    CA: Themed Entertainment Association, 2009).
51 Deckard, "King Kong Project."
52 Ibid.
53 Vicki Vaughan, "MCA Teases Disney With Movie-Studio Ad," *Orlando Sentinel*,
    19 Mar. 1986.
54 Ibid.
55 Barry Upson, interview with author, Napa, CA, 10 Mar. 2014.
56 Gary Goddard, note to author, 9 Apr. 2014.
57 Phil Hettema, interview with author, Pasadena, CA, 7 May 2014.
58 "USH Opens A-Team Live Action Stunt Show," *The Los Angeles Times,* 27 June 1985.
59 Sean Grady, "Universal's High Tech 'Vice' Show," *The Los Angeles Times,* 27 June 1987.

CHAPTER 5

The SUNSHINE STATE

 ## SEAWORLD

FOR JAY STEIN, UNIVERSAL CITY was a good start, but if he wanted to grow the MCA Recreation Group, then he needed to think bigger. He began with an agreement to run tours of the Washington, D.C., mall and Arlington Cemetery in 1970. Stein was trying to build up a track record for managing other National Park assets where tours would be an integral part of the experience, such as Yellowstone and the Grand Canyon. This led to an agreement to manage the Yosemite Valley. The Recreation Group also looked at managing the Kennedy Space Center in 1967, buying Marineland in 1969, and developing a resort in Colorado in 1972.[1] Stein even looked at a possible partnership with Kirk Kerkorian, the owner of the MGM Grand Hotel in Las Vegas.

The one destination that Lew Wasserman was especially interested in was SeaWorld. On March 21, 1964, a group of UCLA graduates opened the 22-acre marine park in San Diego. Milton C. Shedd, Ken Norris, David DeMott, and George Millay started out with six attractions. It turned out to be a huge success right from the start, with more than 400,000 visitors within the first 12 months.

By the early 1970s, SeaWorld had expanded to two parks, San Diego and Ohio. Then came a park in Orlando in 1973. SeaWorld was the leader in its segment of the business. Buzz Price said of a SeaWorld acquisition, "MCA wanted it as a desirable building block for their position in the attractions business."[2] Wasserman and Jay Stein felt that adding the marine parks to the studio tour would firmly establish MCA as a major player within the industry. Better still, the marine park would be complementary to the Studio Tour and not in competition with Disneyland.

Wasserman got his chance to buy SeaWorld in October 1976. MCA was flush with cash from the success of Steven Spielberg's *Jaws,* and they made a hostile bid for SeaWorld. They began by purchasing 8% of the available shares of stock and then offering $22 per share for the rest. The total value of the offer was $35 million. Buzz Price said, "This put the management into a state of shock because they were frightened by the perceived image and style of the men in black suits at MCA."[3] David DeMott, SeaWorld president and chief executive, said of the offer, "They really low-ball."[4]

To fight off the merger, SeaWorld hired investment banker Kidder Peabody and went looking for a white knight, according to Buzz Price. A letter from Milton C. Shedd, chairman of SeaWorld Inc., stated "more could be obtained for our shareholders than pursuant to the MCA offer—and possibly on a tax-free basis."[5] They found their white knight in Harcourt Brace Jovanovich (HBJ), a publishing company. When HBJ made a slightly higher offer than MCA, the management at SeaWorld was relieved. It was their feeling that HBJ would be so busy with its publishing business that they would leave the marine park's management alone.

When MCA heard of the new offer, they considered whether to submit another bid. Mel Ziontz, who represented MCA in its acquisition efforts said, "When some of Lew's people said MCA should make a higher offer, Lew started screaming! He said he wasn't going to get in a bidding war and be made to look like a fool and pay more than the company was worth."[6] Jay Stein argued that it would be worth it and pressed Wasserman to make a deal. Wasserman refused. MCA dropped out, and HBJ bought SeaWorld for $65 million, or $30 per share. Upon reflection, Jay Stein suggested, "I only knew Lew to indirectly acknowledge a mistake one time, 10 years after the fact, but it was huge. He said 'Maybe we should have bought SeaWorld.'"[7]

As it turned out, HBJ was not a hands-off owner. After HBJ took over, they installed a management team of finance people. They decided to compete head-on with other theme parks and move toward more live entertainment and away from their strength, animal shows. "Everybody wants to be in show business," Buzz Price said. Mr. William Jovanovich would tell them to paint the fences orange and other hands-on directives, many of them capricious and authoritarian."[8] They also overbuilt. When they opened a new park in San Antonio, Texas, it was 100% complete. With all the money gone, maintenance suffered and it was tough to add anything new. Even marketing dollars were cut.

Wasserman was not done yet. He started looking at other parks to acquire. In December 1979, he made a bid of $11.47 million for Cedar Point, an Ohio amusement park. Harold Haas, MCA's treasurer, said, "It's a business with which we're familiar. We see Cedar Point as a good investment."[9] The Cedar Point board rejected the MCA bid. When gas prices and interest rates shot up, Wasserman's taste for amusement parks subsided.

MCA even made another attempt to buy SeaWorld when the marine parks were once again up for sale in August 1989. HBJ was in trouble and subject to an unfriendly tender in the United Kingdom. To raise cash, they decided to put SeaWorld up for sale. This time, there were plenty of suitors. MCA was interested. So was Anheuser-Busch. Also bidding on the marine parks was a team of ex-managers lead by George Millay, Jan Schultz, and Bob Hillebrecht.

Buzz Price was hired by MCA to take a look at the properties and to make an assessment. He found the parks dirty and the workers rude. He felt that the only way to save the parks was to double the current levels of capital investment.[10] Price recommended a bid of $700 million for the parks, but MCA learned from the last experience and put in a bid for $900 million. It was still not enough. Anheuser-Busch countered with a bid of $1.1 billion and was successful. The new management understood the problems and immediately invested $2.5 million to build the Forbidden Reef pool. Buzz Price said, "It was the best thing that could ever have happened to SeaWorld. It ended up in strong hands. Had MCA prevailed, SeaWorld would have been subject to four [now five] subsequent changes of ownership at the parent company level."[11] On October 19, 2009, SeaWorld was sold once again, this time to the Blackstone Group, for $2.7 billion.

SHOW ME *a* PARTNER

IN 1964 WALT DISNEY BOUGHT 27,443 acres in Central Florida. He dreamed of building a demonstration community dedicated to imagination, technology, and showmanship. Instead, his brother Roy O. Disney and his successors tossed aside Walt's city idea and in 1971 opened a vacation empire.

Now that Disney had something going in Florida, Lew Wasserman thought it prudent to hire Buzz Price to take a look at the Orlando market. Price came back in 1972 and said that it was too early for Universal to make a move into Florida. Wasserman trusted Price and put any thoughts about Florida aside.

"We really started on Florida in 1974, about the time we were doing the Collapsing Bridge," Terry Winnick said. "Jay was thinking about going to Florida." With Walt Disney World and SeaWorld nearby, Stein wanted to be where the action was, and there was no question that Orlando was the place. Walt Disney World Resort was becoming the most popular vacation destination in the world. Barry Upson said, "Disney had established the fact there was a really strong market. That was the rationale for buying the property."[12] To learn about the Florida market, Stein sent Winnick to meet with architect and planner Robert Lamb Hart, who worked on the master plan for Walt Disney World and Epcot Center.

Stein decided to clone Universal City and place it next door to Disney in Florida. Disney owned the theme park sector, SeaWorld owned the marine park sector, and Universal owned the industrial tour sector. All he had to do was to convince Lew Wasserman that buying land in Florida would be a good investment.

Wasserman was not interested. He did not think there was enough demand for production space to justify a second studio, and the interest rates were continuing to rise, making such an investment risky. Also, he did not want to compete directly with his friends over at Walt Disney Productions. If MCA was going to make a move into Central Florida, somebody had to be the champion. Jay Stein took up the challenge.

To convince Wasserman that a Universal studio and tour in Florida was a viable idea, Stein decided to design a park that would get his bosses excited. Terry Winnick drew up Stein's plans for the first version of the Florida studio and tour.

Winnick said, "It was Hollywood but new and improved. The emphasis was on what a tour needed but we considered every aspect of filming because Jay wanted to make sure that whatever we did in Florida was an improvement not only on what the tour was doing but from a filming stand point, because he knew he had to get filming to go there. Nobody was going to come there if there wasn't something going on."[13]

Unlike Hollywood, Stein could not exploit an authentic back lot that had seen decades of filmmaking. Winnick said, "The original plans called for a front lot walking tour with shows for entertainment and a back lot with "super-duper version of the Tram Tour."[14] The soundstages would have allowed guests to peek at actual productions. Just in case production did not come to Florida as Stein expected, Winnick was prepared to "stage" productions for the visitors' enjoyment.

The Florida back lot would be approximately 60 acres, making it the largest in the entire film industry. Different cities and settings would be represented along the lot's 22 streets. Destinations included an Oklahoma oil field, the Alps, and the Everglades. The trams would encounter many of the same special effects seen in Hollywood, plus a new derailed roller coaster effect and a minefield. The 40-acre front lot entertainment center would have the same kind of shows as Hollywood. Of the four soundstages, two would be reserved for the tour.[15]

The Florida film and television industry used to be hot in the 1960s. Shows like *Flipper, Big Ben,* and *The Jackie Gleason Show* were hits. However, those days were long gone. To figure out how much space should be set aside for production, Stein turned to Bill DeCinces, manager of back lot operations and somebody who knew more about production facilities than just about anybody in Hollywood. Surprisingly, he said, "There is not much need for it. Florida is not going to turn into a film magnet."[16] At most, the market could support maybe two soundstages. This meant the studio tour had to be the real moneymaker. This also meant the studio idea was starting to edge toward competing with Disney.

Stein took his proposal to Wasserman and Sheinberg for their approval. Barry Upson said, "During that first presentation, they let Stein get about half way through and then stopped him. They said, 'We don't like this.'" Then they started to rip Stein apart. Wasserman told Stein, "You and a couple of executives have put this thing together and I don't have any confidence in your judgment. I don't know what the hell you think you are doing, and until you get a partner that agrees that this is a good design it is not going anywhere."[17]

At the time, MCA was in a partner phase. The attitude around the office was "if [an idea] is so good, somebody will want to do this with us," according to Terry Winnick. "It doesn't matter if it is Discovision, it doesn't matter whether it was Spencer Gifts, it doesn't matter if it was the tour. Why should we take all the risk? If it is that good, show me a partner."[18] Wasserman made Stein an offer. If he could find a partner willing to go 50–50 with MCA, he could then build his studio and park in Florida.

Wasserman liked the way things were in Southern California. Winnick said, "Walt [Disney] set out to build a theme park. Universal did not start out to build a theme park."[19] The Florida landscape was littered with the carcasses of failed tourist attractions such as Little England, World Peace Academy, Winter Wonderlando, Bible World, Hurricane World, Tarzanland, Western Fun World, and Night World. Universal was always happy to pick off just enough visitors to make a tidy profit with a minimal investment. Now Stein wanted to spend a lot of MCA's money. All he had to do was find somebody as excited about the idea as himself.

 ## *The* **SUPERBLOCK**

AT MCA, IF SOMEBODY GAVE YOU AN OPENING, you took it. Jay Stein knew what he had to do and started to put the parts together to close the deal. He needed the perfect location at a rock-bottom price. He needed the right people to make something great happen. He still needed a financial partner.

At the time, Stein's planning and development department consisted of Terry Winnick. Stein needed more help, so he called Barry Upson, the man he replaced back in 1967. Upson was running the San Diego Zoo in 1978 when Stein asked, "Do you want to come back and see if you can get it right the second time?"[20] Upson said yes and was put in charge of the fundamental planning. Upson said, "I think the decision was being competitive because that is the frame of mind we had in Hollywood. The tour in Hollywood grew so rapidly it was clear we were taking a bite of Disney and that gave us the motivation to think about being competitive in Florida."[21]

Wasserman gave Stein permission to look for no more than 400 acres. That was the same size as Universal City. Wasserman's rationale was they had not used up all of the Hollywood land yet, so why would Stein need more property in Florida. This was not going to be Walt Disney World.

In November 1978, a real estate broker from Winter Park, Florida, named Allan E. Keen got a call from an old college friend. This friend wanted to introduce a client who was looking for 250–400 acres in the Orlando area. There was one stipulation. Keen could not know the identity of the client. Keen agreed because the referral came from somebody he knew. He went shopping.

By late January 1979, two men from his mystery client came to Florida to check out what he found. Without disclosing their employer, Terry Winnick and Barry Upson drove around the region with Keen looking at properties. The men saw a site near the entrance to Walt Disney World, and they both agreed that it was the best location. However, others suggested it was too close, so they moved on to the number two site.

The Major Realty Corporation, a large real estate concern that was owned by the Bass family of Fort Worth, Texas, owned the next property on the list. The property was known as the Superblock. It was approximately 10 miles north of Walt Disney World and closer to Orlando. Upson said, "The Superblock was a very attractive place because it had utilities out in the streets already."[22] The property was zoned for a large shopping center, so the land use entitlements would not be an issue.

The still-anonymous client gave the go-ahead to negotiate a deal. All was going well, and an agreement was drafted and about to be signed until the seller insisted on knowing who the buyer was. Wasserman wanted to stay behind the scenes and declined. The stalemate lasted for months. It was not until April 1979 that Keen learned that his client was MCA. As a result, he went straight to Florida Gov. Bob Graham to intercede. The governor called Al Lawing of Major Realty and told him that the project would be good for the local and state economy. It worked.

Barry Upson recalled the day when Lew Wasserman and Sidney Sheinberg finally relented and allowed Stein to buy property in Central Florida. The group of men was standing on top of the Sheraton Twin Towers shortly before the papers were signed. When it opened in 1973, the Sheraton was the first major resort hotel along that portion of International Drive. Across the street was the Superblock. Upson did a spiel about their plans for the property and then waited for their response. After a few minutes, Wasserman blessed the project and Universal Studios Florida was born.

On November 22, 1979, MCA announced that they intended to buy 312 acres for $4.5 million. Very few details were released at the time. Herb Steinberg said they were considering an East Coast version of their Hollywood facility. He suggested that it would be "purely a tourist attraction right now" and that "production facilities might be considered down the road."[23] Steinberg recalled, "When we opened the tour back in 1964, we didn't know it would become as wildly successful as it has" and quick to remind everyone that Universal Studios Hollywood had become the third-largest tourist attraction in the United States behind the two Disney theme parks. "We are the world's single largest retail outlet for film," Steinberg boosted. "People take more pictures here than anywhere else."[24] Stein still needed to find a partner.

 # BIGGER *and* BETTER

MCA COMMISSIONED A STUDY in 1980 to determine the potential interest in a Universal Studios Tour in Florida. The Magic Kingdom at Walt Disney World had been open for almost eight years and Epcot Center had not yet opened. The study found that 69% of Walt Disney World guests would be interested in visiting Universal. The men wanted to see the immersive action attractions, such as the recently opened Battle of Galactica. The women wanted to see the makeup show. The researchers learned that those over the age of 50 did not care much for Jaws, but they certainly did like to shop and eat. It seemed that everybody liked the shows involving audience participation. They also learned that what attracted people to Universal was the charisma of Hollywood and the desire to see how movies or TV shows were made.

After the study, MCA was becoming publicly bullish on the tourism market in Orlando. "By 1985, Orlando will be the biggest tourist destination in the world," according to Herb Steinberg. "It's projected that more than 40 million visitors a year will come to that part of central Florida. As the biggest, busiest studio in the world, Universal wants to be where the action is."[25] When asked about the film production facilities, MCA was a little more cautious. "Nobody knows what the character of the films produced there will be or if any pictures will be made there," according to Steinberg.[26]

In June 1981, MCA purchased an additional 111 contiguous acres from Gulf Oil for $8 million. One of MCA's first regulatory hurdles was to seek an exemption from a lengthy and expensive six-county environmental review of its project. Walt Disney World property was outside of the jurisdiction of city of Orlando, Orange, and Osceola Counties. It was managed by a unique quasi-public-private agency called the Reedy Creek Improvement District, set up by the Florida Legislature shortly after Walt Disney's death in 1966. Walt Disney Productions had complete control over what they could do with their property. MCA was subject to rules governed by the city, the county, and the state.

The Florida Department of Community Affairs had determined that the project would have regional impacts and that MCA would be liable for conducting studies before they could proceed. The studies would have to cover a six-county region and would cost millions of dollars and many months. MCA executives were livid. They suggested to the agencies that they would walk away from purchasing the property if this was a requirement. MCA felt they had other options and could buy land near the Orange County Civic Center in southwest Orange County or near the Walt Disney World interchange and I-4. The city realized it would lose out and quickly exempted MCA, stating that the property had already been approved for development. Peter Alexander described the property at the time "where palmettos and scrub brush stood, every so often one of the group would pull out a pistol to shoot a snake."[27]

On July 24, 1981, MCA finally announced plans for a "bigger and better" version of its California facility called Universal City Florida. The $170 million facility would include a complete production studio with dressing rooms, prop warehouses, soundstages, and a back lot with 18 sets. The sets would vary from a Pacific Island village, an old European town, and the Sinai Desert. Just like Hollywood, a tour and entertainment center would complement the studio operations. Long-range plans called for a 300-room hotel, restaurants, a museumlike display of Universal Studios biggest box office hits, and an enclosed 5,000-seat amphitheater. They said that site preparation would begin in 1982 and their hope was to open in late 1984.

The press had a field day speculating on MCA's motivations. Some said that MCA was trying to get away from all of the unions embedded in Hollywood. In 1980, a series of strikes damaged the bottom line. Others suggested that there was a shortage of soundstages due to the growth of home entertainment options. The opportunity was there.[28]

When Universal announced it was building the studio tour, there was always the question of whether this would this be a working studio or a theme park. The general feeling was that visitors wanted to see the real thing. Authenticity was very important. Tony Hoffman of A.G. Becker Inc. said, "I'm not so sure that if you take that kind of theme park out of Hollywood, they're going to have the same kind of impact." Other analysts were more optimistic. Harold Vogel of Merrill Lynch, Pierce, Fenner & Smith Inc. said, "I don't see it being a major increase in the company's earnings anytime this decade, (but it's) a nice addition to the MCA group of companies."[29]

Gov. Bob Graham was especially pleased with the news. He said, "Florida has a special interest in the motion picture and television industry," and the project was "an important signal to the movie industry and the rest of the country and the country's business community."[30] The 22 local labor theatrical craft unions were excited about the announcement. *The Los Angeles Times* stated, "The big winner in the Universal decision appears to be Florida, which has aggressively sought to bring more movie production into the state."[31]

INTEREST *in the* SUBJECT

NOW THAT MCA HAD PUBLICLY COMMITTED to building a new facility, it was crunch time for Stein to find a partner. In the one-story Jack Webb bungalow on the front lot across from the MCA Tower, Stein set up shop. He hired Alden Butcher and Metavision to create a slide show "using a combination of existing stuff and conceptual renderings," according to Terry Winnick. "It had music and special lighting. It used 16 projectors, state-of-the-art. It was used for potential partners and other sponsors."[32] Bob Ward drafted many of the drawings, and Jay Stein's future wife, Susan O'Malley, was responsible for finding corporate sponsors.

Sidney Sheinberg suggested they start with Paramount Pictures. He had claimed that the men who ran Paramount, Michael Eisner and Barry Diller, were his "two best, most trusted friends." Because of this personal relationship, he said, "It would have been unthinkable that we would have discussed this first with any company other than Paramount."[33] The two studios had most recently done business when they formed the USA Network in 1980.

A July 29, 1981, meeting was set up at the bungalow on the Universal lot between representatives from both studios. Confirmed at the meeting were Sidney Sheinberg and Jay Stein from Universal, Paramount chairman Barry Diller, and his executive vice president Arthur Barron.

Although Michael Eisner and the Disney legal team have denied it over the years, Paramount president Michael Eisner was also in attendance. According to Jay Stein's agenda, Eisner was there. Another person at the meeting, MCA development executive Peter Kingston, said, "Michael Eisner was very definitely there. That's the only time I've met the man. He asked very intelligent questions. I was very impressed by his grasp of the subject and equally his interest in the subject. He wasn't there to waste his time."[34]

Even Barry Diller agreed with Universal's side of the story. When Sidney Sheinberg's lawyers looked into filing a suit against Disney, they discovered that Barry Diller, who had moved on to Twentieth-Century Fox, and Michael Eisner had been feuding over the theme parks. Diller had insisted that Eisner was at the meeting.

Over the next 2 hours, MCA representatives presented a slide show of color renderings and blueprints, going through their early plans street by street and running through the numbers. In the end, MCA and Paramount were not able to come to an agreement. *The Los Angeles Times* speculated that Charles Bluhdorn, chairman of Gulf & Western, Paramount's parent corporation, killed the deal.[35] Sheinberg, Wasserman, and Stein were disappointed by Paramount's decision.

Over the next few years, they approached RCA, Taft Entertainment, Lorimar, and the Bass Brothers of Fort Worth, Texas. Ironically, after the Bass Brothers learned of the opportunities in Florida, they became owners of 25% of Disney stock and helped to force future Disney CEO Michael Eisner to increase investment in the Walt Disney World property, thereby setting up the battles to come.

Jay Stein was still looking in 1984 when he made a presentation to Michael Milken, the junk bond king. Instead of investing in the park concept, Milken used the confidential information to convince casino owner Steve Wynn to buy just under 5% of MCA's stock. Wasserman was furious.[36]

After knocking on so many doors, a discouraged Sheinberg said, "I think there was a kind of feeling 'why is MCA looking for a partner if this is so good? Why don't they do it themselves?' We had simply decided that we did not want to expand into Florida all on our own credit."[37] Stein would have to continue looking for that all-elusive partner.

1 Harrison A. Price, Harrison Price Company, "Confessions of an Itinerant Consultant," speech to Universal Creative of Universal Studios Recreation Group, 24 June 1999, Series III, Box 60, Folder 116, Harrison "Buzz" Price Papers, Special Collections & University Archives Department, University of Central Florida Libraries, Orlando, FL.

2 Harrison "Buzz" Price, *Walt's Revolution by the Numbers* (Orlando, FL: Ripley's Entertainment, 2004).

3 Ibid.

4 Kathryn Harris, "MCA Takes the Cautious Road as Competitors Plunge Ahead," *The Los Angeles Times,* 22 Nov. 1981.

5 "SeaWorld Officials Move to Thwart MCA Takeover," *The Los Angeles Times,* 2 Nov. 1976.

6 Connie Bruck, *When Hollywood Had a King: The Reign of Lew Wasserman, Who Leveraged Talent into Power and Influence* (New York: Random House, 2003).

7 Ibid.

8 Price, *Walt's Revolution.*

9 Martin Baron, "MCA Seeks 11% of Ohio Theme Park Operator," *The Los Angeles Times,* 4 Dec. 1979.

10 Harrison "Buzz" Price, Harrison Price Company, to Frank Stanek and Tony Young, "Progress Memorandum Re: SeaWorld to Frank Stanek," report number 706, 3 Aug. 1989, Series I, Box 53, Folder 1119, Harrison "Buzz" Price Papers, Special

Collections & University Archives Department, University of Central Florida Libraries, Orlando, FL.

11 Price, *Walt's Revolution.*

12 Barry Upson, interview with author, Napa, CA, 10 Mar. 2014.

13 Terry Winnick, interview with author, Las Vegas, NV, 25 Feb. 2014.

14 Peter Alexander, interview with author, South Palm Beach, FL, 21 Oct. 2013.

15 Karen Lachenauer, "The Clone That Will Be Universal," *The Los Angeles Times,* 25 Oct. 1981.

16 Alexander, interview with author, 21 Oct. 2013.

17 Ibid.

18 Winnick, interview with author, 25 Feb. 2014.

19 Ibid.

20 Upson, interview with author, 10 Mar. 2014.

21 Ibid.

22 Ibid.

23 "MCA Announces It Has Bought Property in Florida," *Orlando Sentinel, 22 Nov. 1979.*

24 Vernon Scott, "Universal Considering Central Florida Tourist Attraction," *Tampa Tribune,* 10 June 1980.

25 Ibid.

26 "MCA Says Future Uncertain for Making Films in Florida," *The Los Angeles Times,* 24 July 1981.

27 Susan G. Strother, "Theme Park Sprouted from a Field of Dreams," *Orlando Sentinel,* 3 June 1990.

28 Pamela Hollie, "MCA Sets Sights on Florida," *The New York Times,* 29 July 1981.

29 Harris, "MCA Takes Cautious Road."

30 John Wark, "MCA Raises Curtain on Orlando Stardom," *Orlando Sentinel,* 25 July 1981.

31 Pamela Moreland, "MCA to Build Universal City Florida," *The Los Angeles Times,* 22 Nov. 1979.

32 Winnick, interview with author, 25 Feb. 2014.

33 Ellen Farley, "Behind the MCA-Disney War in Florida," *The Los Angeles Times,* 23 Apr. 1989.

34 Ibid.

35 Hollie, "MCA Sets Sights on Florida."

36 Bruck, *When Hollywood Had a King.*

37 Hollie, "MCA Sets Sights on Florida."

CHAPTER 6

The BATTLE BEGINS

ONE LARGE, RAVENOUS RAT

IN THE EARLY 1980S, things were not going smoothly at Walt Disney Productions. At the time, Disney was best known for its theme parks, bad live-action films, and rereleases of old animated classics. Disney's new president, Ron Miller, was trying to move the stagnant studio forward, but the conservative chairman, Card Walker, hampered him. Miller was responsible for Disney's entry into the home video market, Tokyo Disneyland, Touchstone Films, the Disney Channel, and many other innovations. However, a behind-the-scenes power play by Roy E. Disney, son of the company's cofounder, Roy O. Disney, was brewing.

In 1984 Walt Disney Productions became the target of numerous takeover attempts. One person taking a serious look was Lew Wasserman. Miller and Wasserman were old friends. A meeting was set up between Miller, Wasserman, and Disney's new chairman, Ray Watson. It seemed like a deal was possible. The only thing left was deciding who would be president of the new company.

Watson wanted Ron Miller to get the job. Wasserman preferred his right-hand man, Sidney Sheinberg. When Sheinberg recognized that he could be the deal breaker, he declined the job in favor of Miller. However, Wasserman would not be deterred. He continued to insist that Sheinberg should get the job.

Felix Rohatyn, the investment banker advising MCA, told Wasserman, "Do it. A year from now you'll get rid of Miller and make Sid president."[1] Wasserman did not take his advice. MCA could have likely purchased all of Disney for $1.5 billion at the time, but Wasserman opted not to. Barry Diller said of his friend, "It was Lew's inflexibility that caused him to blow deals he should not have blown. He and Jules [Stein] had built the best company. They should have owned the world. And had they made this deal with Disney, everything would have been different."[2]

Then on September 23, 1984, after a very public management coup, Michael Eisner became chairman/CEO and Frank Wells became president. It was not long before Michael Eisner would start to test his old friends at MCA. It began with a conference call shortly after Eisner took over at Disney. Then came the announcement to the shareholders on February 7, 1985, about a studio and tour at Walt Disney World. To reassure stockholders, Eisner told the gathering that the studio theme park would be very different from any other Disney park. "Sensitive to the cost overruns at Epcot, we decided to build Disney-MGM Studios with a much-smaller capacity, while leaving room to expand in the face of demand," he said.[3] Moreover, Eisner said, it "meant that it could be less-finished in its look than our other two parks." He also suggested that the price of admission might be less than the Magic Kingdom and Epcot Center. Disney's park would be half the size of the one envisioned by Universal. Eisner figured it would take Universal at least four or five years to build their park, even if they found their partner right away. Eisner wanted his park built in three years.

All of this was happening while MCA was trying to jump-start the Universal City Florida project. Lew Wasserman met with Florida Gov. Bob Graham in October 1984, while they were both in Los Angeles. Wasserman suggested that Florida loan MCA $150 million from the state's $8 billion pension fund to build the studio and tour. In exchange, MCA would build a bigger studio and park than they originally announced. The pension fund would hold the first mortgage on Universal's 423-acre property as security. Wasserman also suggested that the state invest $35 million per year for five years to produce films in Florida in exchange for a cut in the film's profits. Wasserman reminded the governor that Universal had already invested $40 million in developing its Florida property, and if Graham were serious about making Florida the Hollywood of the East, this would be his best bet.

Graham was receptive to Wasserman's proposal. However, to make it happen, the governor would have to push a bill through the state legislature. It quickly became apparent that this would not be an easy task. A Tallahassee lobbyist and former Disney employee named Bernie Parrish began pressing Florida legislators to kill the bill even before it could come to a vote.

Shortly before the Florida Senate vote on the Universal proposal, Michael Eisner wrote a letter to Sheinberg and Wasserman. Although Eisner denied any personal involvement in the efforts to kill the deal, he did outline Disney's advantages over Universal, including "our land, existing infrastructure, marketing commitment, hotels, monorail, research and development organizations . . . and sources of financing." Eisner added, "We do not want to hurt you. If differences remain, let us keep them private as befits our companies as members of the same industry." Nevertheless, Parrish was successful in killing the bill on June 1, 1985.

On July 8, 1985, a month after the Universal bill died, Disney revealed even more details for its Disney-MGM Studio Tour. They carefully studied what Universal had done in Hollywood to find ways to create an even better experience for the guests. The initial list of attractions for the $300 million park included two stunt shows (*Slapstick* and *Epic*), the audience participation Video Theater, and a tram/walking tour of the production facilities.

Eisner knew that "by launching a studio tour at Walt Disney World, Sid [Sheinberg] would later argue, we were invading Universal's turf."[4] However, he felt that Disney was the company who should be outraged. He argued, "It was Universal that was seeking to capitalize on Disney's efforts, by proposing to build a theme park in Orlando just a few miles from Walt Disney World. It was obvious that they'd chosen their site in an effort to feed off the millions of visitors who were already traveling to Orlando to visit our parks."

Although the entertainment industry was known for being a cutthroat business, Sidney Sheinberg felt Eisner's actions crossed the line. He argued, "This is not the same as two companies competing for a movie or TV slot. The studio tour business had been something we had developed over 25 years. This business doesn't exist anywhere else in America to my knowledge."[5] Sheinberg said, "When it came to our horrible realization that they (Disney) were going to do what they were going to do, there was a horrible sense of personal and corporate betrayal."[6]

A report in *Newsweek* suggested the feud was becoming more personal than business driven. According to the magazine, "MCA and Stein both feel scorned; the former because it failed to woo Eisner from Paramount, the latter because Eisner once declined to hire him for a Disney job."[7] Eisner recalled, "The day before it was announced that Frank and I would be going to Disney in 1984, I received a call from Sid Sheinberg, the president of Universal. He'd heard the rumors that I might be headed for Disney."[8] Sheinberg told Eisner, "Taking the Disney job is the stupidest thing you could possibly do. It's still in play. Eventually, it's going to be taken over by one of the raiders. You'd be crazy to go there." Eisner chalked it up to sour grapes and suggested in his autobiography *Work In Progress,* "If I did accept the Disney job, Sid knew that we would be very aggressive competitors with Universal not just in movies but in theme parks."[9]

Erwin Okun, Disney senior vice president for corporate communications, tried to shrug off MCA's claims. He said, "Universal's arguments are built totally on sands of fantasy. They have been planning their park since 1981. Now we have opened ours quite successfully, and I think they are, right now, sucking on particularly sour grapes."[10]

Sheinberg called Eisner an "egomaniac" with "a failure of character."[11] With regard to the 1981 discussions, he said, "It's like having discussions with a brother or a cousin. These kinds of disclosures are made in the strictest confidence. They are not made on the assumption that one day it is going to come up and bite you."[12]

MCA was so upset about Disney's announcement that it threatened to pull out of Florida. Sidney Sheinberg told the *Orlando Sentinel*, "Disney's ability to decimate you by acting in a predatory way is chilling. Do you really want a little mouse to become one large, ravenous rat?"[13] He warned that if Universal left Orlando, it would become a "company town."[14]

SATURDAY AFTERNOON
in GLENDALE

HOW DID MICHAEL EISNER COME TO BELIEVE that he could outwit his competition by building a studio and tour in Florida first? It started on a scorching September Saturday afternoon. With the temperature nearing 100°F, Eisner, Frank Wells, and Eisner's 14-year-old son Breck paid a visit to Walt Disney Imagineering (WDI) for the first time. The new leadership at Disney had a great deal of experience with motion pictures and television, but the theme park sector of the business was very new to them, and they were keen to learn all they could.

The room at WDI was filled with elaborate scale models of attractions. Walt Disney believed that models were the best way to develop an attraction, and the tradition continued with his successors. During the visit, they were pitched on potential projects, such as Star Tours and Splash Mountain. Eisner recalled, "Among the most promising was a pavilion for Epcot devoted to the history of movies and featuring Audio-Animatronics figures—lifelike replicas of famous actors re-creating memorable scenes from their movies."[15]

Long time Imagineer Marty Sklar said, "When Epcot opened in October 1982, two years before Eisner and Wells came to Disney, our creative team at Imagineering began an analysis of subjects and stories we felt were missing from the Future World area, and countries we especially hoped it include in the future at World Showcase."[16] He wrote, "In our own assessment, we found a glaring omission: there was no pavilion related to show business. Yes, the park itself was all about entertainment and fun—but what about exploring television, the Broadway stage, or how movies are made?"[17]

According to Sklar, "We worked on a plan to have people go outside EPCOT, but we couldn't figure out how to handle the parking and other problems."[18] Eisner recalled, "The more we talked about the attraction, the more we recognized that it had the potential to become a separate, gated park."[19] Eisner told the Imagineers, "Let's develop this a little more."[20]

Eisner and Wells had learned that attendance at Epcot Center had dropped off sharply after the initial excitement in 1982. The leadership at Disney was struggling with a very expensive park that had the perception that it was a permanent world's fair. The park was gaining the reputation of being boring. Mickey Mouse and the other familiar Disney characters were not allowed in the park. They could only be found at the Magic Kingdom a short monorail ride away. This turned off families with small children. To attract more people to Orlando, Disney launched national television ads for the first time.

Within days of starting at Disney, Eisner and Wells met with Sid Bass and investor Richard Rainwater to discuss options to monetize the Florida property. The Bass family had just ended a two-year joint venture with MCA "to cooperate and act jointly with respect to their respective holdings" in Major Realty Corp., which owned land adjacent to MCA's site for the new park. One idea floated at the meeting was building a third gate at Walt Disney World. Another theme park might keep guests on property longer. "The idea was to encourage them to increase their length of stay. It was two to two and a half days and we wanted to get it up to three or four days," according to Wells. The new leadership started looking around for ideas.

Publicly, Walt Disney Productions had been saying that they welcomed Universal. After all, SeaWorld opened in 1973 and there were plenty of other local attractions. Internally, Eisner knew that Universal would compete directly with Epcot and cannibalize the education-based park. Thomas Elrod, vice president for marketing at Disney said, "I can't believe that there won't be some losers."[21]

The management team at Disney was afraid that visitors would skip Epcot and drive down to Universal. The whole purpose of the Walt Disney World expansion was to keep people around an extra day or two. Instead of visiting Epcot, they would visit Universal.

Momentum gathered for a Disney response when long-time executive Dick Nunis met with Michael Eisner and Frank Wells to discuss the five-year master plan for Walt Disney World. Nunis had been suggesting for years that Disney open production studios in Florida. "After Walt's death, we decided it would be a fantastic thing to bring Hollywood to Florida," Nunis said. "We tried the idea with Card Walker [then president of Walt Disney Productions], but we couldn't get the studio executives to agree to it so we decided not to do it." He tried again when Ron Miller took over the company, but with the same result. Both Walker and Miller were hesitant to reinvest because of the high initial price to build Epcot Center. When Eisner asked Nunis, "Dick, we've got a lot of land in Florida. Do you think we could put a studio tour there?" Nunis paused and replied, "Would you like to see the plans?"

Michael Eisner may have sensed weakness in his old friends. He knew they had been looking for a partner for years without success. He sensed they needed him more than he needed them. Marty Sklar, head of WDI, said, "The widespread belief was that the success of Universal's tour in Hollywood was dependent on the fact that real production took place on those studio back lots. How was a park outside Orlando, Florida, to make that same marketing statement, which Michael believed was a must?"[22] Theme park designer and former Disney Imagineer Gary Goddard was more blunt. He said, "[Eisner] wanted to block Universal. He thought if he could get a studio tour going first they wouldn't bother coming."[23]

Eisner was confident that if Disney built it, Hollywood would come. "Some artists, I thought, would jump at a chance to relocate," he said. "By comparison with Los Angeles, Florida offered less-expensive housing, no state income tax, and a more-relaxed lifestyle."[24] Bob Allen, director of the facility, said, "We can build more stages as the demand increases. We have plenty of land. It wouldn't surprise me if we needed more stages within the next five years."[25]

Disney's production facilities were slated to open with four soundstages. The largest would measure 30,000 square feet with a second stage at 15,000 square feet. There would also be two smaller 7,500-square-foot stages. As a way to attract productions, Disney touted its state-of-the-art light rigging system. The light pipes were lowered with computerized wenches to waist level. Rough focus is done, and only the final lighting has to take place on ladders. The technology saved time and money. The studio would also open with seven warehouses full of props. Rounding out the studio would be a back lot, postproduction areas, craft and specialty shops, and a theater that would show daily outtakes from on-site productions to visitors. A new access road would be built to make it easy to approach from the freeway.

Jeffrey Katzenberg was not so sure. He was in charge of animation, and he felt that most of his animators would not want to be exiled in Florida to work in the demonstration animation facility. Although most of the movie and television soundstages would be open to the public via catwalks high above the action, Eisner quickly learned that he would also need to build some hidden soundstages if he wanted to attract any major productions.

The **DYNAMIC DUO:** *Spielberg and Drabinsky*

THE MEN AT MCA WERE STILL REELING from Disney's announcements about Florida and trying to figure out how to compete or even to get into the game. Just like a classic Hollywood drama, sometimes the future needs a little push. Although Stein had yet to find a partner and Sidney Sheinberg was still cool to the idea, he respected the effort that Stein was giving. Like all great Hollywood producers, Sheinberg could recognize talent and was good at connecting the right people. If Stein was going to persist, then maybe he needed a powerful creative ally at the studio—somebody Sheinberg could trust to make sure Stein did not throw all of MCA's money away. Sheinberg turned to director Steven Spielberg.

Late one night, Peter Alexander and Craig Barr were animating Bob Gurr's giant King Kong figure for the tram tour in a soundstage on the back lot. In came Spielberg and his bodyguard Larry, a former Navy SEAL, riding on their golf cart. The director was impressed with the fluid, realistic motions of the gorilla's giant head and wanted to find out what was going on.

As he approached the programming console, Spielberg said, "I heard you guys know what you are doing." Alexander replied, "I always knew what I was doing."[26] Then it hit the director. The two men knew each other. In fact, the two were college roommates and Spielberg was the best man at Alexander's wedding. They had not seen each other in six years.

Spielberg said, "I didn't know you were doing this." Alexander replied, "Yeah, you want to see Kong do his thing?" They gave the director a demonstration of the figure going through a range of motions. When they were done, Spielberg said, "This is pretty good." Then Spielberg asked Alexander to go over to Disney to see what they were doing with Star Tours. Spielberg said, "I just had a little discussion with George Lucas and George said, 'Well, it's too bad you're hooked up with Universal because they don't know what they are doing.'" The next day, Alexander was called into Sidney Sheinberg's office for a "Spielberg Visit Debriefing Meeting." Sheinberg got a call from an excited director who was not only impressed with the Kong figure, but the entire attraction. This endorsement was very important to Sheinberg. His confidence in these expensive attractions was growing.

Alexander followed up on Spielberg's suggestion—he went on Star Tours and thought the attraction was amazing. Disney had just spent $40 million. King Kong in California was only going to cost $7 million. When Alexander got back, Spielberg said, "If you guys can do this . . . why don't you see what you can do with *Back to the Future?*" This was the beginning of Spielberg's long relationship with the Universal theme parks. With Spielberg's backing, Stein knew he had the power to get things done and to out-Disney Disney. Wasserman and Sheinberg would certainly support him now.

Stein had Spielberg's support, but he still needed to find a partner to help finance the project. Jay Stein's dream of a resort to rival Walt Disney World in Florida was starting to feel just out of reach. He really believed he had everything he needed to blow Disney away and to turn Universal Orlando into the go-to destination for Central Florida tourists.

No matter how hard he tried, and he did try, Stein could not find anybody willing to take the chance. Not only that, Terry Winnick suggested, "Jay did not want to find a partner because he did not want to listen to anybody."[27] Stein's luck was about to change during a pitch meeting with Garth Drabinsky of Cineplex Odeon.

Cineplex Odeon was a Toronto-based entertainment company that was 50% owned by MCA. Wasserman and Sheinberg respected and trusted Drabinsky. During the meeting, Peter Alexander would describe the various attractions and Drabinsky would shout out, "Home run!" Phil Hettema described Drabinsky as "a showman and had a big vision for taking a big leap to do something over the top, which was not Sid and Lew's deal."[28] He told Stein he was interested in becoming his partner. According to Terry Winnick, Drabinsky was the catalyst. For everyone who worked for Stein, it was a relief. Alexander said, "Jay [Stein] lived and breathed the Florida project. It would not have happened without Drabinsky."[29]

On December 9, 1986, MCA announced that Cineplex Odeon was on board. The hope was to open the studio production facilities by 1988 and the theme park the following year. Construction costs were estimated to be $175 million to $290 million. MCA expected as many as 6 million guests that first year. Sidney Sheinberg said, "We have every expectation that we'll do well. We will have something that takes a back seat to no one's tour."[30]

In reference to Disney's plans, Sheinberg suggested that MCA would "successfully compete with any other theme parks that might seek to mimic or capitalize on the highly successful experience we have developed."[31] Terry Winnick said, "Disney took the tram and they took the visitors center, our makeup show, the back lot tour, the soundstage. They took the stunt show and made it Indy. So we took theirs. We wanted to make the Disney version of the Universal Studio tour."[32]

IT IS *a* LITTLE WAR

AT A LAVISH ANNOUNCEMENT CEREMONY in Florida on March 27, 1986, Eisner, Frank Wells, and actor/comedian Bob Hope arrived in a 1920s automobile and stood upon a 1930s-style movie set. Eisner told the press that the Disney-MGM Studios theme park would be set on 100 acres near Epcot Center and was expected to open in late 1988 or early 1989.

Florida Gov. Bob Graham welcomed Disney's announcement about the theme park, but he was even more excited about the production facilities. One of the priorities of his administration was to try to establish Florida as a motion picture production alternative to California. Disney coming to the state was considered a major achievement. Jeffery Katzenberg, Chairman of Walt Disney Pictures and Television, publicly agreed: "We also hope our production facilities will be a catalyst for the growth of a satellite motion picture and television industry in Central Florida. We have been much impressed by the state's program to encourage production there."[33] Katzenberg suggested that Disney would ramp up annual production to 15 or more live action films, 15 or more television movies, and 6 cable movies, and he could use the additional studio space. He also quietly mentioned that MGM was not planning to use the facility for production, regardless of what the governor said.

It was very important to Michael Eisner that the rest of Hollywood take Disney's new production facilities in Florida seriously. He could only beat Universal at their own game if people were able to experience real productions under development. To that end, Disney opened a satellite animation studio with a staff of 71, where guests could watch them work while looking through plate glass windows from elevated platforms. Overhead were monitors explaining what was going on. To provide additional context, a 22-minute feature narrated by Walter Cronkite and Robin Williams walked guests through Disney animation history. Disney also produced three Roger Rabbit shorts to be shown in the theater as part of the program.

For live-action productions, Disney's East Coast studio opened with three soundstages. The largest stage was 15,000 square feet and the other two were 7,500 square feet each. Disney took out full page ads in *Variety, The Hollywood Reporter, Millimeter, Electronic Media, Wrap,* and *Film and Video Production* magazines, stating, "If you want expert opinions on where to shoot your next feature, ask your production manager and your children. Anything you can do in Hollywood, New York or Texas, you can do better and cheaper in Orlando. And Disney World is also a great place to spend your allowance."[34] To lure projects, Disney touted a state-of-the-art, fully computerized light grid system that greatly reduced the time to reset lighting, a large pool of experienced technicians and talent, and all of the equipment a production would need.

However, it was a struggle. The soundstages remained surprisingly quiet. Tony Alley, a representative for the International Alliance of Theatrical Stage Employees, said, "The sound stages Disney has now aren't entirely conducive to filmmakers. Stars don't always like tourists looking down into Disney's sound stages to watch them work."[35] Many producers had complained that Disney was asking for "too many concessions to tourists and don't offer enough to producers."[36] By the spring of 1990, Disney was starting to hint that four more soundstages were under development, and none of those would be part of the Disney-MGM Studio theme park.

Eisner tried to placate the creative community. He said, "The heart of this company is motion pictures." But he added, "The studio, if not for the attraction, would go under or we'd be on our knees to the government."[37] Disney public relations man Charles Ridgway was hopeful and said, "I think the fact that there are two studios being developed here probably makes it more likely that significant movie and TV industry will develop here."[38] Suddenly, Universal opening a studio up the street was a benefit to Disney. Over time, Eisner felt confident that the production facilities could stand on their own. He was wrong.

Over at Universal, Jay Stein's reaction toward the new Disney park and studio was more blunt. "I think they're very vulnerable," he said. "It IS a little like war. It means that when you invade you make damn sure that your army is big enough and strong enough to win." He suggested that Disney was "offering their guests approximately one-third of what we're offering."

Stein was not alone in his assessment. Bradley Braun from the University of Central Florida said, "The big question is can they [Disney and Universal] maintain the momentum after the novelty wears off?"[39] Tom Powers of Goodkin Research said Disney might benefit by opening first, but most people associate Universal with motion pictures more than they do Disney.

Jay Stein promised, "Across the board we're going to deliver a more-impressive entertainment experience. [Universal] needs to create and deliver an entertainment experience that is so different and superior that we can assure ourselves that we're going to capture enough segments of the market to make this thing profitable."[40]

YUPSCALE ENTERTAINMENT

THE BATTLES BETWEEN UNIVERSAL AND DISNEY would not be limited to Florida or the parks in Southern California. In 1987 Michael Eisner decided to bring the fight right to Universal's front door.

Walt Disney believed his company could not only entertain, but that it could also change the way people experienced the public realm. He proved this with Disneyland and tried to apply those lessons to a wide range of projects, including a demonstration city, a ski resort, and an arts college. Those projects would become his all-consuming passions during the last years of his life. It did not take long for Eisner to realize that he now held this power in his hands. He was ambitious, and he was anxious to use the power. One day Eisner told John Titian of Tishman, who was building two hotels near Epcot at the time, "John, I'm 44 years old. I've made more money than I ever dreamed of. Now I want to be on the cover of *Time* magazine. By using the most controversial architects in the country, I will establish Disney as a serious patron of the arts."[41]

In the fall of 1985, Disney formed a partnership with James W. Rouse's acclaimed Enterprise Development Company. James Rouse was an incredibly successful, well-respected, and socially conscious developer. Some of his best-known projects include the planned community of Columbia, Maryland, and festival marketplaces, such as Faneuil Hall in Boston, South Street Seaport in New York, and Baltimore's Harborplace.

Rouse had been an admirer of Walt's talents for placemaking from the beginning. In a keynote speech before the 1963 Urban Design Conference at Harvard University, he said, "I hold a view that may be somewhat shocking to an audience as sophisticated as this: that the greatest piece of urban design in the United States today is Disneyland." It was this mutual respect that Eisner used to bring the companies together.

The two companies began to look for opportunities to build family-entertainment centers at key urban locations. "We want big population-based cities," according to Charles E. Cobb Jr., CEO of Arvida Disney Corp.[42] There were three projects that made it to the development stage: Texposition in Dallas, Navy Pier in Chicago, and the most controversial, Disney-MGM Backlot Studio in Burbank. He suggested, "If we do it right, it's going to have a major impact not only on the urban core of a city we select but on the whole region."[43]

The projects would have something for everyone by combining a festival marketplace, a Disney entertainment complex, and a regional shopping center. During the day, the festival marketplace would attract both locals and visitors and become the regional shopping and dining destination of choice. Disney officials were quick to point out, though, that the complex was not a mini-theme park and there would be a wide variety of entertainment, rides, shopping, and dining options to attract visitors. At night, the atmosphere would change to satisfy the adult seeking fine dining, "yupscale" entertainment, unique lounges, and venues such as the Adventurer's Club. Most important, the overall environment would be so delightful people would visit just to be there.

Michael McCall, Enterprise's development director, said the partnership would be good business. "While Disney's per caps and profitability reigned supreme, Rouse's attendance records were extraordinary, yet garnered by a mere fraction of private capital investment."[44] "A 'synergistic slam dunk' was the strategic order of the day; a product whereby Rouse throngs spent Disney-level dollars, as a result of a modest investment, when compared to the then-record-setting expense of Disney's EPCOT."[45]

The Texas and Chicago projects did not make it past the drawing board, but the Burbank project in 1987 would become a new battleground between the two companies. Burbank was the hometown of

The Walt Disney Company and so close that Wasserman and Shein-berg could see the location for the project from their office windows. What they heard and saw only made them mad.

For 12 years, Burbank had been looking for someone to build a regional shopping center on a significant piece of vacant property on Third and Magnolia, right in the heart of "Beautiful Downtown Burbank," as comedian Johnny Carson used to say. At one point, Ernest W. Hahn Inc. had an agreement with the city to build a conventional $158 million mall, but the deal fell through. When Robert R. Bowne, a Burbank City Councilman, heard the news, he suggested, "Why don't we let Disney dream a dream for Burbank?"[46] That is exactly what the leadership of Burbank set out to do.

Without telling other members of the City Council, Council-woman and former Mayor Mary Lou Howard contacted Michael Eisner and invited him to have lunch with her and Burbank City Manager Bud Ovrom. During the 2-hour lunch, Eisner sketched out on napkins and tablecloths some of his ideas for what to do with the property. Eisner remembered, "I was having a fabulous time. That's what the creative process is all about."[47]

Disney proposed to build The Disney-MGM Studio Backlot at an estimated $150 million–$300 million. WDI was in charge of the design, Disney Development was in charge of the project economics, and the Rouse team was responsible for filling the place with retailers. It was expected to attract as many as 15 million visitors a year. That was more than Disneyland or the Magic Kingdom. The city hoped that the complex would generate $1 million–$3 million in new taxes annually.

The 40-acre project would have featured a man-made lake, a fantasy hotel, and restaurants that changed decor with the season. Other features included an animation production studio and a radio and television media center. The 18-inch "Burbank Ocean" would top the six-story parking garage, and a massive waterfall would screen the structure from those passing by on the nearby I-5 freeway.

To expedite the project, city officials negotiated a property agreement with Disney at the bargain price of $1 million on May 5, 1987. City hall watchdogs claimed that the offer was too low and suggested the property was worth closer to $50 million. MCA officials were also troubled by the deal. They claimed that they were denied the opportunity to bid on the property.

Even more sinister, after the deal was announced, Jay Stein claimed that Disney executives offered to drop plans to build the Burbank project if MCA would abandon the Florida project. Stein described the communications as "blackmail tactics." Sidney Sheinberg would not disclose who made the offer. He said, "It doesn't serve our purposes at this point to reveal who made the communication, to whom it was made, and how we learned about it." Cineplex Odeon's Garth Drabinsky, MCA's partner in Florida, confirmed, "The communication was made to the venture."[48] The Walt Disney Company denied the charge. In June 1987 MCA filed suit to overturn the Burbank deal.

It was a surprise to many Hollywood observers when a month later Sidney Sheinberg and Michael Eisner were spotted at the Registry Hotel near Universal having breakfast. Disney vice president Erwin Okun said, "It was a breakfast that Michael called for, because he thought it would be constructive, but part of the agreement was that neither of the two of them would discuss it publicly."[49]

The development agreement with Burbank allowed Disney exclusive rights for six months to develop its plans and then an additional six months after approval from the City Council. If either side was dissatisfied after one year, the city could solicit other development options. It would not take that long.

By October 1987, Disney was claiming that it had problems attracting a major retailer and that they were scaling back their plans. Internally, writer Michael McCall said they "overshot the target by misunderstanding the dynamics of translating down theme park attractions to the commercial environment dominated by malls, and transforming developer-driven retail merchandising up to the level of attractions."[50] When Michael Eisner learned in February 1988 that the cost of the Disney project had skyrocketed to more than $618 million, he admitted, "I would say it's some time off before we break ground, a couple of years maybe."[51] On April 8, 1988, Disney sent a letter to Burbank officials withdrawing from the agreement. When asked for his assessment, Sidney Sheinberg said, "I don't want to talk anymore about anything that we feel toward Disney. We love everybody. Peace, love, and friendship."[52]

ESTIMATES *in the* BILLIONS

WITH THE MATTERS IN BURBANK SETTLED, it was time to announce to the world that Universal Studios was ready to compete directly with Disneyland. In 1988 Jay Stein announced a three-year expansion that was expected to cost $142 million. New attractions would include the Star Trek Adventure, *Earthquake,* Back to the Future: The Ride, and the E.T. Adventure.

Stein proudly told the press, "I have never seen the numbers of what this property [the hill] is worth, but I have read several estimates in the billions."[53] He was right. Universal City had become an important asset for MCA. The company valued the 400-acre property as worth only $6 million to reduce property taxes, but a more-accurate market value was in excess of $1.2 billion.[54] Much of the value centered on the park's 4 million annual visitors.

The Universal tour had a reputation as a place to visit once, or with out-of-town guests, but not a park to frequent like one did at Disneyland. At the time, roughly 78% of Universal's visitors were from outside of Southern California. The mix at Disneyland was closer to 50–50. That was the driving force behind the expansion. When asked if MCA could catch Disney, Stein said, "Absolutely."[55] Sheinberg agreed, "With these mega-additions, the Universal Studios Tour will complete its evolution from a 1964 'industrial tour' to what we believe will be among the most exciting and innovative recreational attractions in the world."[56]

To succeed, MCA had to overcome three obstacles: not enough parking, not enough land that was not already dedicated to production, and residential neighborhoods adjacent to the studio that were getting angrier and better organized every time MCA wanted to expand.

The solution was a parking structure. Not just any parking structure. Tucked up against a rugged hillside that was used as a backdrop for the 1950s television Western *Laramie*, MCA built a brand-new, $58 million, seven-story parking structure. At the bottom of Laramie Canyon was an acre and a half of land. By building an inverted pyramid, they created 4.5 acres of new land for the Entertainment Center and 20 acres of new parking that could hold 2,850 cars. The parking structure sat conveniently in the middle of the property, thereby avoiding conflicts with the neighbors.

"The bottleneck always has been parking," said Stein. "We have always believed the attendance [potential] was there, but we lacked the ability to accommodate the autos and buses. Now we'll be able to handle them."[57] The park was now able to handle as many as 5.5 million visitors per year.

On the top of the structure would be the next marquee attraction in Hollywood: Back to the Future. This presented its own problems. When both theaters were running, the building would shake equal to a magnitude of a 3.7 earthquake. The structure had to be specially engineered to deal with the pounding.

To bring a bit of the back lot experience within touch of Hollywood visitors, the Streets of the World opened on June 18, 1988. Jay Stein said, "Research shows people want to get off the tram and wander through back-lot sets, and they never were able to do that, and now they can."[58] The restaurant and retail area was meant to absorb some of the crowds that would be heading for Back to the Future. The project cost $20 million.

"Streets of the World was an attempt to kind of cram in as much flavor as we could into an area that was too small," according to Phil Hettema. "We all made ourselves believe it. There were a lot of interesting conversations. We had to go back and assign a film to every facade." Baker Street was based on turn-of-the-century London with the Strand

Hotel, the Alpha Inn, and Sherlock Holmes apartment. On the other side was Moulin Rouge Street with the Cafe Moustache and the Hotel Casanova. In between was the *Irma La Douce* courtyard dedicated to Shirley MacLaine and Jack Lemmon. Facing the Wild West arena was a celebration of America in the 1950s and 1960s. Mel's Drive-in was straight out of *American Graffiti,* and Faber College came from *National Lampoon's Animal House.*

Parking and creating land from nothing was easy. Dealing with the neighbors was an entirely different matter. During one land-use study, planner James A. Nelson asked neighbors what type of development they would like to see. Their response was no to more things like the Parting of the Red Sea and yes to "a bookstore, a sidewalk café where they can sit and watch the tourists, a newsstand. They want an Irvine Ranch Market, more restaurants, a dinner theater, a place to dance, a library."[59] He learned that local residents enjoyed the Cineplex, but they also wanted more entertainment options for before and after the shows. Many residents were shocked that Universal would even bother to ask their opinions. Polly Ward, president of the Studio City Residents Association said, "This is absolutely the first time a major entity has come to the community first."[60]

To entertain all of these new guests (and hopefully some of the local residents), Universal introduced its most ambitious audience participatory show to date. The $7 million *Star Trek Adventure* opened on June 18, 1988, in the new, 1,200-seat Panasonic Theater in the Studio Entertainment Center.

Under the direction of Phil Hettema, the show was similar to earlier participatory shows where volunteers were used in various roles, videotaped, and then their work inserted into a 7-minute mini-drama. The video would then be played back to the audience. The difference was the sheer scale and complexity of the show. Based on Paramount Pictures' *Star Trek* television series and movies, the story pits the Federation crew against a warship full of Klingons. Only when both parties team up against a common enemy do they learn the lesson of cooperation.

The action took place on five different sets based on the movies. The sets included the bridge of the USS *Enterprise,* the transporter room, the engine room, a Klingon Bird of Prey, and on the planet Akumal 7. The sets were moved using a Broadway-style tracking system. During the transporter room segment, four guests were engulfed in an energy field and "beamed" down to the planet. The illusion was created using the time-tested Pepper's ghost effect with a box on a sliding track. British illusionist John Pepper created the effect in the 1860s using a large, disguised window placed diagonally across a stage. Behind the window was real furniture. Under normal lighting, the window is fully transparent showing only what is behind the glass. However, when objects were lighted off stage, the images would reflect off the glass, making them appear in the same space as the real furniture. George Lucas's Industrial Light & Magic designed the special effects, and the show was capable of being repeated up to 10 times daily.

When the show opened, it was originally 1 hour and 10 minutes long. "The most miserable hour and a half of my life was the first time that show ran," said Phil Hettema. This was unacceptable for a theme park show. By the time each show had ended, there was less than 10% of the audience still in the seats. Gary Goddard was brought in to cut the show down to an acceptable 27 minutes of live taping. The footage was edited into a 7-minute show using the Ultramatte, a "real-time look-ahead auto assembly edit system." Phil Hettema said, "Our video edit system is the only one like it in the world. It enables us to shoot this entire story out of sequence and instantly play it back edited into the correct sequence combined with stock footage we created, plus sound effects and scoring." As a bonus, the edited video was available for sale for $30 after the show. The volunteers' names were placed in the credits, making this a must-have souvenir.

The show used a lot of volunteers, who loved being part of the action. Twenty-three visitors were selected to don costumes and makeup while three more were chosen to work as stagehands. One child was made up as "puppy lizard," a Klingon pet that was "a cute dragon/dog, bigger than a St. Bernard that has scales and hair and sharp teeth."

Hettema said, "It's been a blast because it [the show] combines so many different things. We've worked with [creator] Gene Roddenberry and the *Star Trek* people on special effects and sound effects. It's been like producing a movie and theater and a Broadway show at the same time."[61] He also recognized, "The bottom line was it was technically impressive but there wasn't much of a show there."[62] However, it was the next step in the evolution of the audience participation show going back to Stage 70. Although attendance remained at 4.2 million in 1987 and 1988, the park was preparing for the next year, when a seismic event would hit Universal Studios Hollywood.

The DISNEY-MGM STUDIOS THEME PARK

ON MAY 1, 1989, the race to open a studio and tour in Florida was over and Disney won. Michael Eisner proudly cut the ribbon on the Disney-MGM Studios theme park. At the last minute, the park's name was changed from the Disney-MGM Studio Tour to strengthen the image of the tourist side of the park. The cost of the 135-acre park had ballooned to an estimated $500 million–$550 million. Disney hoped that attendance would be between 3 million and 5 million a year.

Guests visiting the new theme park entered a fantasy re-creation of Hollywood Boulevard circa 1930–1940. Randy Printz of WDI said, "We want to immerse you in that belief that you've landed in Hollywood in the Golden Age." Michael Eisner suggested, "The overall design for the park was an attempt to evoke old Hollywood, rich in detail and atmosphere. Architecturally, we drew on the graceful curvilinear style of the 1920s—Streamline Moderne, an offshoot of Art Deco—in part by re-creating Hollywood landmarks ranging from the Brown Derby restaurant to Grauman's Chinese Theatre."[63]

Bob Weis was responsible for the park's design and said, "I was not a fanatic about Hollywood. I was always interested in the movies, but this project has made me a fanatic." For research, he "spent a long time walking through Hollywood, looking at landmarks, theaters, museums. I stood back and tried to figure out the original form of each building. I bought a lot of merchandise and photos, and did a lot of movie watching."[64] His goal was to take "aspects of Hollywood that have disappeared and given them new life. We've brought the glamour back." Weis strove for a messy vitality that was uncommon for a Disney park. It was more like visiting Universal Studios in Hollywood. "We worked hard to get the right kind of hodgepodge," Weis said. "Hollywood was an entrepreneurial, energetic place. We've glamorized the entrepreneurism and exuberance."[65]

Dick Nunis described the studio park as "a Disneyland theme park done Hollywood style. You can expect to see Hollywood Boulevard probably better than Hollywood Boulevard is today."[66] Even Roy E. Disney was impressed. He said, "I walked through the park at the annual meeting. It's just spectacular. So much better than anything we've done before."[67]

Washingtonian palms line Hollywood Boulevard; at the end of the street is a full-size reproduction of the iconic Grauman's Chinese Theatre (1927), acting as a beckoning hand. Like its Hollywood prototype, movie stars were invited to enshrine their handprints in cement to be placed in the courtyard. The first stars to take advantage of this privilege were actors Darryl Hannah and Paul Reubens (as Pee-Wee Herman).

The proposed Epcot pavilion that started this competition, The Great Movie Ride, was the centerpiece attraction. The elaborate dark ride is a celebration of famous moments in the movies laid out on a 90,000-square-foot soundstage. The 20-minute *Indiana Jones Stunt Spectacular* is an almost direct copy from the *A-Team* and *Miami Vice* stunt shows at Universal Studios Hollywood. Disney's Foley (sound effects) demonstration was called the *Monster Sound Show.*

The other big attraction was the 2-hour Backstage Studio Tour. Because Disney had little in the way of actual production going on, it had to be creative. After boarding the shuttle, guests rode past the craft and wardrobe shops. Then they turned onto the back lot and passed through the Residential Street set featuring the home from *The Golden Girls* television show. Leaving Residential Street, the trams entered the tour's special effects spectacular, Catastrophe Canyon. An earthquake in an oil field set off a chain reaction that included pyrotechnics and a water tank that unleashed 76,000 gallons of water over the trams.

The trams continued to the New York Street set, where a huge forced-perspective backdrop of the city skyline dominated the end of the street. Because of the lack of activity on the back lot, the Imagineers littered the street with trash to add a touch of authenticity. This went against the training for virtually everybody at Disney. Pam Parks from Disney said, "When they first put the trash out, the cleaning crews came through at night and picked it all up. They had to bring it back and glue it down."[68]

Just like the Universal tour, guests got off the trams after New York Street for a break. The rest of the tour was by foot. Disney's version of the audience participation special effects demonstration was based on the ABC mini-series *The Winds of War* (1983). A naval battle was staged in a special effects tank, using volunteers as actors. To the delight of the audience, the volunteers were thoroughly drenched and then their images were inserted into stock footage and played back.

The walking tour continued into a corridor that ran alongside four working soundstages. Through a plate glass window, guests could peer down on the action below in the rare instance that somebody was actually using the facility. One stage had been dressed for the *New Mickey Mouse Club* television show. The fourth soundstage was filled with props. A walk past the postproduction shops led to the Walt Disney Theater, where guests were shown clips and trailers.

Another audience participation show was *Superstar Television*. During this show, volunteers got to act in ABC shows such as *General Hospital* and *The Golden Girls*. There were stage shows, including *Dick Tracy Live Stage Spectacular* and *Here Comes the Muppets Stage Show*. Star Tours, a ride that debuted in Disneyland, also was added to the slim roster.

Disney claimed that the Disney-MGM Studios theme park was not a direct copy of Universal's Florida plans. But it was obvious that it was an attempt to re-create the studio at Universal City, with the guest's point of view as the first priority. Actual production was secondary.

The park was a commercial success from the moment the front gate first opened. Michael Eisner recalled, "Our biggest problem was dealing with demand. Within several hours of opening the gates for the first time, we reached capacity and had to begin turning people away from the parking lots."[69] He added that the studio park was "a new concept, a new idea."[70] Of course, that did not sit well with Jay

Stein. He said, "I don't even understand that kind of comment. We have been doing it for 25 years." [71]

SOUND FAMILIAR?

JAY STEIN WAS SO FRUSTRATED he decided to try and shame Disney by showing Universal's original 1981 plans to reporters of *The Los Angeles Times*.[72] Terry Winnick had just come back from a battle with cancer and began putting together a book for Stein with everything they had done and everything that Disney had done. Winnick said, "Don't confuse what we were trying to do in '78, '79 with what Disney was doing. Disney stole our idea. They copied us." He added, "Disney built a bunch of stuff based on what they stole from us, which was the old Hollywood and special effects that were done related to major motion pictures."[73] The Disney production studio "was bullshit. It was a theme park and everybody knew it."[74]

Stein claimed that Disney "borrowed 65% to 70% from the 1981 plan."[75] He complained, "I just think that when you work as hard as we did in trying to get this program and studio tour off the ground, and this is a project that I have worked on for 20 years, then you see someone come along and take your ideas and . . . incorporate them in their project and say that this was their idea, (that) this was conceived by the Imagineers, that just makes me angry."[76]

A prime example was Catastrophe Canyon at Disney-MGM. For Universal City, Florida, Winnick had put together a major attraction on the studio tram tour called the Hollywood Canyon. According to Terry Winnick, the original idea was inspired by real locations in Los Angeles. He was designing the first four homes of a subdivision called Lake Hollywood Estates for Howard Cole and Howard Cohen. The homes overlooked the Lake Hollywood reservoir. While working on the project, Winnick realized that the lake was actually just below the famous Hollywood sign. He told Stein, "What we ought to do is to have the [Hollywood] dam break and the water come through the Hollywood sign and then come down into Hollywood Hills." Stein loved it. It would combine technology already being used in Hollywood for the Collapsing Bridge and the Flash Flood set.

The trams would have entered a canyon with a large-scale model of the Hollywood Dam high above the famous Hollywood sign. Suddenly, a powerful simulated earthquake would shake the tram using the gimbal system from *Earthquake* at Hollywood. Overhead, power lines would snap, and the ground beneath the tram would seem to crack. Both effects were also in use in Hollywood. Buildings would start to collapse all around the tram, the street would buckle, and the dam would burst, sending 250,000 gallons of water toward the tram. Along the way, there would be plenty of explosions. At the last second, the water would disperse and the visitors would be safe. Stein liked it.

Then the tram would pull away and cross the Florida version of the collapsing bridge. The next scene was themed after John Wayne's *Hellfighters*, the 1968 tribute to legendary firefighter Red Adair. Once again, an earthquake would shake the tram, causing boulders to fall down and an oil truck to slide into a gas tank, creating a massive explosion. Winnick said that Disney not only stole the idea for its attraction from Universal, but it even borrowed from Steven Spielberg's early television film *Duel* (1971).[77]

Another example was the Foley demonstration. Universal had proposed to bring audience volunteers on stage to create sound effects for a short film. The joke was that the film was set at a tempo no volunteer could maintain. Like Hollywood, the results would be played back to the audience.

Universal also planned to bring its existing *Star Trek* audience participation show to Florida. Volunteers would be given costumes, scripts, and a chance to perform in scenes that would be edited into a short film. Their competitor had Superstar Television, where a tour brochure described how "you'll be escorted to a backstage 'Green Room,' where you'll be given costumes, scripts, and stage instructions."

The similarities were not limited to the attractions. The entrance plaza for Universal's Florida park would have featured a stylish palm-lined Hollywood Boulevard of the 1930s and 1940s "designed to re-create the exciting golden era of Hollywood," according to the slide show given to *The Los Angeles Times*. Both Disney's and Universal's Hollywood Boulevard plans emphasized Art Deco and Streamline Moderne architecture.

As in Hollywood, visitors to Universal Studios would have boarded a tram and driven through a back lot with a New York Street, Hollywood Boulevard, and a street of residential facades from popular TV shows and movies. When Disney-MGM opened, it had a Hollywood Boulevard, a New York street, and a residential street. When Disney built the MGM Studio, "they had a tram and tram-driven effects," Terry Winnick said. "They had a front lot and a back lot and the back lot was tram-driven. Give me a break."[78]

The Los Angeles Times followed up with independent theme park designers to compare the plans for both parks, and many would only speak off the record. What they found were plans that were similar, and "two of them said that the similarities were 'too close for just coincidence' and 'extreme.'"[79] Dave Schweninger, president of Sequoia Creative, did go on the record and said, "I can't deny they're very similar." However, he cautioned about any malicious behavior. He said, "People all over the country don't have a lot of facts and breadth (knowledge about the movie business) and what they perceive is the palm trees, the architecture, all those kinds of things. They know there are sound effects and they want to see them [created]."[80] When Jay Stein heard of Schweninger's comments, he countered, "They [Disney] could have done sound effects a million ways. . . . There is nothing that is generic to a studio tour."

1 Connie Bruck, *When Hollywood Had a King: The Reign of Lew Wasserman, Who Leveraged Talent into Power and Influence* (New York: Random House, 2003).

2 Ibid.

3 Michael D. Eisner with Tony Schwartz, *Work In Progress* (New York: Hyperion, 1998).

4 Eisner with Schwartz, *Work In Progress.*

5 Vicki Vaughan, "MCA Smells a Rat in Disney's Plans for Studio Tour," *Orlando Sentinel,* 15 May 1985.

6 Ellen Farley, "Behind the MCA-Disney Tour War in Florida," *The Los Angeles Times*, 23 Apr. 1989.

7 "A Real Kongfrontation," *Newsweek,* 10 June 1990.

8 Eisner with Schwartz, *Work In Progress.*

9 Ibid.

10 Jeffrey Schmaltz, "Nastiness Is Not a Fantasy in Movie Theme Park War," *The New York Times,* 13 Aug. 1989.

11 Eisner with Schwartz, *Work In Progress.*

12 Farley, "Behind the MCA-Disney Tour War.

13 Vaughan, "MCA Smells a Rat."

14 Ibid.

15 Eisner with Schwartz, *Work In Progress.*

16 Marty Sklar, *Dream It! Do It!* (New York: Disney Editions, 2013).

17 Ibid.

18 Ibid.

19 Ibid.

20 Ibid.

21 Anders Gyllenhaal, "Orlando Hotels Creating New Kingdom," *Miami Herald,* 16 Jan. 1984.

22 Sklar, *Dream It!*

23 Gary Goddard, interview with author, North Hollywood, CA, 12 Jan. 2014.

24 Eisner with Schwartz, *Work In Progress.*

25 Vicki Vaughan, "Disney Lot Starts on its Tour Studio," *Orlando Sentinel*, 28 Mar. 1989.

26 Peter Alexander, interview with author, South Palm Beach, FL, 21 Oct. 2013.

27 Terry Winnick, interview with author, Las Vegas, NV, 25 Feb. 2014.

28 Phil Hettema, interview with author, Pasadena, CA, 7 May 2014.

29 Alexander, interview with author, 21 Oct. 2013.

30 Vicki Vaughan, "Entering Stage Left: MCA Studio Race Is On As Disney Builds Its TV, Film Production Complex," *Orlando Sentinel,* 10 Dec. 1986.

31 Ibid.

32 Winnick, interview with author, 25 Feb. 2014.

33 Ibid.

34 "Walt Disney Co. Isn't Sparing Any . . .," *Orlando Sentinel,* 18 July 1988.

35 Vicki Vaughan, "Disney Plans New Sound Stages," *Orlando Sentinel,* 25 Apr. 1990.

36 Ibid.

37 John Hill and Vicki Vaughan, "Movie Studios Hold Key for Walt Disney," *Orlando Sentinel,* 2 May 1988.

38 Farley, "Behind the MCA-Disney Tour War."

39 Dan Tracy, "Fast-train Plans Pick Up Steam Local Officials Still Have Questions, Reservations," *Orlando Sentinel,* 1 May 1989.

40 Schmaltz, "Nastiness Is Not a Fantasy."

41 Alan Lapidus, *Everything by Design: My Life as an Architect,* (New York: St. Martin's Press).

42 Merwin Sigale, "Disney, James Rouse Explore Entertainment, Retail Venture," *The Miami News,* 7 Oct. 1986, 8A.

43 Ibid.

44 Michael McCall, "Rouse Meets the Mouse," *Entertainment Magazine,* Jan./Feb. 2002.

45 Ibid.

46 Greg Braxton, "Disney Dazzled Burbank with its Vision for Backlot," *The Los Angeles Times,* 8 June 1987.

47 Ibid.

48 Kathryn Harris, "Disney Did Offer Deal on Parks to MCA, Cineplex Chief Says," *The Los Angeles Times,* 8 May 1987.

49 Kathryn Harris, "Eisner, Sheinberg Silent on Power Breakfast Agenda," *The Los Angeles Times,* 28 July 1987.

50 McCall, "Rouse Meets the Mouse."

51 Kathryn Harris, "MCA Purchase Not in Plans, Disney Insists," *The Los Angeles Times,* 19 Feb. 1988.

52 Ellen Farley, "A Rivalry of Titanic Proportions," *The Los Angeles Times,* 24 Apr. 1988.

53 Rick Sherwood, "The Future of Universal's Playground," *The Los Angeles Times,* 24 Apr. 1988.

54 Kathryn Harris, "MCA Takes Cautious Road as Competitors Plunge Ahead," *The Los Angeles Times,* 22 Nov. 1981.

55 Sharon Bernstein, "MCA Takes on the Mouse," *The Los Angeles Times,* 3 June 1990.

56 Sherwood, "Future of Universal's Playground."

57 Ibid.

58 Ibid.

59 Bob Pool, "King Kong," *The Los Angeles Times,* 12 Dec. 1988.

60 Ibid.

61 Phil Hettema, interview with author, Pasadena, CA, 16 Jan. 2014.

62 Ibid.

63 Eisner with Schwartz, *Work In Progress.*

64 Edward L. Prizer, "Hollywood Dream Comes Alive in Orlando," *Orlando Magazine,* May 1989.

65 Ibid.

66 Ibid.

67 Ibid.

68 Ibid.

69 Eisner with Schwartz, *Work in Progress.*

70 Adam Yeomans, "Disney Will Speed Up Expansion of Studio Theme Park," *Orlando Sentinel,* 1 Aug. 1989.

71 Ibid.

72 Farley, "Behind the MCA-Disney Tour War."
73 Winnick, interview with author, 25 Feb. 2014.
74 Ibid.
75 Farley, "Behind the MCA-Disney Tour War."
76 Ibid.
77 Winnick, interview with author, 25 Feb. 2014.
78 Winnick, interview with author, 25 Feb. 2014.
79 Farley, "Behind the MCA-Disney Tour War."
80 Ibid.

CHAPTER 7

From INDUSTRIAL TOUR *to* THEME PARK

BRING *in the* LOCALS

EARTHQUAKE: THE BIG ONE was originally supposed to be one of the marquee attractions at Universal City Florida but would debut in Hollywood instead. Based on Universal's blockbuster hit *Earthquake!* (1974), the show was meant to take advantage of a jittery Southern California population with fresh memories of the devastating Sylmar earthquake of 1971. "The earthquake subject matter was no accident, believe me," said Nick Winslow, an economic consultant. "Universal just had to look at its data to realize it's not getting its fair share of locals, and the *Earthquake!* show [would bring] in locals."[1]

The original plan was based on the Hollywood Canyon show for Universal City Florida. Peter Alexander was in charge, and he was not so sure that the dam breaking was such a good idea. He said, "Having been around engineering enough, I knew that thing is going to dump 250,000 gallons of water and it is coming down 200 feet, so when it hits the bottom it is going to destroy everything in its path." Stein did not believe him and hired an engineer. After careful consideration, the engineer agreed with Alexander and the concept was scrapped.

Peter Alexander used the delays to refine the concept. He started with Walter Mirisch, who was going to produce the Universal sequel. Mirisch told the ride designer that the next film was going to be set in San Francisco. Alexander asked if there was a scene in a BART station. When Mirisch said yes, a theme park attraction was born.

The underground transit station provided the perfect environment for an 8.3 earthquake that Alexander could safely manipulate. The tram entered a "live" set that resembled the interior of a subway station. All of a sudden, the lights flickered and the ground started to shake. The roar of the earthquake was courtesy of Universal's Sensurround sound technology.

To increase the sense of danger, the first concept showed the street above collapsing next to the tram. That was not scary enough. Then somebody suggested that a trolley fall into the station. Larry Lester found his opening and suggested that he could rig a tanker truck to slide down the collapsing street and burst into flames feet away from the visitors. They would feel the heat.

Making matters worse was a runaway BART subway train barreling toward the tram. It would jackknife and barely miss the tram. As suddenly as the earthquake started, it would stop. Then 60,000 gallons of water dropped from tanks on the roof, creating a 15-foot waterfall on the station platform very close to the trams. David Codiga was the project manager, and Larry Lester was creative director. Codiga started as a show coordinator on *Miami Vice* and eventually rose to executive vice president of Universal Creative.

Earthquake: The Big One opened in Hollywood on March 18, 1989, inside a 25,000-square-foot, custom-built soundstage. Soundstage 50 replaced *The Tower of London* (1962) set. The film starred Boris Karloff and Basil Rathbone and is best remembered as Vincent Price's horror film debut. The set was used as the concentration camp in *Judgment at Nuremberg* (1961), an amusement park in an episode of *Murder She Wrote,* and a village on another planet in *Buck Rogers in the 25th Century.*

In 1988 the castle was torn down, and steel pilings were sunk 25 feet into the ground and locked together by beams weighing 8,000 pounds each. All of this was necessary for the building to withstand the quake's 60,000 pounds of force. Another consideration was making the building safe, just in case a real earthquake struck Southern California.

Although the 2-minute *Earthquake* show was estimated to cost $14 million, it had a positive effect on the bottom line. Attendance topped 5.1 million visitors in 1989, boosting attendance by 25% over the previous year.

With most of the creative energy focused on Florida, Universal Studios Hollywood had to be happy with a few minor tweaks in 1990. Phil Hettema retooled *The Wild Wild Wild West Stunt Show,* and Jay Stein renamed it *The Riot Act Stunt Show.* In this version, a stunt coordinator on a horse and his partner would begin to describe how stunts were performed in the movies, when Ma Hopper and her boys Cole and Clod would interrupt them. The trio would then take over as the stunt crew, and mayhem ensued. At one point, Ma would fall off a balcony, and then stumble into a well, setting off a bomb. The grand finale literally brought the house down in a stunt reminiscent of one done by silent star Buster Keaton. The *Universal Insider* claimed, "You will see Hollywood's finest show you the tricks of their trade ... how they survive knock-down, drag-out gunfights, crackling bullwhips, whirlwind fistfights, saddle-busting horseplay, and more." The title of the new version of the show only lasted a year, but the script remained unchanged for many years. Barbara Epstein was the show director, and Alex Plasshaert was stunt coordinator, with consultation from Hal Needham, one of the true greats of the stunt industry.

The tram tour got a new temporary addition. To celebrate the success of the Universal film *Back to the Future 2* (1989), the iconic Courthouse Square was redressed to appear as Hill Valley in 2015. The show featured a mock electrification of a guest, who would be struck by a special-effects lightning bolt and reappear as a spark-encircled skeleton.

In an attempt to cater to younger children, Hettema added Fievel's Playland. MCA was proud of Fievel Mousekewitz from *An American Tail* (1986). The studio claimed that the animated film was "the highest-grossing animated film ever released." Sidney Sheinberg said, "We're not intimidated by Disney—we've got a mouse that is more important than theirs."[2] All of the props were oversize, and children could slide down a 15-foot banana peel, climb through an old shoe, or run through a maze of tunnels shaped like Swiss cheese. Along with the play area was a live stage show featuring the world's largest puppet at 16 feet and operated by two puppeteers.

Despite the new additions, attendance dropped to 4.6 million in 1990 and remained the same in 1991.

WE ARE GOING *to* OUTDO THEM

ONCE MICHAEL EISNER ANNOUNCED that Disney was going to build a studio-based theme park with a back lot tram tour in Florida, Universal had two choices. They could come up with something quick or sell off the Florida property and retreat back to Hollywood. Although the studio and tour was not a high priority to Wasserman and Sheinberg, it became one when Eisner decided to meddle. Phil Hettema said, "It's classic Jay [Stein] in so many ways, because on the one hand Jay's ambitions are why that park [Florida] exists. It was his fierce competition with Disney that he was able to leverage brilliantly because Michael Eisner announced they were going to do a studio tour when Universal had already talked about it."[3] Everyone in Hollywood knew that Lew Wasserman was very competitive and usually won. It was time to teach the youngster over at Disney a lesson. MCA was now in it to win it.

Eisner underestimated Wasserman, Sheinberg, and Jay Stein. If Eisner intended to preemptively copy Universal's studio and industrial tour, then MCA would simply build a bigger and better theme park and beat Disney at its own game. "It isn't just the redesigning," Stein said. "It was the addition of new attractions and shows, expanded streets and restaurants, that were not contemplated in 1981. It all relates to the fact that Disney took what we had, and we had to fish or cut bait."[4] Stein made it very clear. "The one that wins Orlando wins the world."[5]

Peter Alexander said, "They stuck it to us, then we are going to outdo them."[6] The first step was signing Steven Spielberg on as creative consultant. According to the *Orlando Sentinel,* Spielberg would collect 2% of the gross revenues from Universal Studios Florida, including tickets and concession sales, in perpetuity.[7] It was worth it. Barry Upson said, "Universal Studios Florida would not exist except for Spielberg film rights." [8]

Jay Stein then started to gather a handful of people. Bob Ward was the designer, architect, and master planner. Barry Upson also worked on the master plan and was the executive. Peter Alexander was the show guy and would tell Ward and Upson how big the show buildings needed to be. Terry Winnick and Larry Lester were the Universal veterans. Richard Crane had to get everything built, and Molly Rose watched the budgets and schedules. The team recruited studio veteran Henry Bumstead and his team to help design authentic backlot facades. The group was set up in the Hewlett-Packard building north of Universal City on Lankershim Boulevard. They also met at the Black Tower or in Jay Stein's living room.

"The original concept for Universal Studios Florida was to move an expanded and improved Universal Studios Hollywood to Orlando," Barry Upson said. "Lew [Wasserman] and Sid's [Sheinberg] rejection of that idea plus the intense re-work of Universal Studios Hollywood at that time delayed the Universal Studios Florida planning for a couple of years. When we got back to it, early attraction concept ideas led us to the core theme of 'Ride the Movies' in Universal Studios Florida. The rich movie set street environments reinforced that basic guest experience." Looking back in 2014, Barry Upson said, "I feel the fundamental concept has held up extraordinarily well for 25 years."[9]

It was up to Peter Alexander and his tiny crew to come up with something that would work. He said, "We weren't going to compete with Disney. We did not have Mickey Mouse." He knew "the only way we could compete against Disney with essentially the same product [a studio tour] in the same market [Orlando] was to 'out-Disney' them. That meant bigger, better rides." Alexander felt if they did not go big they would be slaughtered and the park would close within two years. "I had the arrogance of youth," Alexander said. "So we got to go big."[10]

Alexander had worked at Disney and learned, "The thing about Disney was it was very soft and family but it was big production value. It is kind of nice but it doesn't have any edge."[11] Finding that edge was how Universal was going to win. Terry Winnick was confident. He said, "The Pirates of the Caribbean is for wimps. Climbing the tree house, that's for wimps. Space Mountain, big deal. We got King Kong, we got *Earthquake!*, we got Back to the Future, we got Jaws. We are going to terrorize these people. These are going to be rides that are going to scare the [expletive] out of people. This is not for wimps."[12] At one meeting, Jay Stein told his team, "If they got 5,000 square feet of hot dogs, we're going to have six and if they got an inch diameter hot dog and it's the best hot dog they got then we're going have a better hot dog."[13]

The design team studied everything at Disney. Peter Alexander said, "Once we were in the Florida market and they already had a bigger, better version of Universal Studios tour, we had to out-Disney Disney. Florida would never have the authenticity of Hollywood. It was never going to become a film hub."[14]

The theme park was not going to be an easy project. Alexander said, "The thought of designing and building custom rides was both new and staggering to Universal management. They had never before built any kind of ride, let alone a Disney-quality experience."[15] When Sidney Sheinberg learned that each major ride would cost approximately $25 million to $30 million, Alexander said, "He looked ashen, but being a fearless executive, he green-lighted them anyway. We were in an 'arms race' with Disney, and he knew that the only way to win was with bigger and better weapons."[16]

With Disney proposing to build its version of Universal Hollywood Studios in Florida, Universal needed to find a different angle. Bob Ward recalled the team asking themselves, "Why not allow visitors studio access to explore the back lot on foot rather than see it from the tram? Which led to the heretical thought: What would happen if we got rid of the tram?"[17] If there were no tram, visitors would be free to wander. It would be easy to hide the large show buildings with the rides inside. Universal knew how to build back lots. Barry Upson said, "Our basic m.o. has been to show people how movies are made."[18]

"We started with the theme that we were a working movie studio," Peter Alexander said. "Thus, when you arrive at Universal, the first thing you do is walk through the 'studio gate.' Now it so happens that the original Universal Studios in Los Angeles never had a studio gate. To get on the Universal lot, you just drove past a guard shack and waved at the guard named Scotty. However, since Scotty passed away, we decided to 'borrow' the Paramount Studio main gate for Universal, Florida, and a replica (somewhat improved) of what is there today."[19] Out front was a globe bearing the Universal logo. At 24 feet, the globe could have been a lot bigger, but then the logo would not have fit in visitor photos.

The front lot would be the first area that visitors would experience. The buildings would be rows of soundstages. Some would be real, to meet Universal's production needs, while others would house rides and shows. Soundstages made perfect theme park show buildings. Little money had to be spent on theming the exterior, while inside the shows could be inexpensively updated frequently.

Human behavior meant that most visitors would instinctively turn right. That is where Alexander placed the entrance to the "back lot." The back lot was based on a loop, which was first developed by Randy Duell for Six Flags Over Texas. Duell also designed the Studio Entertainment Center at Universal Studios Hollywood. The benefit of the loop was that it was impossible for visitors to get lost. The downside was that the attraction you may most want to visit is on the other side, and a long walk away. The World Showcase at Epcot Center was based on the same concept.

The architecture in the back lot would look like exterior shooting sets. "We wanted a real, working studio," said Bob Ward. "Each area had to work as a theme park and a shootable street set."[20] Stein respected Ward and let him do what he needed to do with the exteriors. Movie set designers Henry Bumstead and Norm Newberry also worked with Ward. The outside sets matched the locations for the rides. They acted like a preshow to the preshow.

Peter Alexander said, "If you walk behind a set, as you often do when you are standing in line for a ride, you'll see the structure that holds it up—unlike Disneyland—because that's what you see when you walk behind the facade of a shooting set in Hollywood. It's all Movie Magic at Universal, and everything in the park flows from that theme."[21] While the Disney parks strove to eliminate any visual contradictions that would disrupt the story they were trying to tell through environmental design, Universal seemed to celebrate the chaos that is inherent on a movie back lot.

The HORSE RACE

WITH THE BASIC LAYOUT SETTLED UPON, the next challenge would be to come up with the right mix of rides and shows. Terry Winnick said Universal was all about "selling authenticity and current hit movie experiences. Do you want to see an oil truck blow up or do you want to see King Kong?" He added, "We were going to beat Disney at their own game."[22]

Of course, the press was quick to turn the contest into a horse race. They made comparisons between Universal's new park and the Disney-MGM Studios. Universal Studios reportedly cost $630 million compared to Disney's $500 million investment. Universal was roughly twice the size of its competitor at 256.6 acres and supplied 7,000 parking spaces, while Disney provided 4,500. Universal would hit capacity at 40,000 visitors, while Disney could only handle 25,000 visitors. Upon reflection, Peter Alexander said, "In the long run, it was good for both companies and good for the theme park business, because the state-of-the-art of theme park attractions took a huge leap forward."[23]

Jay Stein knew that Disney was going to open its park first if for no other reason than the regulatory environment. The Reedy Creek Improvement District regulated development within Walt Disney World. The district had broad powers and could expedite Disney's requests. Universal had to deal with the city of Orlando.

Stein wanted to get the park up and running before June 1990. The world's largest event for selling travel to the United States from abroad, the International Pow Wow, was coming to Orlando. The three-day conference rotated from various cities around the United States, and the main sponsors tended to dominate the agenda. Disney was responsible for bringing the event to Orlando, and Stein wanted to crash its party.

Tensions were beginning to run high. Stein was pushing his team to the breaking point. In late 1988 Peter Alexander called a meeting of the principal players. Alexander knew how complex these things were and told Stein, "None of this [expletive] stuff is going to work."[24] Terry Winnick was brought in to help. Barry Upson suggested, "Let's extend it a year and be easy on ourselves and develop a proper product."[25] Stein was so frustrated with Upson that he threw him out of the meeting.

To try to push things along, Stein hired Mike Bartlett as project manager. After getting up to speed, Bartlett realized just how ambitious Universal's plans were. Alexander reminded him that Universal had to go big because Disney was only 10 miles away. Bartlett knew right then that they would never be ready. What Bartlett did not know was Sidney Sheinberg told Stein that MCA did not want to be embarrassed. Stein was lining up the team's support, and Bartlett would be the sacrificial lamb and tell Wasserman and Sheinberg not to get their hopes up.

Steven Lew said, "Many of our attractions are first-time undertakings and, because of their complexity, we are allowing plenty of lead time to enable us to prepare an opening that will go smoothly."[26] As the opening date came closer, the team would gather once a day to see what needed to be done. Phil Hettema described the meetings as "a blood bath from Jay."[27] A primary target was Keith James, the director of production for the entire park. The entire show team worked for James, and when Stein would demand the impossible or unfairly place the blame on one of the team, James would step in and defend them. Hettema described James as "the most professional executive on the project and largely responsible for the ultimate success of the park product."[28]

Gary Goddard said, "The lack of an engineering staff working on highly advanced prototype ride systems was the critical piece missing."[29] Keith Rainey was the sole ride engineer for the entire park. He had one assistant to get the whole park operating. Stein's insistence on rushing would come back to haunt him.

The production facilities would be the first thing to open. In October 1988, the *New Leave it to Beaver* series with Jerry Mathers and

Barbara Billingsley began production on one of the soundstages. Other productions using the studio facilities included *Parenthood*, a movie directed by Ron Howard and starring Steve Martin, Mary Steenburgen, Jason Robards, and Rick Moranis, and *Psycho IV* starring Anthony Perkins. Universal proudly boasted in a press release that its new facility was "the largest motion picture and television production studio outside of Hollywood." Within the first year, 13 feature films and 500 television episodes would go before the cameras at Universal Studios.

Not long before the park's grand opening, Jay Stein got a new partner. Cineplex Odeon was struggling under a mountain of debt in 1988 due to overexpansion. On March 22, 1989, it sold its share of Universal Studios Florida to the Rank Organisation of Britain for $150 million. Rank owned the Hard Rock Café chain and had interests ranging from vacation resort properties to a partnership with Xerox. From MCA's point of view, the deal was good for them because Rank had better connections for European expansion. Sidney Sheinberg said of their old partner, "Did it turn out to be more expensive than we thought? Obviously. Did it become too big for Cineplex? Yes."[30]

PRODUCTION CENTRAL

BECAUSE THE IDEA OF UNIVERSAL STUDIOS FLORIDA was to allow the guests to walk through the lot unhampered, the first act for the show naturally would be the front lot of a movie studio. The typical guest services are disguised as the Publicity Department, Studio Payroll, Sound Transfer, and Projection Maintenance. The architecture echoes the California-style architecture of the studio bungalows. Offices for the administrative staff are placed inside replicas of two Hollywood nightclubs, the Mocambo (1941) and Ciro's (1940).

Once past this area, guests enter Production Central. Here, the architectural statement is industrial. Soundstages line a grid of streets. Inside the soundstages are shows and rides that can easily be switched out with new characters and stories to keep the park fresh.

Susan Lustig was the very capable producer responsible for two of the shows. On Stage 40 was *Alfred Hitchcock: The Art of Making Movies*. A signature element at the Hollywood park was the audience participation special effects demonstration. The new mantra of bigger and better meant that Orlando would get the most elaborate show yet devised.

Classic Hitchcock film posters lined the walls of the queue, and visitors were handed a pair of 3-D glasses to be used later in the show. Just like Hollywood, the show was broken up into multiple rooms to expedite larger crowds. An actor posing as the second unit director named Alexander hosted the show. He guided the visitors through each of the rooms.

In the first room was a 9-minute montage of film clips narrated by Alfred Hitchcock. Toward the end, the host would tell the audience that they were in for a special treat. For the first time anywhere, an audience would see the ending from *Dial M for Murder* (1954) the way it was intended to be shown: in 3-D. The film was shot in Dino DeLaurentiis's studio in Wilmington near the Port of Los Angeles. Alexander said, "Every time it rained we thanked ourselves there was not sound" because of how cheap the studio was built.[31]

Suddenly, the film seemed to stop, and the screen appeared to be torn to shreds from behind by an attacking flock of birds. The 3-D effects ended with the birds setting off explosives and fireworks. A shadow-bird would land on a perch and then morph into the shadow of Alfred Hitchcock.

Inside the next room was the main show. Peter Alexander said, "We want to capture the terror, romance, and suspense of *Psycho*."[32] The set consisted of a scaled-down model of the *Psycho* house and a full-scale section of the Bates Motel. The show began with the first-ever 3-D film featured at Universal, in which actor Anthony Perkins talked about some of the special effects used in the making of Hitchcock's *Psycho* (1960). For example, during the infamous shower scene, Hitchcock decided that by using the camera in place of Norman Bates's knife, the scene would be much less graphic, but far more effective.

The film would end, the lights would come on, and a reproduction of the shower scene set would be revealed. The set had breakaway walls, a shower that pivoted, and a large truss that lowered with a number of pre-positioned cameras. An actress was brought out to play the role made famous by Janet Leigh, and an audience volunteer played the Mrs. Bates/Norman character. The demonstration took the audience, shot for shot, through the scene. At the conclusion of the demonstration, Anthony Perkins returned to the screen and told the audience, "Maybe the best thing to show you more about the shower scene is to just show the scene itself," and the scene just shot would appear on the screen.

The final room was filled with props and interactive displays. One of the largest sets was the life-size torch from the Statue of Liberty similar to the one used in *Saboteur* (1942). Volunteers were selected to demonstrate how composite shots were made using matte paintings. Another display featured part of a carousel used in *Strangers on a Train* (1951) to show how rear projection screens can create the illusion of traveling at high speeds.

The display inspired by *Rear Window* (1954), starring Jimmy Stewart, was very popular. Visitors were asked to look through binoculars at a set that resembled the apartment building seen in the film, and find the killer in one of the windows. Also on display was a hotel set model from *Vertigo* (1958) and a wax mannequin of Alfred Hitchcock. Visitors trying to stay out of the heat could sit in a director's chair and watch clips from *Alfred Hitchcock Presents*. Next-door was The Bates Motel Gift Shop, with souvenir shower curtains available for sale. The show was renamed the *Alfred Hitchcock's 3-D Theatre* a few years later and finally closed on January 3, 2003, to make way for the *Shrek 4-D* attraction.

If the Hitchcock show was a way to reveal visual special effects, the *Murder, She Wrote Mystery Post Production Theatre* was a way to explain an additional aspect of the moviemaking process, the role of executive producer. Visitors would have to make creative decisions, such as choosing the bad guy, the guest star, the plot, and some of the special effects for an episode of the long-running television show starring Angela Lansbury.

Murder, She Wrote Mystery Post Production Theatre was also Florida's version of the Foley demonstration. Volunteers would create the sound effects for a video clip, and the results were played back to the audience. The show clocked in at 35 minutes, making it the longest show on opening day. Both of Lustig's shows opened in full working order on opening day. The theme park attraction was closed in 1996, just after the television show had ended its 12-season run.

The first ride many guests would encounter was the motion simulator ride The Funtastic World of Hanna-Barbera. When the team pitched the simulator ride to the founders of the legendary animation studio, they heard that Universal was working with Steven Spielberg. That was enough for them. Not only did Universal pick up the theme park rights, but live action films resulted. Universal started making deals using the parks as bait.

The Hanna-Barbera show was meant to target the entire family. The first simulator ride was the Tour of the Universe at the CN Tower in Toronto, Canada, which opened in 1985 and closed in 1990. The most famous was Star Tours at Disneyland, which opened in 1987.

Universal's ride would be different. Peter Alexander came up with the idea of a motion theater. In a conversation with Barry Upson, Alexander said, "You know these theme park attractions don't make any sense. It's like every time you want to change out and put a new television show on you have to buy a new television." The motion theater provided greater flexibility to remain current. We could just change out the film," Alexander said. "Change out some of the props and we would have something new." Alexander cited one other advantage to the motion theater. He said, "The problem with traditional dark rides like E.T. is it is literally cast in concrete, and if it doesn't work it is too darn bad."[33] History has shown Alexander to be correct. The theater has been retrofitted three times.

unofficial **TIP**
In a strange twist, after the ride closed at Universal in 2002, The Funtastic World of Hanna-Barbera became a featured attraction at the Paramount theme parks.

The Funtastic World of Hanna-Barbera was the first ride film done completely using computer-generated imagery (CGI). The film was created and directed by Mario Kamberg and produced by Sherry McKenna. In the preshow, William Hanna and Joseph Barbera lead an animation demonstration. It quickly turns into a chase as the cartoon villain Dick Dastardly has kidnapped Elroy Jetson.

Guests then moved into the main theater, where they found a seat in 1 of 12 motion-simulation bases built by Ride Trade. Each base sat eight guests. During the 7.5-minute film, they flew through Bedrock, the world of Scooby-Doo, and the Jetsons' hometown. At the show's exit was an interactive play area with elements themed to the Flintstones, such as Pebble's playhouse.

Another little bit of Hollywood was the Boneyard. Just like the Prop Plaza in Hollywood, visitors could get up-close to famous props for a photo. On display was the chariot from *Ben Hur,* a carriage from *Gone with the Wind,* one of the sharks from *Jaws: The Revenge,* a shark fin from *Jaws 3-D,* and props from *The Flintstones.* Later on, the Kawasaki KZ1000-P21 police motorcycle from *Terminator 2: Judgment Day* joined the rest of the props. The Boneyard lasted until 2008, when the Universal Music Plaza Stage replaced it. The permanent stage was a re-creation of the famous Hollywood Bowl.

In California, the tram tour was central to the tourist experience. In Florida, it was a secondary attraction called the Production Studio Tram Tour. Remember, at Universal Studios Florida, it was important to remind guests that they got to walk through the entire studio, unlike Disney-MGM, where they had to take a tram. The queue for the 15-minute tram ride was at Sound Stage 19. Inside the building were displays of filmmaking equipment. Along the outside wall were plaques honoring all of the productions filmed at the studio.

Before the trams left Production Central, they drove past the exterior of some of the soundstages and the wardrobe department. From there, they drove around the lagoon through San Francisco/Amity and World Expo. Once past the sets of *Psycho IV,* the Hollywood area, and the Boneyard, they returned to Sound Stage 19. Before the tour ended in 1995, other sets would become part of the tour, including a cabin from television's *The Swamp Thing.*

If visitors wanted to see an actual production and maybe even participate, they only had to visit the Nickelodeon Studios. The children's television network agreed to locate at Universal Studios Florida in November 1988. The first production was the *Super Sloppy Double Dare* show in June 1989.

The 40-minute guided walking tour began on the second floor of Soundstage 19. Once past the *Blues Clues* room, the visitors would walk through a viewing tube that allowed them to peek into an actual soundstage. The next stop was the Control room, where they saw a video about the television network. Next door was Soundstage 18 with another viewing tube, which gave the guide a second opportunity to talk about a current production. Soundstage 17 held the Game Lab, where visitors could audition to be on a show, and the Gak Kitchen, where they could experience slime. Visitors also walked past the wardrobe and makeup departments. Peter Alexander was pleased with Nickelodeon Studios. "That worked because those were real shows."[34]

In 1992 the network buried a time capsule in front of Sound Stage 18 that included items chosen by viewers. Some of the items included a Nintendo Game Boy, a copy of *Nickelodeon Magazine*, a *Home Alone* VHS tape, clips of Nickelodeon station IDs, and various other toys. The time capsule was to be opened on April 30, 2042. However, Nickelodeon Studios did not last that long. The tour closed on June 15, 2001, and the Game Lab lasted until April 2005. The time capsule was reburied at the Nickelodeon Suites Resort in Orlando.

For many early visitors, the unexpected highlight of their trip would be a personal encounter with a celebrity impersonator. Many of Hollywood's iconic stars wandered the back lot areas. On opening day, the roster included Mae West, the Marx Brothers, W.C. Fields, and Marilyn Monroe.

Actor Ron Schneider was put in charge of the celebrity impersonators. He was living in Florida after working at Disney and saw the Bates Mansion built on a hill in a vacant lot near his home. For a while, that was the only sign of construction. He was able to utilize Universal's attitude of "we can afford to be rebels, non-conformist, anarchists" to the fullest.[35] He said that is why the Blues Brothers fit so well at Universal Studios. "Our first mini-concert is pulled straight from the trunk of the Bluesmobile; two stand-up mics hooked up to speakers on the car roof, with a music track coming from the cassette player in the dashboard," Schneider recalled. "Nothing but a few

*un**official* **TIP**
On November 9, 2006, Universal Orlando announced that Sound Stage 18 would be redesigned to become a 1,000-seat permanent venue for Blue Man Group. The new venue opened June 1, 2007.

songs at first, but Dan [Joliet Jake] and Keith [Elwood] invest it with as much personality as possible, and the guests eat it up."[36] He said, "In the back lot's New York area there was an abandoned construction platform right next to the front stoop of a brownstone apartment. The stairs, the sight lines, the elevation . . . it all seems ideal!"[37] The Blues Brothers show would remain one of the very few things unchanged since the opening days.

NEW YORK

A WALK THROUGH THE SETS OF NEW YORK, Hollywood, or San Francisco was like taking a stroll through the back lot in Hollywood. Barry Upson said, "You will find many in our industry that think the term *theming* is really overused in almost every facet of our life and has become a cliché. However, true theming is still critical to successful park development and operations. Good park theming is seeing to it that everything in the park contributes positively to its central story line and to a compelling, cohesive guest experience: no jarring, non-thematic events, services or facilities are allowed. This is easier said than done, but it is vital to success."[38]

Upson felt it was important to present an authentic experience. "Since most, if not all of Universal's attractions are based on a final film product or selected compelling components of the process [stunts, animals, screen tests, and so on], there was never really a line between 'real' and 'entertaining'—the attractions had to be both," Barry Upson said. "The studio environment is also always 'real' in its own way."[39]

Bob Ward and Norm Newberry designed the facades at Universal as actual backdrops for productions. "Movie sets are designed differently than normal buildings," Peter Alexander explained. "They have more depth to them because they are always in the background; they are not the star. They are a little bit out of focus, so they won't read unless they are deeper. So the corbel or whatever architectural detail is always bigger on a movie set, so that is the way Universal Studios is designed."[40] Ward felt the sets needed to be realistic, and he protected them from budget cuts.

In the New York area, movie references are everywhere. There is the Kitty Kat Club, a reference to *Cabaret;* the Priscilla Hotel from *Thoroughly Modern Millie;* and the Hudson Street Home for Girls from *Annie.* O'Rourke's Bar & Grill was named after a minor character in *The Godfather,* and Louie's Restaurant was where Michael Corleone killed a fellow gangster and a police captain.

Some of the key members of the Universal staff are honored with their names on the windows of the *Metropolis Tribune* and other building facades. Displayed prominently at the end of the New York Street, overlooking the lagoon, is a tribute to Lew Wasserman. Wasserman's head, without his trademark glasses, was placed on top of a large statue of Abraham Lincoln. The biggest tribute was reserved for Jay Stein. At the top of a tall column in the center of Gramercy Park is a herald archangel with Stein's face.

Across the lagoon is a rare patch of green modeled after the East Green section of Central Park. It is a relaxed little space with trees, grass, fake boulders, and multiple winding paths along the edge of the lagoon. It was the connection between Hollywood and Expo Center. At the edges of the park are self-guided demonstrations on filmmaking techniques. For example, visitors can aim their cameras at strategically placed backdrops to simulate the illusions created through matte paintings and miniatures.

No matter how hard Universal tried to stay true to its roots as a working studio, writer Jeremy Thompson saw a downside to this technique. He said the New York sets were "experientially empty, and consist of nothing more than a series of very elaborate facades to wander through and disguise the area's two main attractions. . . . It's no surprise that there's almost always some party, parade, or special seasonal event going on at Universal Studios Florida, otherwise it could be one of the most lifeless major theme parks in the world."[41]

When King Kong first opened on the tram tour in Hollywood, he instantly became a huge hit and the symbol of the Universal Studios experience. He was in your face, a bit scary, and you got a good laugh when it was all over. There was no way there would be a Universal Studios Florida without King Kong.

The "bigger and better" version of the Hollywood attraction was conceived at a lunch in 1987 at the Rive Gauche Café in Sherman Oaks. The men were mulling over the problem of turning a 2-minute experience into a full-fledged theme park ride. "We thought, 'What could top running across Kong?'" recalled Alexander. "Then we thought, 'He could pick you up, shake you around and then throw you down.'"[42] Bob Ward had seen the film *Nighthawks* (1981), where actor Rutger Hauer was on the 59th Street Bridge. Ward remembered that there was an aerial tram that traveled alongside the bridge. What if the guests were in a gondola suspended high above the ground? That would make them feel vulnerable.

Alexander said, "That's really good, Bob, but we need more of a story. I knew that just an 'attack' by itself would not be enough to 'out-Disney Disney.'" He suggested, "OK, here's the story . . . you are in the queue line . . . and you hear Kong has escaped. You board the Roosevelt Island tram to be evacuated, but in the first scene, you see that Kong has laid down a path of destruction before you . . . then you round the corner . . . and there he is on the bridge. He stops your tramcar, then picks it up, but a helicopter shoots at him and he throws down the tramcar. Then, since our basic theme was 'behind the scenes in Hollywood,' TV monitors turn on inside the tramcar, and you find that your whole experience has been filmed and that you—the guest— have actually just 'starred' in a *King Kong* film. Later, our Advertising VP David Weitzner's team coined the term 'ride the movies' to describe Kong and the other 'super rides' we developed."[43]

Stein hired Gary Goddard and Landmark Entertainment Group to help develop the concept and script. They also produced the sound track and film components. Goddard felt Stein liked working with consultants because they could be easily motivated through coercion.[44]

The story line was simple and compelling. The show was set in New York. WWOR radio is playing while the visitors are in the queue dressed as a New York subway station. WWOR was a real MCA-owned radio station in New Jersey. Suddenly, there is a breaking news report claiming that King Kong has escaped and the only safe haven is Roosevelt Island. To get there, visitors needed to ride an aerial tram over the East River. Before riders could arrive safely, they would confront King Kong. Jay Stein coined the name Kongfrontation.

The show was staged inside one of the world's largest soundstages. The six-story building was 71,000 square feet, or the size of two football fields. In Hollywood, many times it is the backgrounds that make the impossible seem plausible. "The setting for Kong had to be brilliantly designed to allow the 37-foot-tall creature to appear at his best," said Peter Alexander. "For that task, I asked Henry Bumstead [Bummy to his friends] to design the set, and under his supervision, with Tom Reidenbach's help in turning my layout into a fully functional plan, Kong's world took shape."

The most difficult set to build was the scale-model reproduction of the 59th Street Bridge that had to fit inside of a 60-foot tall building. Alexander said, "Bummy's forced-perspective miniature bridge did the job, aided by yards and yards of 'Gerritts black velour' [a kind of jet-black curtain that magicians use for 'black art' tricks such as levitation]. It made the horizon disappear and helped allow the guests to lose sight of how high off the ground they really were."

The ride system proved particularly difficult. Not only did the vehicles need to look something like the real Roosevelt Island Tram cars, but each of the four cars required a "traveling motion base" that would create the illusion that Kong was picking up the tram and then throwing it down. Alexander asked two firms to develop designs that would accomplish this never-before-seen show action. One, Intamin of Switzerland, developed a ride vehicle suspended by cables at each of the four corners. The second, Arrow Development of Utah, created a device that acted like an accordion bellows on top of the tramcar. Arrow won the job, and then it was up to Universal to provide it with the specs that would define the tramcar's motions.

A key question was: How fast should the tram drop when King Kong "threw it down" at the end of the ride? To determine the force, Alexander said, "We developed a harness rig to 'fly' a person. We suspended the rig from the top of (45-foot-tall) Stage 24 at Universal Studios. Somebody had to be the test pilot, and since nobody else volunteered, I took the first drop."[45] Unfortunately, a miscommunication caused the engineers to drop him at full free-fall, and then jerk him to a sudden stop about 3 feet from the cement stage floor, resulting in a double hernia operation some months later. From that, they learned that they didn't want to make King Kong a free-fall coaster type of experience.

The next big challenge was to get the computer system that controlled King Kong to "talk" to the ride control system. To create the illusion that the big guy was picking up the tram, he needed to place his hands inside the ride envelope (directly under the tramcar). That meant that Kong's actions had to work in synch with the ride's bellows (which were actually doing the work of picking up the 50-passenger car).

Kong's producer, Craig Barr, and his team spent months inside the curtains at the center of the attraction—the control room—getting the two systems to work with each other.[46]

Like many of the other major attractions on opening day, Kong had his issues. Because of a power outage hours before the park opened, the master software program forced technicians to trigger the ape's movements manually.

Gary Goddard was responsible for *Ghostbusters: A Live Action Spooktacular*. The 11-minute live show stayed true to the Ivan Reitman film. With that in-your-face attitude that appealed to Jay Stein, Goddard placed the audience in a free business seminar to learn how to start up their own Ghostbuster business. Up front was a re-creation of the Temple of Gozer from the film's finale. The massive, 100-foot-wide set rivaled the one in the original film, which was the largest set ever built on a Hollywood soundstage.

When the show opened, the emphasis was on comedy and audience participation. The show began with a tour guide on stage talking about her disbelief in ghosts. Then familiar characters from the film, such as

unofficial **TIP**
Kongfrontation closed on September 8, 2002, to make way for the Florida version of Revenge of the Mummy. It seems a giant gorilla tossing your tram was not enough of a thrill.

Slimer, Gozer, and the Stay Puft Marshmallow Man, would magically appear from nowhere. Goddard employed a Pepper's ghost to allow the 13 mechanical ghosts to interact with real human actors. Built across the entire width of the stage between the actors and the audience was a ¾-inch-thick slanted glass window. With a brightly lit stage, the actors appeared as they normally would. Above the audience was a balcony where mechanical "ghosts" were located. When show lights illuminated these figures, their reflections appeared on the half mirrored window next to the actors. The illusion was so well constructed that the audience never realized that there was a piece of glass at all.

The original plans called for an elaborate, $400,000 preshow that was cut at the last minute. The success of the show allowed for the preshow to be installed a couple of years later. The script was also revamped a few years after opening. This time the Ghostbusters only show up in the final 2 minutes. The show closed in 1996.

SAN FRANCISCO *and* AMITY

THE SAN FRANCISCO/AMITY SECTION would be home to two of the most highly anticipated attractions, *Earthquake: The Big One* and Jaws. Both of these attractions were attempts to take a 2-minute experience in Hollywood and stretch it out to a full-scale attraction.

The San Francisco set is an impressive collection of structures modeled after real buildings. The largest structure is the Ghirardelli factory (1853) with its iconic sign atop the building. Many of the other buildings reflected the theme of the main attraction, *Earthquake: The Big One*. Inside of Richter Burger Co. is a replica of the Louis Agassiz statue that fell headfirst into the ground during the 1906 San Francisco earthquake. A miniature Fisherman's Wharf was placed along the central lagoon, and cable car tracks were embedded in the main path. Nearby is the Buena Vista Café, an almost-exact copy of a 1916 boardinghouse famous for creating the first Irish coffee. The Cannery at Del Monte Square in Fisherman's Wharf was the inspiration for the Wharfside Cannery.

Although *Earthquake: The Big One* was slated to open with the rest of the park, a power outage hours before opening knocked out some of the software. Instead, the attraction opened on October 9. For those who arrived on opening day, its absence was yet another disappointment.

When the attraction did open, visitors discovered it combined preshow elements from the special effects demonstrations used in California and the immersive tram experience. The show began in a large room with a set piece in front of a blue screen. Actor Charlton Heston appeared on-screen to demonstrate how *Earthquake* was filmed. As in Hollywood, volunteers acted out scenes and the results were shown on large screens above the stage. Then the audience was led to the "Oakland" subway station to a train that resembled a stripped-down Bay Area Rapid Transit train.

Peter Alexander had suggested the train go in a loop, but Sidney Sheinberg wanted to save money and suggested that it go one way and then back up. His rationale? It is Hollywood, after all. Alexander said, "At Universal there was always a budget. At Disney, it really didn't matter. Everything was 40¢ on the dollar compared to Disney. We had virtually no engineering staff."[47]

Once everyone was loaded, the train moved forward through a dark, confined space and entered a San Francisco subway station. The ride experience was similar to the Hollywood version. Just as in Hollywood, at the end of the demonstration the magic is stripped away and the inner workings are revealed.

As impressive as *Earthquake* was, the real draw was Jaws. Just like King Kong, the shark was the Universal Studio Tour in the minds of many. Alexander and his team had to take another 2-minute experience and create a stand-alone attraction. Originally, Alexander wanted to make the Jaws experience just one part of a much-longer boat ride. He hired former Imagineer Bill Martin to lay out the ride. When Jay Stein saw the plans, he suggested that Alexander toss everything and just make an all-Jaws ride.

The story line was straightforward and simple. Guests would board an inflatable tour boat for a peaceful ride around Amity Island, when suddenly something would go incredibly wrong. The first sign would be chatter on the boat's radio; then the boat would pass another tour boat as it sank into the lagoon. Floating in the water was a mouse ear hat from Disney. Suddenly, a 3-ton, 24-foot great white shark would bear down on the guests. The captain would fight back with a grenade launcher and escape the shark's first pass. However, the unrelenting shark would continue to attack.

Universal hired Ride & Show Engineering Inc. to fabricate and install the ride. John Zovich, William Watkins, and Eduard Feuer were former Imagineers and worked on the *Miami Vice* stunt show as well as the *Earthquake* ride system. The show was technically complex. Jaws was breaking new ground; nothing like this had ever been attempted before.

"The boat driver was an example of a staff person contributing to the show experience," Barry Upson said. "It was like the tour guides."[48] They piloted their boats around a 7-acre lagoon filled with 5 million gallons of water. It took seven different sharks to create the various action sequences.

Alexander asked Sidney Sheinberg if he had any suggestions about the finale. "[Sidney Sheinberg] comes up to me with that cigar in his mouth, and says, 'In every shark picture, the shark blows up in the end.'" Alexander said, "So I found someone who could make a shark blow up every 60 seconds."[49] That meant building an underwater explosion effect simulator. This included a submerged shooter for shooting props (shark flesh) and red dye–colored water that would float to the water's surface.

Peter Alexander programmed the size of the flames. "I wanted to make it intense and scary, but not dangerous; so I kept making Ron turn the fire up higher and higher," he said. "When it got to the point where the heat was actually painful, we dialed it back just a bit. So the impact on the audience was amazing: some people thought they were actually getting burned, but I knew from personal experience that it was safe, even for prolonged exposure."

Another breakthrough effect was the shark grabbing the boat and spinning it around. At least, that was the plan. Like the "meat machine," the effect was frequently broken. Alexander said, "I could not recall a single time I rode the attraction and everything worked."[50]

On August 23, 1990, Universal closed down the ride to figure out what went wrong. In a 40-page filing, Universal sued Ride & Show Engineering in Orange County Circuit Court for poor workmanship. Steven Lew, president of USF said, "We are angry. We are disappointed. There are numerous design flaws."[51] He added, "We have suffered tremendously. They did not deliver on what they could deliver on. In the interim, we had to discover and correct problems at our own expense."[52]

By December, Universal had tossed in the towel. The park announced that the Jaws attraction would not reopen until 1992. Tom Williams said, "We are undergoing a comprehensive engineering effort that will translate [into] an opening that has yet to be determined."[53]

Throughout 1991, Universal aggressively tried to get the attraction running; however, by 1992 it had given up. It was determined that the existing version was fatally flawed, and Universal had to start over.

After an investigation, Universal claimed that Ride & Show was at fault. The park suggested that the problems were due to improper testing of the materials for stress while being underwater. Even though Ride & Show said it had tested the components underwater for months, Universal claimed that Ride & Show had used all the wrong materials. None of it was waterproof. It turned out that Ride & Show used non-waterproof parts in the water and then everything started to fail. On April 4, 1991, a settlement was reached with Ride & Show Engineering.

Show director Adam Bezark summed it up this way, "You can imagine how complex it must be to get one giant mechanical water-craft to swim up and bite another giant mechanical watercraft which is MOVING with absolute precision, hundreds of times per day." Ride & Show claimed that Universal was making the company the scape-goat for the problems caused by an economic turndown and higher gas prices. "We feel very strongly about the quality of the products we build," Mark Messersmith of Ride & Show said. "But since they are not experiencing the kinds of attendance they expected, they are pointing fingers at us. We are little guys. We are just a small vendor trying to do our job."[54]

The story line in the revised version of Jaws came from *Jaws II*. The show was set two years after the first movie, as the town of Amity exploited the notoriety it gained after the first shark attack. The tour took guests past the actual spots where the shark had eaten the island-ers. Instead of blowing up, this time the shark met his demise through electrocution. Alexander was confident that this effect would work and be reliable. He said, "Shark bites wire and starts a fire. We knew how to do fire."

After Alexander left Universal, it became Bezark's job to get things working. Bezark said, "My role was to bring the whole thing together: fine-tune the script, program the boats and sharks, work out the effects timings and lighting, oversee the new sound track and train the per-formers, etc." Intamin rebuilt the track. Regal Marine Industries fabri-cated the boats. Universal went straight to the experts at Oceaneering Technologies to build the heavy-duty hydraulic machinery. The only things to remain in the new version would be the general layout of the ride, some of the sets, and some of the gags like the mouse ears.

In September 2005 Jaws went down to seasonal status, operating only during busy weeks. This was due to the rising costs of fuel because the attraction used a lot of gas for fire effects. Universal reopened the attraction on February 4, 2007, due to numerous complaints of its part-time closure. A complete closure would be devastating to the park. It was valuable to Universal because of its capacity, reported at 2,500 people an hour; that's phenomenal by thrill ride standards. A typical major ride at most theme parks would do well to handle 1,800 people an hour. For the reopening, the ride had been improved, the queue had been cleaned, the boats had been repainted, and the sharks now thrashed around and had been bloodied up and repainted to make them feel much more realistic. However, the fire effects had been reduced.

On December 2, 2011, Universal announced that Bruce the shark would no longer be terrorizing guests as of January 2012. Tom Schroder said, "Jaws has been an amazing attraction and an important part of our history. We know that Jaws holds a special place in the hearts of our guests. But we always have to look to the future and dedicate ourselves to providing new, innovative entertainment experiences for our guests."[55] Soon Harry Potter, an even greater force, would replace the shark. Park officials did suggest that a tribute to the shark would make its way into the new theme.

Joining Jaws and *Earthquake* was a show for the younger guests. The *American Tail Live Show* was based on Steven Spielberg's animated fantasy adventure *An American Tail: Fievel Goes West*. Within the first year, *Beetlejuice's Rock and Roll Graveyard Revue* replaced the show, making *Fievel* the very first opening-day attraction to close.

EXPO CENTER

EXPO CENTER WAS THE HOME for the park's fantasy rides, E.T. Adventure and Back to the Future. Back to the Future was not ready for opening day and would open in 1991. Inside the Cinemagic Center was the *Animal Actors Stage*. The animal show was the same as Hollywood's and starred Lassie and Mr. Ed look-alikes.

More than any other ride at Universal Studios Florida, E.T. Adventure was directly aimed at Disney's strength: family rides. "For me, the E.T. Adventure ride in the Universal theme parks is the next evolution of the original motion picture," Steven Spielberg said. "In a very real sense, it's the only sequel to the movie." Spielberg was looking for a "warm and touching" attraction.[56]

Peter Alexander knew this was going to be a difficult project and felt the pressure. He said, "Relationship stories like E.T. that rely on 2-hour-long films to create their emotional impact are not easily translated into 6- or 8-minute theme park rides, so designing a ride or show that captured the essence of the film presented quite a challenge."[57] The ride was destined to be Universal's family-friendly, high-capacity ride like Disney's It's a Small World or Pirates of the Caribbean.

Goddard also had a suggestion for the destination. He thought Universal should do a modern take on Tom Sawyer's Island at the Disney parks. "You have to take a raft to get there and you have to take a raft to come back," he said. "You can't just walk there. For E.T. you take the bike ride and land on the planet. The planet is a completely interactive place. You get off the bike and it's cool."[58]

As a result, Universal hired a Swiss company to build a platform suspended under a track with nine BMX bicycles mounted on top of the platform. In the front bicycle's basket is an E.T. figure that reacts to the goings-on throughout the ride. He hides when scared and is magically gone when the riders reach the finale.

Before the riders board their bicycles, they watch a brief preshow starring director Steven Spielberg. Unlike the multiple television monitors in use today, the original preshow was displayed on a large single screen. Spielberg was sitting in a movie theater watching E.T. and paused to tell the riders that they were actors in the sequel and were wanted on the set. The preshow was changed in 2002 to celebrate the film's 20th anniversary.

The elaborate queue is part soundstage set and part redwood forest. To add realism, redwood scent is pumped into the room, and a permanent full moon lights the path. On occasion, an audio-animatronic figure named Botanicus rises from the forest floor and talks with guests.

Once at the loading dock, riders take a seat on one of the bicycles, and the 15-minute chase with a surprise ending begins. The objective is to escape from the police and NASA and take E.T. to safety. Along the way, riders fly over a city, giving the ride its Peter Pan moment. Below is a massive model made up of 3,340 miniature buildings, 250 cars, and 1,000 streetlights. Above are 4,400 stars.

Determining that final destination was a struggle. Alexander asked himself, "Once you jump on the bikes and then you are riding, where do you go?"[59] In the film, the children fly to E.T.'s spaceship. Alexander felt that would be anticlimatic. Instead, he wanted the visitors to fly all the way to the Green Planet, E.T.'s home. After all, E.T.'s mission in the film was to gather plants for his ailing planet.

But what does the Green Planet look like? Alexander asked Steven Spielberg. Spielberg told him that it had to be a positive, organic environment. The director felt that most science fiction planets were weird, dark, cold, and unpleasant. He suggested that Alexander read William Kotzwinkle's E.T.: The Book of the Green Planet: A Novel. That turned out to be a pointless exercise. Instead, Alexander found inspiration from the ocean. He said "the bottom of the ocean is pretty cool" and if you "think underwater it's organic and it's beautiful." He remembered, "When I was a kid I had surfed in California, and when the waves were flat on, my friends and I had done a bit of diving. I always remembered thinking how the plants and coral rock formations on the ocean floor seemed like an alien landscape." He collected materials to show his art directors "and with that simple inspiration, they went crazy designing the 'friendly' 'alien' Green Planet."[60] The designers created a whole cast of eclectic characters, such as Cloud Bearers, Water Sprites, Jumpums, and Tickly Moot Moots.

As for the finale, Spielberg told Alexander, "Remember E.T. is a personal story. So at the end, the guests need a personal moment with him." Alexander asked, "What if he knows your name? What if E.T. knows everyone's name, and thanks them by name for bringing him home?"[61] That was exactly what Spielberg was looking for.

Universal hired Birket Engineering to develop the goodbye system. As guests enter the ride, they are handed a bar-coded passport with their name. The computer was preprogrammed with 5,808 names. While boarding the ride vehicle, the employee collects the passports and passes them over a window scanner. The system identifies the vehicle as it leaves by reading a radio-frequency tag mounted to the top of the vehicle. As the riders approach the finale, an animated E.T. figure turns and greets them by name.

To add additional emotional punch, composer John Williams crafted a custom score for the ride. Today, E.T. Adventure is the only original attraction still operating in the park.

HOLLYWOOD

THE FINAL STOP ON THE LOOP around the Universal Studios Florida lagoon is Hollywood. The Hollywood Boulevard is lined with highly detailed facades of famous Los Angeles buildings, including Montmartre Café (1922), S.H. Kress & Co. (1935), the Hollywood Playhouse (1921), Schwab's Pharmacy (1935), the Brown Derby (1929), and the Max Factor Building (1931). The level of detail was above and beyond anything that Disney had done at its studio park. Instead of using forced perspective like Disney's version of Hollywood Boulevard, these facades are full-size backdrops ready for motion pictures.

When the park opened, there was only one attraction in the Hollywood section. Inside of the Pantages Theater (1929) was the 25-minute *Phantom of the Opera Make-Up Show*. The sometimes humorous and at times morbid show took visitors behind the scenes to demonstrate the latest makeup techniques used in Hollywood. Many of the elements were lifted from *The Land of a Thousand Faces* show in

Hollywood. A custom sound track performed by the London Symphony Orchestra was produced for the show.

Guests entered a lobby dressed as the Paris Opera House. On display were some of the monsters that made Universal Studios famous. Along the walls were tributes to Lon Chaney Sr., Jack Pierce, Lon Chaney Jr., Bud Westmore, Alfred Hitchcock, and the Munsters. Other items included an original Lon Chaney mask and the body of Regan from *The Exorcist* (1973).

unofficial **TIP**
The makeup show would be constantly updated but remain true to origins. The name would also frequently change. In 1993 the show was known as *The Gory, Gruesome & Grotesque Horror Make-up Show.*

Academy Award–winning makeup artist Rick Baker was hired as a consultant, and one of the stand-out demonstrations was his mechanical changing face of the werewolf used in *An American Werewolf in London* (1981). Visitors were also shown the lifelike gorilla masks that Baker created for *Gorillas in the Mist* (1988).

Of course, there was plenty of blood and gore. One memorable demonstration was how they made roaches appear to come out of an actor's mouth in *Creepshow* (1982). *The Fly* (1986) was the inspiration for another illusion when a 200-pound, 5-foot-tall fly crept out of its pod and walked onto the stage. At one point, an actor would burst through a mirror, get within 5 feet of the nearest guests, and then disappear. Nobody was safe.

Outside the theater, embedded into the sidewalks, were plaques identical to the famous Walk of the Stars on Hollywood Boulevard. Along with movie and TV personalities with a connection to Universal were plaques dedicated to Universal executives deemed essential to the Recreation division, including Bob Gault, Robert Ward, and Tom Williams.

In an attempt to keep people in the park well into the evening, Universal Studios Florida debuted with the *Dynamite Nights Stunt Spectacular*. Based on a *Miami Vice* theme, stuntmen piloted high-speed boats and personal watercraft on the central lagoon, blowing up a boathouse, ships, and even a seaplane. According to Peter Alexander, the only thing spectacular was the failure of the show. He said, "We were not used to running a big ride park. For the stunt show in the lake, boats that were supposed to sink and then float would just sink. We did not have the engineering staff that Disney had."[62] The show closed on February 17, 2000.

NOT *a* VERY GRAND OPENING

IT IS COMMON PRACTICE IN THE THEME PARK INDUSTRY to soft open before a grand opening. Universal also calls this a technical rehearsal. It gives the operations team a chance to gain experience and test the rides in real-world conditions with ordinary visitors. Due to the scheduled opening date, Universal had to compress its break-in period to just a few weeks. The first visitors through the gates arrived on May 21, 1990. Because the park knew that a lot of stuff was not working, it only charged half-price admission to avoid any disappointment.

June 7, 1990, will live in the memories of Universal staffers as a day of infamy. The forecast called for a 91°F day with the humidity reaching 93%. The day started well. The opening ceremony took place at 8 a.m. Joining Jay Stein and the other MCA executives were Steven Spielberg, James Stewart, Michael J. Fox, Bill Cosby, Sylvester Stallone, Robert Wagner, Morgan Fairchild, Anthony Perkins, Sissy Spacek, and Beau Bridges. A time capsule was buried with Hollywood memorabilia, including the knife and shower curtain used in Alfred Hitchcock's *Psycho*. The intent was to dig up the time capsule during the park's 25th anniversary in 2015.

Stein, Alexander, and the rest of the team knew they were not ready for the invitation-only event. The limited soft opening exposed many problems. According to Ron Schneider, "The night before Universal Studios Florida opens, everything seems really quiet and peaceful. Since all of the attractions are either indoors or behind the scenes, whatever desperation is going on (and there is plenty) is hidden from view."[63]

Terry Winnick had been designing MCA attractions longer than anybody, and he said, "It was never going to be ready. That was the same story that Jay heard from me every year when I was all by myself. You are approving it in January, and you want me to open it in June, and I am sleeping in a motor home. My crews are working 24 hours a day, and Jay's attitude was, 'We're going to open it because we said we are going to open it and we need to open it, and we will fix it afterward.'"[64] Winnick felt that Stein "did not realize how big of a disaster he was about to experience."[65]

Nearly every major attraction failed. By the end of the day, more than 1,000 guests stormed Guest Services and demanded refunds. Kongfrontation was struggling. The "talk back" system was still not working properly. There was no way to be certain that Kong would not malfunction and stick his hand into the tramcar and nail somebody in the third row or that the tramcar would not break off Kong's hand in the process. Alexander was concerned that someone might get seriously hurt.

Steven Spielberg came to show off Kongfrontation to Bob Pittman and his entourage from Time Warner. Spielberg was not fond of heights and suggested that he wait for his guests at the exit. Alexander pulled Pittman aside to explain the situation. Pittman nervously laughed and rode the attraction without incident. He remembered Alexander's warnings and years later hired him to work for him. It would take another week to get Kongfrontation working properly.

Earthquake! was having programming issues. Larry Lester was able to fix those after the first couple of weeks. Jaws was a nightmare. Bob Ward may have had it the worst. He was on the Jaws ride with

Sidney Sheinberg and his wife when it broke down. After 30 minutes, they brought out a rowboat to rescue the passengers.[66]

During the preview day, only four attractions worked as planned. The E.T. Adventure was truly a magical ride. It was the only major ride that worked flawlessly on opening day due to the work of show producer Jane Jackson, a Disney veteran. Lines grew to more than 2 hours. *The Murder She Wrote* and *Hitchcock* shows also opened on schedule. And the *Ghostbusters* show opened without a hitch. Gary Goddard was an outside consultant, and his contract was for a turnkey production. Universal built the building and Goddard promised to have the show ready by opening day. Goddard said, "opening date is opening date," and if he missed the deadline, he would have been severely penalized.[67] Throughout the day, they kept asking Goddard if he could run the show again just to give people something to do.

Time magazine called the park "Universal's Swamp of Dreams." "One TV station aired footage of Park President Tom Williams bravely confronting angry guests outside *Earthquake!*; another shows the growing mob waiting to register complaints at the Guest Relations Office," Ron Schneider recalled.[68] The *Orlando Sentinel* reported, "They came, they stood, they left mad."[69]

The marketing team went into panic mode and began to hand out one free ticket for a future visit for every paid ticket. All of the advertising changed to avoid mentioning the broken attractions. USF vice president of marketing Randy Garfield said, "We felt it was a good business decision to merchandise only those products you can actually deliver on."[70] The staff was trained to reply to unhappy customers with the suggestion, "Please do not agree with the guest that we should not have opened on June 7 as advertised. We couldn't allow them to arrive only to find our gates locked."[71] MCA executives held out hope that the park would reach the first-year goal of $5 million to $6 million. Steven Lew said, "Twelve months is a long time, and this market is somewhat seasonal. We feel that when King Kong starts growling, when that banana breath starts blowing . . . we are going to hit a high stride."[72]

Michael Eisner was diplomatic in his response to the new theme park. For a long time, he believed that MCA would never get the financing to build the project. He felt that Wasserman and Sheinberg were not really committed to opening an attraction in Florida. "At one point, my assistant Art Levitt and I climbed over a fence at 3 in the morning to see if any dirt had actually been moved at their site 4 miles from Walt Disney World," he said. "All we saw was a small construction permit sign in the middle of the property."[73]

When construction finally started, Eisner said, "I resigned myself to the fact that the prospect of an aggressive competitor was an incentive to redouble our own efforts and not take our success for granted."[74] In his autobiography, *Work in Progress: Risking Failure, Surviving*

Success, Eisner found comfort in advice from David Sarnoff, founder of both NBC and RCA. Sarnoff said, "Competition brings out the worst in people and the best in products."

Publicly, Tom Williams tried to put forward the best face possible. "When we built this place, it was the first time we built a theme park. We know what we did right. We know what we did wrong." Randy Garfield added, "We're a real, working studio, we aren't a theme park. Our back lot sets aren't just cutesy streets. They were designed to be used for filming. Visitors can see something being shot here virtually every day on our sound stages."[75] Terry Winnick was more blunt: "The hardest thing we had to do initially in Florida was to convince the public that we were not MGM-Disney."[76]

Even though attendance was 60% below projections, MCA's new partner, the Rank Organisation, was publicly supportive. Rodney Rycroft said, "I think we will just watch the situation carefully and continue to have confidence that the operators [MCA] will bring it up to levels that we had hoped for in due course. That may just take a little longer than we originally hoped."[77]

Despite the Florida park's rough start, Stein's loyalty to the company was rewarded; in October 1990 he was named chairman and CEO of the Recreation Services Group. Ron Bension was named president and COO.

◼ **BACK** *to the* **FUTURE**

IN HOLLYWOOD, YOU ARE ONLY AS GOOD AS your last movie. String too many duds together, and you might find yourself back waiting tables. Jay Stein was getting nervous. Even with the bump up in title, he knew he was in the crosshairs. After the disastrous launch of Universal Studios Florida, the pressure was on to find a hit. Once again, Steven Spielberg came to the rescue. Back to the Future: The Ride opened on May 2, 1991, and turned Universal Studios Florida around.

A roller coaster was considered early on, but it was decided that the technology moved too quickly to tell the story. It was also too low-tech for the ambitious team at Universal. Instead, inspiration struck Alexander while daydreaming. "One day, I was sitting in a conference room with a bunch of execs and I got this picture in my mind: DeLoreans, in a steep, domed IMAX theater," he said. "Each DeLorean would ride on top of its own simulator motion base, and by cutting off the sight lines to the rest of the theater, guests inside each car would feel like they were flying."[78]

"I think that there's always going to be roller coasters, but this is the next generation of rides," Terry Winnick said. "With a motion vehicle you can create all kinds of environments and experiences, in the sea, in the air, traveling through time." He described the experience "as close to virtual reality as you're going to get today. You can't see below, above or to either side. You can only see and hear what we want you to hear."[79]

When Alexander went to Jay Stein to tell him of his idea, Stein immediately dismissed the concept. "If that was going to work somebody would already be doing it now. It's too good of an idea."[80] Stein bet Alexander $1,000 it wouldn't work.

With that additional incentive, Alexander went to work. To prove that the concept had merit, he fashioned a foam-core mock-up of a DeLorean ride vehicle. Bob Ward described the mock-up "sort of like when you carve up a refrigerator box as a kid." Then they rented the OMNIMAX theater at Caesar's Palace in Las Vegas and placed the mock-up inside. Alexander and Craig Barr got in the mock-up, and Alexander said, "We felt pretty stupid."[81]

Barr was also a nonbeliever and bet Alexander an additional $20 that it would not work. "However, as soon as the lights went down and the film rolled, Craig put a $20 bill in my outstretched palm," said Alexander. "What we saw from inside the foam-core mock-up was amazing. Just by cutting off sight lines and isolating our vehicle from the stationary parts of the theater, we produced the sensation of flying." [82] Alexander got the green light and a budget of $25 million to produce the ride. He also claims that Stein has yet to pay off their bet.[83]

Then came the search for the right kind of motion simulators. Before Alexander worked at Disney and MCA, he worked at Hughes Aircraft. He immediately contacted friends at the Singer Corporation, a company that manufactured flight simulators.

"An industrial design firm in Pasadena [Smith-Bruni Design] mocked up the seating and look of the DeLorean ride vehicles," Alexander said. "The trick there was to make a two-passenger DeLorean into an eight-passenger ride vehicle, and yet still make it look like a DeLorean. I remember we designed the unit (again, Bill Watkins engineered it) to pull 1G, although after I left, my boss Jay Stein cranked it up to pull more than that."[84] Alexander was the first of three show producers assigned to the ride.

Next up was Phil Hettema. He focused on getting the motion vehicles to work and placing them in the dome. He said, "It is a very complex operation because you are distributing people to three levels into 24 different vehicles." To test the concept, they rented out the OMNIMAX theater at the Science World dome in Vancouver. Hettema stitched together all of the off-the-shelf footage they could find, plus a few minutes of early CGI wire-frame footage. They created a wire-frame city where they could drive down alleys. It was during this phase of the testing that they realized they could make the vehicle appear to fly backward. This became an important element in the final version. However, the CGI format did not work. Hettema said, "The strategy for producing the film just did not pan out."[85]

Then came Sherry McKenna. She was brought in as media producer for the whole park, with a focus on Back to the Future and Hanna-Barbera. McKenna brought in Douglas Trumbull of Berkshire Motion Picture Corp. Trumball was the award-winning special-effects wizard behind such films as *2001: A Space Odyssey* (1968) and *Blade Runner* (1982) and directed *Brain Storm* (1983) and *Silent Running* (1971). Trumball had worked on the very first motion simulator called Tour of the Universe at the CN Tower in Toronto. The attraction opened in 1985. That ride loaded from the rear and had a similar layout as Star Tours. It was built on a Boeing 747 simulator base built by Rediffusion Motion Platforms.

After McKenna came Terry Winnick to finish the project. Because Universal was committed to the 84-foot OMNIMAX format, Trumball needed to deal with one of its idiosyncrasies. To take into account the curved screen that provides a 270-degree image, all of the miniature sets had to be built with curved surfaces. Flying through the Ice Age and Jurassic period sets were custom cameras.

The OMNIMAX format used a special IMAX 70-millimeter film, which was 10 times larger than the standard 35-millimeter frame used in regular movie theaters and three times larger than the standard 70-millimeter process used on some epic films. Instead of the film being projected from the rear of an auditorium, it was projected from the center of the audience area through a fish-eye lens onto the domed screen.

The 4.5-minute film cost $16 million to produce. Trumball chose to use motion control photography to make the models look real. It was one of the first OMNIMAX films to use stop motion photography. No digital or computer animation was used. This would also be the last big optical effects shoot done in Hollywood and the biggest. Terry Winnick said, "We had to invent the technology, including the projection system, which didn't exist when we began."[86]

In anticipation of record crowds, the ride was presented in two identical theaters connected by a central queue area. The IMAX dome screens were 84 feet in diameter. The screens covered twice the area of an average OMNIMAX screen. Each screen was made of flat, perforated stainless steel sheets and weighed 12 tons. They were the largest of their type in the world. They took six months each to construct and were treated with a powder-coated painting process that made them more reflective than the average movie screen.

Twenty-three% of the surface of the screens was made of tiny holes to accommodate the massive sound system. The 72,400,000 holes allowed the 11-channel, 10,000-watt audio system to assault the ears. This was considered the largest permanent sound system at the time.

In a normal OMNIMAX movie theater, the audience seating would be steeply raked so that everyone had a view of the whole dome. At Back to the Future, they would be seated in 1 of 12 DeLorean cars on hydraulic motion bases. The cars were on three levels.

An elevator lifted the vehicles 10 feet out of their staging room to a viewing position. The motion bases were mutually arranged with respect to each other, so that a passenger in any vehicle can view substantially the entire screen but not any other vehicle within the theater. Actuators beneath each vehicle move the vehicle in three dimensions in coordination with the projected motion picture.[87]

The sound effects were not limited to the audio system. "We created a process called the frequency injection," Winnick said. "We inject sound waves into each of the cars' hydraulic systems so that we mimic the sense of running over everything from cobblestones to a lava flow."[88]

The timing of the film with the motion of the vehicle was critical. If the motion picture and the movement were not perfectly in synch, many visitors would get ill. "We controlled the movement of camera with the movement of the ride vehicle," Winnick said. "You may be moving 2 or 3 feet, but because the camera was traveling in the opposite or same direction it enhances the sensation so the brain thinks it's moving hundreds of feet up and down. That's what makes it exciting." He added, "Our philosophy was that Back to the Future would be the most complicated and technologically advanced attraction ever attempted."

To make sure the ride was true to the source material, Winnick watched the films 140 times to duplicate the details. The ride was meant to be a continuation of the *Back to the Future* trilogy of films. The adventure began in Doc Brown's new Institute of Future Technology. Many of the props in the queue area were authentic and from the films, including the flux capacitor. Doc Brown has invented a convertible, eight-passenger Time Vehicle that is faster and more energy efficient than his earlier machine. While in line, visitors learn that Biff Tannen, the movie's bad guy, has stolen Doc Brown's time-travel car and has gone back in time.

Riders were told to get into one of the DeLorean time-travel cars so that Doc Brown could guide them through Hill Valley using a remote control. They had to stop Biff so that he did not disrupt the "space-time continuum." During the journey, riders would travel from a high-tech version of Hill Valley in 2015 all the way back to the Cretaceous Period.

A new musical score composed by Alan Silvestri, who scored all three *Back to the Future* films, enhanced the ride. There were in-theater effects to tease the other senses, including wind, cold air, and clouds made of liquid nitrogen.

Operations vice president Rich Costales was concerned about the ride's intensity. He said, "We thought for sure we would get a lot of people throwing up on the ride." Universal hired a physician named Dr. Richard Brown to test the ride movements. He was known in the industry as the "ride doctor." He suggested that a typical reaction after being jolted around was to build up a thirst, so extra water fountains were installed at the exits.

When the ride opened in Florida on May 2, 1991, expectations were high. Inside the 13-story building were two OMNIMAX screens and 24 eight-seat DeLoreans on three levels. On the top level were three vehicles, five on the second level, and four on the bottom level.

The overall budget had reportedly shot up to $60 million, but it did not matter. The ride was a huge hit. Most important, the ride worked perfectly from day one, helping to overcome the park's tarnished image from the grand opening. Peter Alexander recalled a moment at the grand opening when he saw Spielberg and George Lucas exiting the attraction. "George looked furious while Spielberg was grinning ear to ear. Thumbs up all the way baby!"[89]

The Hollywood version opened to the public on June 12, 1993. At the grand opening were Steven Spielberg, Michael J. Fox, Mary Steenburgen, Lea Thompson, and Tom Wilson. The Hollywood ride was also housed in a 13-story building built on the hillside where RockSlide and Battle of Galactica once entertained visitors.

"To match or be better than Disney, that was the goal," said Barry Upson. "When we got Back to the Future functioning properly, [Michael] Eisner saw it and he said it was the world's best attraction."[90] Dennis Speigel, president of International Theme Park Services Inc., a consulting firm in Cincinnati, agreed. He said the ride "was the launching pad for what Universal is doing today," said. "They out-Disneyed Disney. Universal is clearly nipping at their heels in terms of entertainment sophistication and appeal." Looking back, Peter Alexander said, "This was the first time they built a 'ride' with no real production and the value of authenticity found in Hollywood."[91]

Alexander left MCA during the planning for Back to the Future to become a consultant. He was becoming increasingly frustrated with Stein, who wanted more creative control of the parks. He said, "Every time Jay would come up with an idea, I would take it to Spielberg and tell him it was Jay's idea, 'what do you think of that?' and he would go, 'I don't think much of that, what do you think of it' and I would go, 'I don't think much of it either but I am obligated to present it to you.'"[92]

Alexander said Stein "wanted to turn everything into a thrill ride. For example, Back to the Future was scientifically programmed by Douglas Trumball. He carefully matched the movement of the vehicles to the film he produced. It was absolutely in synch with the film. Stein 'over-drove' it and made the vehicles rock, thereby destroying the careful balance. As a result, people were getting sick. In a simulator you get sick when it is not in synch with the film."[93]

Back to the Future was not the only ride subjected to these changes. Alexander said, "Kong was a gentle ride. The experience of being handled by Kong was the ride, and then let's get back to the film. Stein wanted to turn it into a thrill ride. The downforce was so strong the building truss had to be remade to handle the new loads. Jay liked gore."[94]

1 Mary Ann Galante, "Theme Parks Take a Wild Ride to Catch Disney," *The Los Angeles Times,* 28 Jan. 1990.

2 William Gruber, "MCA Exec Takes Swipe at Disney, Mickey," *Chicago Tribune,* 7 May 1987.

3 Phil Hettema, interview with author, Pasadena, CA, 16 Jan. 2014.

4 Ellen Farley, "Behind the MCA-Disney Tour War in Florida," *The Los Angeles Times*, 23 Apr. 1989.

5 Jeffrey Schmaltz, "Nastiness Is Not a Fantasy in Movie Theme Park War," *The New York Times,* 13 Aug. 1989.

6 Peter Alexander, interview with author, South Palm Beach, FL, 21 Oct. 2013.

7 James Bates, "Steven Spielberg Enjoys Rich Deal with Universal," *Orlando Sentinel,* 24 June 2003.

8 Alexander Matzkeit, "The Days of 'Build It and They Shall Come' are Over: An Interview with Theme Park Veteran Barry Upson," *Real Virtuality,* June 2009, tinyurl.com/upsonrvinterview (accessed 23 Apr. 2013).

9 Barry Upson, interview with author, Napa, CA, 10 Mar. 2014.

10 Alexander, interview with author, 21 Oct. 2013.

11 Ibid.

12 Terry Winnick, interview with author, Las Vegas, NV, 25 Feb. 2014.

13 Ibid.

14 Alexander, interview with author, 21 Oct. 2013.

15 Peter Alexander, "King Kong: The Monster Who Created Universal Studios Florida," totallyfuncompany.com/kongmedia/articles/kingkongarticle.htm (accessed 11 May 2013).

16 Ibid.

17 Adam J. Bezark, "Painting with Bulldozers," *The 15th Annual THEA Awards* (Burbank, CA: Themed Entertainment Association, 2009), 19.

18 Susan G. Strother, "Designers' Ideas Took Fine-tuning Orlando," *Orlando Sentinel,* 3 June 1990.

19 Alexander, interview with author, 21 Oct. 2013.

20 Bezark, "Painting with Bulldozers."

21 Alexander, interview with author, 21 Oct. 2013.

22 Terry Winnick, interview with author, Las Vegas, NV, 25 Feb. 2014.

23 Alexander, "King Kong: The Monster."

24 Alexander, interview with author, 21 Oct. 2013.

25 Upson, interview with author, 10 Mar. 2014.

26 Adam Yeomans, "Universal Sets New Tour Date; Changes in Attractions Delay Debut," *Orlando Sentinel,* 21 Nov. 1988.

27 Hettema, interview with author, 16 Jan. 2014.

28 Ibid.

29 Gary Goddard, interview with author, North Hollywood, CA, 12 Jan. 2014.

30 Kathryn Harris, "Cineplex Bows out of Florida Theme Park," *The Los Angeles Times,* 23 Mar. 1989.

31 Alexander, interview with author, 21 Oct. 2013.

32 Susan G. Strother, "Special Effects Flying into Studio," *Central Florida Business,* 1 Jan. 1990.

33 Alexander, interview with author, 21 Oct. 2013.

34 Alexander, interview with author, 21 Oct. 2013.

35 Ron Schneider, *From Dreamer to Dreamfinder* (Clearwater, FL: Bamboo Forest Publishing, 2012).

36 Ibid.

37 Ibid.

38 Upson, interview with author, 10 Mar. 2014.

39 Matzkeit, "Interview with Barry Upson," tinyurl.com/upsonrvinterview.

40 Alexander, interview with author, 21 Oct. 2013.

41 Jeremy Thompson, "Universal Studios Florida," *Roller Coaster Philosophy,* 3 Mar. 2012, rollercoasterphilosophy.com/2012/universal-studios-florida (accessed 15 Sept. 2013).

42 Strother, "Designers' Ideas."

43 Alexander, interview with author, 21 Oct. 2013.

44 Goddard, interview with author, 12 Jan. 2014.

45 Alexander, "King Kong: The Monster."

46 Ibid.

47 Alexander, interview with author, 21 Oct. 2013.

48 Upson, interview with author, 10 Mar. 2014.

49 Strother, "Special Effects Flying into Studio."

50 Alexander, interview with author, 21 Oct. 2013.

51 Susan G. Strother, "Angry Universal Shuts Jaws Until '91," *Orlando Sentinel,* 23 Aug. 1990.

52 Ibid.

53 Susan G. Strother, "Jaws May Not See Action Until 1992," *Orlando Sentinel,* 13 Dec. 1990.

54 Jube Shiver, Jr., "Universal Sues Designer of 2 Theme Park Rides," *The Los Angeles Times,* 23 Aug. 1990.

55 Kristen Stieffel, "Universal Orlando to Close Jaws," *Orlando Business Journal,* 2 Dec. 2011.

56 "Universal Studios Theme Parks Revamp E.T. Adventure," *Orlando Business Journal,* 25 Feb. 2002.

57 Peter Alexander, "Theme Design vs. Architecture," Totally Fun Company, 2005, totallyfuncompany.com/tpdvsarchitecture.htm (accessed 11 May 2013).

58 Ibid.

59 Alexander, interview with author, 21 Oct. 2013.

60 Alexander, "Theme Design vs. Architecture."

61 Ibid.

62 Alexander, interview with author, 21 Oct. 2013.

63 Schneider, *From Dreamer to Dreamfinder.*

64 Terry Winnick, telephone interview with author, 20 Apr. 2014.

65 Ibid.

66 Bezark, "Painting with Bulldozers," 20.

67 Goddard, interview with author, 12 Jan. 2014.

68 Schneider, *From Dreamer to Dreamfinder.*

69 Mary Meehan, "10 Percent Demand Refunds; Lines and Closed Rides Drive Away Customers," *Orlando Sentinel,* 8 June 1990.

70 Susan G. Strother, "Universal Studios Revamps Ads after Rides Don't Work," *Orlando Sentinel,* 15 June 1990.

71 Mike Clary, "First Mouse, Now Bugs Beset MCA Entertainment," *The Los Angeles Times,*19 July 1990).

72 Ibid.

73 Michael D. Eisner with Tony Schwartz, *Work in Progress,* (New York: Hyperion, 1998).

74 Ibid.

75 Strother, "Universal Studios Revamps Ads."

76 Winnick, interview with author, 25 Feb. 2014.

77 Susan G. Strother, "Park Woes May Slow MCA Progress; Analysts Say Wait and See on Universal Studios Florida," *Orlando Sentinel,* 2 Sept. 1990.

78 Alexander Maddux, "Is This Totally Fun, or What?," *Maddux Business Report,* Sept. 1991.

79 Winnick, interview with author, 25 Feb. 2014.

80 Alexander, "Theme Design vs. Architecture."

81 Strother, "Designers' Ideas."

82 Ibid.

83 Alexander, interview with author, 21 Oct. 2013.

84 Ibid.

85 Phil Hettema, interview with author, Pasadena, CA, 7 May 2014.

86 Terry Winnick, telephone interview with author, 23 Jan. 2014.

87 Craig K. Barr and Peter N. Alexander, Ride attraction, US Patent 5,192,247, filed 28 May 1992 and issued 9 Mar. 1993.

88 Winnick, interview with author, 25 Feb. 2014.

89 Alexander, interview with author, 21 Oct. 2013.

90 Upson, interview with author, 10 Mar. 2014.

91 Alexander, interview with author, 21 Oct. 2013.

92 Ibid.

93 Ibid.

94 Ibid.

CHAPTER 8

MATSUSHITA,
1991–1995

A **MAJOR STRATEGIC RELATIONSHIP**

THROUGHOUT ITS HISTORY, MCA aggressively looked for opportunities to diversify and grow by acquiring other companies. Over the
years, the company bought Universal City, Decca Records, Spencer
Gifts, G.P. Putnam's Sons publishing, Columbia Savings and Loan, and
many other companies. They operated the lease for Yosemite Camp
and provided tours of the National Mall in Washington, D.C. MCA
even considered purchasing Marineland in 1969 and operating the
tourist facilities at the Kennedy Space Center in 1967.[1]

Then in 1968, MCA became the target. Westinghouse Electric Co.
and MCA came to an agreement to merge, but that effort was blocked
by the Justice Department. The objection appeared to center on the
merging of MCA's television production with Westinghouse's ownership of television stations. Another deal was announced between
Firestone Tire and Rubber Co., but negotiations broke down before
the deal could be finalized. A couple of decades later, in 1990, MCA
was once again the target.

It began when Sony acquired Columbia Pictures in 1989. The Japanese electronics firm wanted to be sure it had a source for content
to feed the various devices it intended to sell. Then came the merger
of Time Inc. and Warner Communications the same year. This time,
the marriage created a company capable of producing and distributing content in virtually any medium. The entertainment industry
was beginning to feel the effects of globalization, the need for greater
financial resources, and market share. Lew Wasserman said, "Companies are going to merge, become stronger, particularly in the area of
vertical integration. I think it's inevitable."[2]

Concerned with where the business was going, Wasserman began merger discussions with Martin Davis, chairman of Paramount Communications. At the same time, Sidney Sheinberg had super agent Michael Ovitz of Creative Artists Agency trying to broker a deal with the Matsushita Electric Industrial Company of Osaka, Japan. In a *Vanity Fair* exposé, Bryan Burrough and Kim Masters wrote, "Shrewdly anticipating a culture clash between staid Matsushita and the Holly-woodites—particularly Wasserman's lieutenant, the outspoken Sidney Sheinberg—[Michael] Ovitz kept the parties as separate as possible throughout the negotiations." They added, "Sheinberg says he didn't object; he trusted Ovitz despite a moment when doubts arose. As the deal neared its conclusion, Sheinberg says, the MCA faction went to New York to talk price. When they arrived, they were immediately told that the range would be lower than expected."[3]

The negotiations were a success. In November 1990, Matsushita acquired MCA in a $6.6 billion deal. To retain the services of Wasserman and Sheinberg, the Japanese offered to let them set their own compensation.

In many ways, the merger seemed like a natural fit. Matsushita was a leader in manufacturing audio and video equipment under consumer brands such as Panasonic, Quasar, and Technics. MCA was a leader in producing content that would be used by Matsushita's consumer electronics subsidiaries.

Controlling both the creation and distribution of entertainment seemed to be the future of Hollywood. Matsushita wanted to buy a Hollywood studio in reaction to Sony's purchase of Columbia Pictures. "The conviction that MCA must enter into a major strategic relationship did not come to me quickly or easily," Sidney Sheinberg said. "However, the expansion of our businesses and the changes that have occurred on the world entertainment scene have convinced me that entering into such a relationship is nothing short of a duty we owe our shareholders, our employees, our creative colleagues and indeed all those with whom we enjoy relationships." For the first time, the men at MCA were not fully in control of their own destinies.

The STUDIO CENTER

WHEN THE STUDIO TOUR BEGAN in 1964, it was always meant to be secondary to production. It was a nice way to make a bit of money as long as it did not get in the way. During that first year, the front lot was the tour's entrance. By 1965 a stop on the front lot was a large part of the tour. The trams would stop and guests were guided through the wardrobe department, dressing rooms, and soundstages. After the first couple of years, Stage 32 would become a regular stop for guests to walk through. With the growing crowds, Stage 30 was added as a second venue in 1970. Stage 30 had been the original home to *Leave it to Beaver* (1957–1963) and *The Munsters* (1964–1966).

To provide a consistent show and give the studio a chance to plug its latest products, Terry Winnick put together the *Special Effects Stage* in 1977. Actor and friend of the tour Robert Wagner hosted on film a show that demonstrated how chroma-key (blue or green screen) technology was used in productions. Volunteers from the audience were selected to act out a scene from *Buck Rogers*. Just as before, the trams would pull up in front of the soundstages and visitors would disembark to see the show or to use a restroom. After the demonstration, they would find the first available tram and continue on the tour.

Looking for something a bit more relevant to modern audiences in the 1980s than Buck Rogers, Sidney Sheinberg called MGM/UA chairman and CEO Frank Rothman and asked if he had any movies he needed to promote. Rothman suggested their new science fiction feature *2010* (1984) might make a good fit. MGM/UA provided the rights, the models, and the drawings for free. Rothman was happy for the goodwill and the chance to have MGM/UA trailers in rotation at the Showcase Theater.

Just like the Buck Rogers segment, visitors would learn how filmmakers used a blue screen to layer images together. However, this time instead of two volunteers sitting in a fake spaceship being rocked by a stagehand, they would be lifted into the air via a sophisticated flying harness rig.

Peter Alexander was put in charge of developing the 8-minute show, and he hired former Disney Imagineer Bob Gurr to develop the sophisticated flying rig. The demonstration was based on the scene from the movie where an astronaut and a cosmonaut race against time to reenter a spacecraft before a nearby planet explodes. The entire project was done from start to finish in only 30 days at a cost of $1.5 million. Two identical stages had to be built, one for each theater.

Volunteers had to be between 5-foot-6 and 6 feet and weigh between 100 and 200 pounds. No one over age 65 or under age 12 was allowed. The volunteers had to be strapped into a body harness and then climb into a spacesuit. The harness was connected to two thin wires controlled by a computer, which lifted the volunteers 7 feet off the ground. Inside of their helmets were headphones through which they were fed instructions from the director. As they moved about in front of the screen, an image of space was electronically blended using laser disc technology and shown on monitors to the audience. Bob Gurr said, "Why, Disneyland lawyers would have a heart attack over the very thought. But Universal was fearless and very serious."[4] Up to 240 volunteers a day could be accommodated, and they received a T-shirt for participating.

By the late 1970s, the Universal Studio Tour was the model of efficiency. The system worked great when attendance on a busy day was approximately 12,000 visitors. However, since the mid-1980s, that number was regularly topping 25,000. It just was not working. Jay Stein needed to expand if the tour was to grow. Terry Winnick said, "Part of the game was to keep them in the park as long as you could, because the longer they stayed, the more they had to eat and the more souvenirs they would buy."[5] As always, a big constraint on growth had been the topography of Universal City. In the past, it was fairly easy to remove more of the hillside and truck the dirt somewhere else, but that was no longer an option due to California's strict environmental regulations. With the hilltop limited as an option, there was only one other place to go. The solution was to expand on the front lot.

Starting March 15, 1991, the tour entrance was moved to the lower lot to a new visitor area called the Studio Center. The facility was so named because it was the actual center of the front lot. Some of the bungalows used by movie producers were removed to make room.

The Starway, a 0.25-mile-long escalator system, connected the Studio Center to the Entertainment Center on the hill. Guests could come and go as they pleased. As visitors rode the escalator, they were entertained by a fictional radio station called KUSH, which played quizzes, snippets of music from Universal films, and safety announcements. This lasted until June 2006 when, in a fit of corporate synergy, the audio track was provided by NBC's *Access Hollywood* television show.

Stages 30 and 32 became a stand-alone attraction and were no longer part of the tour. The Special Effects Stages were designed to expose the sleight-of-hand effects featured in such Universal blockbusters as *Dr. Seuss' How The Grinch Stole Christmas, The Mummy Returns, Gladiator, Jurassic Park, The Scorpion King,* and many others.

The show lasted 30 minutes. Each soundstage was divided into three rooms. Each room had fixed bench seating and soundproof partitions between them. The partitions lifted up after one show ended to allow the audience through into the next room.

Within each of the uniquely themed stages, guests enjoyed a series of hands-on demonstrations that transported volunteering audience members from passive observers to actors seamlessly starring in a variety of Universal films. Technologies showcased over the years included makeup, computer animation, mechanical monsters, models, and miniatures. The final stage was dedicated to Foley sound effects, a technique pioneered by Universal's legendary soundman, Jack Donovan Foley, in the 1920s.

The shows would be constantly updated to reflect current Universal projects. Early shows included *The Magic of Alfred Hitchcock,* like the show in Florida, and *Harry and the Hendersons Sound Effects Show.* The show segments would frequently change to reflect the latest marketing priorities. For a time, the show was renamed *The World of Cinemagic.* By 2010 the *Special Effects Stages* were closed, and the Transformers ride took their place.

Also new to the Studio Center was "Lucy: A Tribute." In August 1989, Gary Morton, Lucille Ball's husband, called Lew Wasserman to see if he was interested in any of the memorabilia that Lucy left behind. Of course, Wasserman said yes. Lucie Arnaz and her brother Desi Jr. also donated items. Museum curator Julia Earp was hired to help identify and catalogue the many items on hand. There were so many items that Earp worked three days a week for nine months to document everything.

The room was in the shape of a heart, and everything in the exhibit was authentic. The only exception was the re-creation of the set from *I Love Lucy*, which was originally located nearby on Stage 24. Along one wall was a display that included the first issue of *TV Guide* with Desi Arnaz Jr. on the cover. There were also 25 more *TV Guide* covers from her personal collection. The air-conditioned museum was a pleasant place to spend time before or after taking the tram to the back lot.

With so many memorabilia items on hand, a duplicate exhibit opened in May 1992 at Universal Studios Florida. Some of the items unique to this exhibit included a pink feather fan and briefcase owned by Lucy, plus Desi Arnaz's sword and straw hat.

Another way to spend time was eating at a new Studio Commissary, an establishment not actually used by studio employees. This restaurant at the entrance of the Studio Tour was a reminder of how the park began. The restaurant replaced production bungalows for Edith Head, John Landis, and John Belushi. The facility would later be licensed to the Chinese fast food chain Panda Express.

BABY STEPS

WITH THE OPENING-DAY PROBLEMS slowly subsiding in Florida, Tom Williams announced that 1991 would be the year for new shows and Back to the Future. Adding shows made good sense. They were a low-cost, reliable way to add capacity fast. For example, the *Blues Brothers Show* created by Ron Schneider takes place on a small stage in the New York area of the park. It features Jake and Elwood Blues, the characters made famous by John Belushi and Dan Aykroyd in *The Blues Brothers.*

Another show was the *Streetbusters*. The characters from *Ghostbusters* were making their second appearance in the brand-new park. This time the guys were in pursuit of Beetlejuice in a musical review using pop songs from the late 1980s and early 1990s. The show lasted until 1993. The 20-minute *Wild Wild Wild West Stunt*

Show was lifted directly from Hollywood and placed in an arena next to the Amity area. It debuted on July 4, 1991. The show lasted until September 1, 2003.

The most innovative new show was the *Screen Test Home Video Adventure* inside the facade of New York's famous Paramount Theater (1927). The facility opened on March 25, 1991, and for an extra $31.75, guests could star in one of two productions and return home with a 10-minute videocassette. *Your Day at Universal Studios* put the guests at the center of the action on a tour of the park and its rides. If a guest was wearing blue, he or she would be given a "touristy" shirt so that the person did not disappear while in front of the blue screen. *Star Trek Adventure* allowed fans to dress in a Velcro Star Fleet uniform and act "alongside" the stars of the *Star Trek* television and motion pictures in a specially produced mini-episode. The edited shows were a result of the Ultimatte editing system that Universal developed for the Hollywood park. Considering that a general admission ticket that year was $30.74, it was a pricey addition to one's vacation. It was the only show not included in the general admission price.

Just across the main pathway from Central Park was a re-creation of the Hollywood Hotel (1904) and the Garden of Allah Villas (1919) apartment complex. In 1991 a short-lived walk-through attraction called How To Make a Mega Movie Deal was opened inside. Visitors would follow the story of a man progressing from a mail room to the executive suites in Hollywood. The attraction closed in 1993 and was replaced by AT&T at the Movies in 1998. The interactive exhibit included various AT&T-based technologies presented in movie style. The building was finally shuttered in 2001.

unofficial **TIP**
Screen Test Home Video Adventure closed on Nov. 11, 1996, and was replaced by the Islands of Adventure Preview Center in 1997. That display closed when the new park opened.

Since 1972, Knott's Berry Farm had been raking in the money every October with Knott's Scary Farm. The creation of John Waite, the park would be transformed in a matter of hours from a family-friendly environment during the day to a not-suitable-for-young-children walk-through horror fest at night. The result was a way to generate huge revenues in traditionally one of the slowest times of the year for the theme park industry. It was a gold mine.

Jay Stein had a big empty park in Florida, and he worked for a movie studio with a reputation for monsters, so borrowing from Knott's seemed like a brilliant idea. Marketing executive Randy Garfield said, "Anyone in this business tries to find a new niche, where the competition is less intense. For us, that's Halloween."[6]

The first Universal Studios Fright Nights ran for three nights in 1991 with one haunted house. Tim Sepielli placed the haunted house in the long-unused queue for Jaws. Schneider recalled, "The house ends with the guests making a circuit around a large cage filled with strobe lights, loud rock music, and a collection of classic Universal Studios Monsters wandering around inside."[7] Just for fun, Ron Schneider added "a lost little girl trapped with the monsters, sweetly asking the way out while clutching a map of the Magic Kingdom."[8]

Ron Schneider was assigned to develop entertainment for the event. Neil Miller rounded out the team. Schneider said, "In laying out his ideas for our first Halloween event, Jay Stein doesn't have much to offer in the way of specifics; but he does say, 'I want a chainsaw massacre in New York.' So it falls to me to script a 'massacre.'"[9] Stein also asked Schneider to develop a small show for a plot of land adjacent to the Hard Rock Café. He came up with the *Graveyard of Rock Stars* and set up 10 large bleachers in front of the Bates Motel. The Bates Mansion loomed over the audience. Beetlejuice was the host, and the show featured such thrills as Mother Bates flying out of the second-story window of the mansion over the heads of the audience or watching a partially decomposed Elvis Presley rising from the grave. The event was a huge hit and would become an Orlando cultural rite of passage for teenagers.

A year later, it was Hollywood's turn. "This is a natural for us," Terry Winnick said. "Universal's history with monsters goes back to 1925 and *The Phantom of the Opera* with Lon Chaney. They were all shot right here on this lot. This is hallowed ground."[10] The first Halloween Horror Nights ran for six nights.

Universal knew it was competing with Knott's. Stein took the challenge to steal some people from Knott's seriously by investing several million dollars on props, sets, and new shows. Three hundred performers were hired to roam the park or work in the Nightmare Alley maze. Magicians Penn & Teller put on a 45-minute show, which was joined by a gory comedy show called *Ghoulia Wild's Roadside Cuisine*. During the comedy show, the hostess pulls a hitchhiker out of the fridge and the livers and intestines fly.

Unfortunately, most of the scares were reserved for the tram ride through the back lot. It was a failure. Winnick said, "You can't scare somebody with a human figure chasing after a 150-foot tram."[11] It did not matter. Each night was a sellout with more than 16,000 visitors.

BACKDRAFT

JAY STEIN PLOWED FORWARD with new shows and rides to attract visitors in 1992. He started with the entertainment department. They created two new shows for both coasts that opened July 4, 1992. *Beetlejuice's Rock and Roll Graveyard Revue* attracted adults and teens, while *Rocky and Bullwinkle Live* targeted kids.

Tim Burton's innovative dark comedy *Beetlejuice* (1988) provided source material that Disney never would have touched. Starting with a host who was one of the most offensive personalities imaginable, *Beetlejuice's Rock and Roll Graveyard Revue* stars a band made up of Universal's classic monsters, including Dracula, The Phantom of the Opera, The Wolf Man, Frankenstein, and his bride.

The 25-minute show combines contemporary music with MTV-style dance steps. The show was hip, edgy, and became dated rapidly. The Hollywood version debuted on a small outdoor stage on the top deck of the Frankenstein parking structure and moved into the Castle Dracula Theater in 1995 before closing in 1999. Frequent updates to the Florida version have given it new life, and remarkably, it continues to entertain guests.

The *Rocky and Bullwinkle Live* show starred popular Jay Ward characters, such as Dudley Do-Right, Boris Badenov, and Natasha Fatale, and the moose and squirrel.

The big new attraction was reserved for Hollywood. *Backdraft* was a spectacular special effects demonstration based on director Ron Howard's film of the same name. The 1991 film followed the exploits of a fire squadron in Chicago. The attraction was everything that Stein loved. People would feel the heat of the fire; they would be scared, tossed, and squirted. Moreover, it featured a Universal film by one of Wasserman and Sheinberg's favorite directors. *Backdraft* officially opened on July 1, 1992.

Phil Hettema was responsible for the $10 million attraction, and it was quite a challenge. Stein wanted an in-your-face re-creation of an action sequence from the film. The entire show and its support equipment needed to fit inside of Stage 30, a 90-foot-by-170-foot space. He had to create a show that could reliably display an unprecedented number of fire effects at least 200 times a day to suck up more than 2,000 guests an hour. "The reason we were able to do *Backdraft* was we had years of experience doing propane explosions going back to Jaws and the *A-Team*," according to Phil Hettema. "We really upped the ante."[12]

Hettema divided the soundstage into three rooms. In the first room, director Ron Howard described what a back draft was and how the film was made. The second room was dressed like a Chicago firehouse. Actors Scott Glenn and Kurt Russell talked about the difficulties the cast went through to make the movie as realistic-looking as possible. At the time, Russell was working on *Captain Ron* in Florida, so he had grown his hair down to his shoulders. Hettema and the film crew found a local fire department that would let them shoot, covered up their logo, and stuffed Russell's mane under a fire chief helmet. As Glenn went into detail on how the filmmakers tried bringing personality to the flames, a live demonstration of a rotating flame effect would spring into action before exploding into a ball of fire within reach of the audience.

The final room was a re-creation of the film's finale in the chemical warehouse built inside of a 500,000-cubic-foot soundstage. Guests stood along a balcony overlooking the set. This was not a passive experience. Right after the unseen director called out "action," a fire would break out in an office. That spark set off more than 40 special effects. Flames shot from walls, sped across structural pipes, ignited gas lines, careened into containers of flammable liquid, and incinerated catwalks that hung suspended above the viewers.[13] Although the guests could feel the heat from the 2,000-degree fires, an invisible air curtain protected them. At one point, the balcony would drop ½ inch, adding to the terror. When the director shouted "cut," the flames died out, and the guests were ushered out to let the next audience come in.

This level of pyrotechnics used so close to the audience had never been attempted before. The building was coated with an inch of fire protection. A special gas line had to be installed, plus an exhaust system that was powerful enough to exchange 200,000 cubic feet of air every minute. Should anything go wrong, the audience was protected by a deluge system that would drop hundreds of gallons of water stored in tanks, flooding the pit area in 3 seconds. The show was not cheap to operate. Each show used 1,000 cubic feet of natural gas, which was enough to power one home for a year.

Hettema described the show "as quintessential Universal as you can get." Ron Bension said, "It's more dense and more complex than any other attraction we've done. As realistic as the film." He boasted, "We could shoot a film in here."[14] Ironically, a few months after the show opened, a fire in the air-conditioning system forced its temporary closure. Guests thought the black smoke was part of the show.

Universal had always struggled to keep people in the park late in the day. In 1992 Disney debuted the very popular *Fantasmic* show at Disneyland along the banks of the Rivers of America in 1992. The show copied the *Conan* show by bringing together a wide variety of special effects commonly found in the movies and television on stage. Universal Studios Hollywood wanted to regain the momentum and created a laser show called *SpectraBlast* to honor the tour's 30th anniversary. The nighttime show included a flying DeLorean (flown in on wires), a UFO (an internally lit inflatable that was dangled from a blacked-out crane arm), fountains, lasers, and pyrotechnics. A cast of eight performers joined the Effects Jockey, and clips from Universal films drove the show's narrative. The show lasted until September 1994.

 # *A* CHILDREN'S PARK

ABOUT A YEAR BEFORE UNIVERSAL STUDIOS FLORIDA opened, Jay Stein called a meeting of top people. "We all thought 'oh boy,' but what he wanted to talk about was the theme of the second park," said Barry Upson. "He let it be known that he wanted the team to start thinking about what we could do for the second park."[15]

Jay Stein bristled when people suggested that Universal had built a theme park in Florida just like Disney. In his mind, Universal Studios Florida was just like Hollywood. It was a working film and television production studio that had visitor attractions. Disney was the one who built a theme park. If Stein was going to compete directly with Disney, he needed an immersive, fantasy-based theme park to join the studio. Then he could turn the Orlando property into a full-service destination with hotels, shopping, dining, and entertainment like Walt Disney World. Only better.

The first ideas for a second park came to Jay Stein within days of Universal Studios Florida's opening. In a 20-page memo dictated to company attorney Tony Sauber, Stein outlined the project that would become Project X. He included a list of characters that he wanted to see featured in the park. Sauber said, "The Disney-type character wouldn't have worked for us. We wanted an edgier, more action-prone, less soft and fuzzy character."[16]

Stein's confidence was boosted by a study from Economics Research Associates (ERA) that looked at the addition of a park targeting children ages 3–12 years old. ERA was tasked to determine the viability of a project in either Los Angeles or Orlando. Until now, Universal was happy to concede that segment of the market to Disney. However, if Stein wanted to truly dominate the theme park market, he needed to find a way to attract more youngsters. Two approaches were looked at: a freestanding park or one inside one of the existing parks.

An example of a successful freestanding theme park for children was Legoland. The park opened in 1968. It was built adjacent to the Lego factory in Billund, Denmark. The park originally opened as a small permanent exhibit to show off the versatility of the little plastic bricks. First-year attendance topped 625,000 people, and the facility rapidly expanded to meet the demand. The combination of family-friendly rides, beautiful gardens, and elaborate displays made of Lego bricks attracted far more than children. By the late 1980s, the park was attracting more than 1 million visitors a year, with two-thirds of those being adults. The formula proved so successful that Lego began looking for international partners and opened new parks in the United Kingdom, Germany, Malaysia, and two locations in the United States.

The popular public television series *Sesame Street* was the foundation for another children's park. Sesame Place opened in 1980 in Lower Bucks County, Pennsylvania. The $10 million, 7-acre park was built adjacent to the Oxford Valley shopping mall. The project was a joint venture between Busch Entertainment and the Children's Television Workshop. When the park first opened, it was very successful.

Like Legoland, it attracted more adults than expected. A second park in Irving, Texas, opened in 1982. However, Sesame Place's popularity quickly faded and the Texas park closed after only two years. Today, SeaWorld Entertainment operates the original park.

A different kind of children's park was Castle Amusement Park in Riverside, California. The facility opened in 1976, with four miniature golf courses and an arcade. Bud Hurlbut, the man responsible for the Calico Mine Ride and the Timber Mountain Log Ride at Knott's Berry Farm, owned the park. Castle Park was less like Disneyland and more like an updated version of the corner kiddie land that was commonly found throughout the Los Angeles region.

In contrast to a freestanding facility, another option was to build something inside the existing parks. Camp Snoopy at Knott's Berry Farm was a prime example. The first of its kind, Camp Snoopy not only succeeded in appealing to younger children, it also kept families in the park longer and was considered a primary attendance inducer. The area was made up of lightly themed amusement park rides, beautiful landscaping, and food tailored to the pint-size customers. Ride waits took into account the short attention span of kids, allowing them to average about two rides per hour. Other attractions included a birthday party room and a game room sponsored by Apple Computer. The success of Camp Snoopy inspired Bugs Bunny World at Magic Mountain in Valencia, California, and Hanna-Barbera Land at Kings Island, Ohio.

It was estimated that a children's park in Hollywood would need about 26 acres and cost about $86 million. If Universal wanted to build in Florida, the park would need to be about 17 acres and cost about $57 million. Buzz Price was confident there was a market and either facility would bring in an additional 750,000 visitors per year.

The Planning and Development group explored ideas for Hollywood. They looked at different concepts, including a family park and a pop culture park. In the end, the potential complexity in securing development entitlement from two different government agencies and the lack of available land in Hollywood pushed the project to the side.

However, the idea of a second gate did take root in Florida. The numbers were there. Orlando had become the number-one vacation destination in the world. Walt Disney World was attracting as many as 28 million people a year, with 12 million going straight to the Magic Kingdom. Universal Studios Florida drew more than 7 million guests in 1991.

MCA was making a dent. Once again, a bit of gamesmanship became an issue. Although no theme park discloses its actual annual attendance, they do work with reporters on estimates. Over at Disney, it was suggested that Bruce Lavell was pulling 2 million visitors from Epcot and giving it to the Studios just to stay ahead.[17]

CARTOON WORLD

"GENTLEMEN, THIS IS PROJECT X," said Jay Stein as he pinned up a map of Disneyland on the wall. "I don't want to rewrite the book. There is our plan. Everybody thinks we are opening our second gate. We are actually opening our first gate. This is going to a 12 million–person park. They think we are going to be building a 6 million–person park. We are going to drive this right up Disney's ass. This is going to be our number one park."[18]

There were not many people in the room during that meeting in 1991. From Universal were Phil Hettema, Dale Mason, Barry Upson, and Norm Newberry. Gary Goddard from Landmark Entertainment and Larry Hitchcock were the two outsiders. Phil Hettema recalled, "Getting through the challenging start at Universal Studios Florida and having an identity and having success and then taking stock and saying, 'OK, no let's really go for it' and broaden the base from the niche audience up until that point. That was Jay."[19]

Stein wanted to build a park that would attract 7 million visitors the first year and then quickly ramp up to 10 million within a couple of years. The eight-person team was housed in a "skunk works" on Magnolia Avenue in North Hollywood. "Jay had the vision to say, 'Let them go' and nobody got in our faces," according to Phil Hettema.[20] It was rare that Jay Stein or Barry Upson came to check up on them. When somebody needed to pitch an idea, they wheeled out their drawings or model for a show and tell. It was a creative atmosphere.

After the experience of the studio and tour, MCA was naturally secretive about the new project. At one point, Jay Stein admitted to the press, "Some of the ideas that are in our mill right now have the potential to be as big as Universal Studios Florida and as big as any of the Disney parks. The kind of size that I am looking for, I'd like to be bigger than Disney."[21]

For a children's park to succeed, Universal needed properties that would appeal to younger visitors. Barry Upson said, "Larger, bolder, and more-recognizable characters were needed to compete and build attendance. This is when 'rights' started to become a major issue." With the right intellectual property rights, Upson said, you can "work on a grander scale, improve the design details, use more complex content or infrastructure, achieve a higher capacity, and use more-sophisticated operations and maintenance." Upson noted, "Securing exclusive rights to strong film properties from any source is more critical now to creating an attraction that cannot be duplicated competitively."[22] A familiar property with a powerful, simple story line or concept can help tie everything together and provide a cohesive guest experience. "Many theme parks simply adopt a movie or television title as a name for a standard iron ride or show," Upson said.

"Universal and Disney built their attractions around the basic premise of the film. There is a world of difference in these two strategies."[23]

Disney was built around characters that they owned. That was not the case at Universal. Securing the rights for use at the theme park was more difficult at Universal due to cast deals, partnerships, and so on. It was up to Tony Sauber to get the licenses.

"I think the fundamental motivation was to take an obviously very successful market in movies and television and make it work in another form," Upson explained. "Since the movies and television shows were promoted heavily, you could latch on to that success and then we would have something going in a three-dimensional theme complex."[24]

Stein wanted a park based on licensed properties, such as the world of Dr. Seuss, Warner Bros. Looney Toons cartoons, and the DC Comics universe, as well as Universal-owned properties. To gain the theme park rights for the various properties, Stein had his team develop ride and show concepts that could be used as a sales tool.

The team's confidence was bolstered on June 18, 1991, when Universal obtained the theme park rights to the Jay Ward characters, including Rocky and Bullwinkle, Dudley Do-Right, and many others. Although Disney had the video rights, they lost the theme park rights to Universal. This was a major win.

As Project X evolved, it became known as Cartoon World. Gary Goddard of Landmark was hired to design the entrance. He would be responsible for more than half the park.

Comic Strip Lane would be Cartoon World's Main Street USA. The front of the park would appear as a "Cartoon/Comic Book/Comic Strip Factory," and guests would enter through the loading dock. Most of the characters would have been pulled straight from the Sunday funnies. The architecture would have been "a series of anthropomorphic buildings," according to Phil Hettema. "The buildings actually had faces and they felt like they were alive."[25]

As guests walked through the turnstiles, they might catch a glimpse of a cartoon character clocking in and going to work. The entrance would narrow to a tunnel acting as a "customs" inspection point with official-looking audio-animatronic guards humorously watching to see what real-world items people are bringing into Cartoon World. On the other side of the front gate was the Entrance Plaza. This is where visitors would find guest services, shops, restaurants, and a little theater showing cartoons.

Inside of the Cartoon World Opera House would be the *Night of the Opera* show, featuring performances by the Carl Stalling Commemorative Cartoon Band. The show would bring together characters from all five lands. At the end of the street would be a plaza and viewing area for the evening spectacular like Disney's daily fireworks.

The Jay Ward characters would be represented in The Northwest Mining Camp. The innovative Dudley Do-Right's Great Northwest Sawmill flume ride would feature logs that appear to be tied together side by side. Just before the drop, the logs encounter a giant table saw, slicing them in half, and forcing the riders to go down separate slides.

Popeye's Island was divided into two realms, Sweethaven Village and the Docks. Sweethaven Village would have been a brightly colored, timeworn town reflecting the look of the cartoons. Food would be available from Wimpy's Boardinghouse & Burger Joint. The main attraction for Sweethaven Village would be Popeye's Adventure Boat Ride. During the preshow for this dark ride, Popeye and his friends would be projected onto a high-definition screen and greet the visitors as they entered. Although Popeye promised that this would be a gentle boat ride, various villains right behind him would be kidnapping his friends. All alone, he would set off to rescue them, telling visitors to follow in a Sweethaven Tour Boat. After the boats arrived at Goon Island, visitors would follow Popeye as he took on the villains and rescued his friends.

The Docks would look more run-down and feature Bluto's Bilge-Rat Barge Wild River Ride, Popeye's Dockside Arcade, and the Roughouse Café. Bluto's Bilge-Rat Barges was going to be "the wildest, wettest, meanest, and maddest river you ever see'd." Unique to this raft ride would be the many ways that the visitors would get soaked, including an "ultra-super spinach soaker" and the "spit shine bilge-rat bath."

The Roughouse Café would be a run-down nautical Victorian structure at the edge of the water, featuring a show similar to the *Hoop-Dee-Doo Musical Revue* at Walt Disney World. The building and the interior would appear to be built from scrap boat parts. Gary Goddard was the creator of both shows, and he was so positive they could work that he made an offer to Jay Stein to finance it himself.

All sorts of ideas were floated early on. There was Casper's Haunted House, a child-friendly dark ride; the Mighty Mouse Theatre, an audio-animatronics show done in the style of an opera; and Mr. Magoo's Bumper Cars, an enclosed bumper car system with one-way streets going through a series of sets.

THE WORLD OF DR. SEUSS

DR. SEUSS WAS ALSO PART OF THE ORIGINAL MIX. This would have been the park's Fantasyland and about the same size as the one at the Magic Kingdom. The major rides would have been a dark ride featuring the *Cat in the Hat* and a boat ride based on *If I Ran the Zoo*. A 3-D animated film called *Horton's Corner* would give families a chance to rest indoors. McBean's Driving Machines would be miniature vehicles like Autopia at Disney, and the Grinch's Sleigh Ride would have been a child-friendly roller coaster. Supporting the major attractions would be children's flat rides like the Caro-Seuss-El elevated merry-go-round; the Oh, the Thinks You Can Think spin ride; the One Fish, Two Fish, Red Fish, Blue Fish boat ride; and the Dumbo-like Flying Pans ride.

SUPERHERO LAND

GODDARD WAS ALSO RESPONSIBLE for Superhero Land. He was a DC Comic book fan from childhood and perfectly prepared for the challenge. He divided the land into two distinct districts. Metropolis would be the "city of light" and reflect the Art Deco architecture of New York and Chicago in the 1930s through the use of bright colors, polished metals, and glass.

Across the bridge from Metropolis was Gotham, described as "the darker side of Superhero Land." The art director reflected the blend of gothic and contemporary art direction seen in the Warner Bros. *Batman* movies. The big attraction in Gotham would have been *Deathtrap*, an innovative show combining a motion simulator with Intaman's Freefall ride. At the climax of the battle between Superman and Lex Luthor, the 18 visitors aboard the "passenger pod" would be propelled backward from a 130-foot drop, undergoing a true free fall experience.

Off in a side alley in Gotham was The Joker's Madhouse. Goddard had come up with something that was part haunted house, part insane asylum, and part carnival of the weird.[26] Guests would enter the building through the giant open mouth of the Joker. His evil eyes would peer down on the people, and he would occasionally squirt the crowd with his lapel daisy.

The ride inside was a combination wild mouse coaster and dark ride. By the time the riders made it to the postshow, they would have escaped through a fiery tunnel and a false ending. This was not a roller coaster designed for the faint of heart. Goddard designed a postshow that was an interactive room-by-room tour through the world of DC Comics villains. Everybody was here, including Gigantica, Mr. Twister, the Penguin, Lex Luthor, Mr. Zero, the Riddler, Catwoman, the Fiddler, and Felix Faust. There would also be some low-cost, teen-oriented carnival attractions that would be heavily themed, such as an octopus ride dressed as Doc Octopus, one of the old-fashioned antigravity rides dedicated to Magneto, and Doctor Doom's Fearfall.

Another show was inside the Hall of Legends. The Mindwarp Chamber was a domed theater with reclining chairs. Visitors would put on a "cyberhelmet" with 3-D lenses and holographic sound. After being scanned, they would be sent into "Super-Reality." However, Brainiac would interrupt the trip. He would have seized the chamber and all who were there as bait, so he could capture the entire Justice League. A screen that covered the entire ceiling would engulf the audience. The 3-D illusion would have put the characters and special effects right in the face of the visitors unlike any other attraction.

The Green Lantern, Captain Atom, Hawkman, and Hawkwoman would do their best to rescue the audience, but Brainiac would capture them. The same thing would happen to Wonder Woman, Cyborg, and the Green Arrow. Even Superman would struggle with Brainiac until he figured out how to get help from the audience. In this 3-D movie, the audience would play an active role by reaching out to grasp the Psicon energy field, which would destroy Brainiac's hold on everyone, and he would be captured.

Goddard wrote to Dr. Hugh Greer at the Santa Barbara Medical Foundation Clinic's Department of Neurology to ask about the scientific basis for the cyberhelmet. The doctor wrote back "strange request indeed," but verified that Goddard was going in the right direction and provided a list of buzzwords to add credibility.[27]

Goddard also designed a thrill ride that started out as Joker's Wild! but shifted toward a battle between Batman and the Penguin. The Bat Wing suspended coaster allowed riders a choice to ride the Penguin's Pen-O-wing fighter or Batman's BatWing flyer. Computers would control the coasters, allowing for near misses as they traveled in and out of three large show buildings filled with large sets for the Riddler's Warehouse, Catwoman's Catabombs, and the Penguin's Palace. Steven Spielberg weighed in at one point and suggested they develop some sort of scoring system and crown a victor at the end. Riders would be encouraged to press a button at specific points to score points. At the end of the ride, the scores would be revealed, and a winner between Batman and the Penguin would be declared.

Rounding out the offerings would have been *The Batman & Robin Action Adventure Spectacular!,* a major stunt show similar to *Miami Vice* in Hollywood. Goddard drafted a script filled with Jay Bangs. Siegfried & Roy's *Beyond Belief* Las Vegas magic show inspired the proposed *Deathtraps! Terrible Traps* and *Fantastic Escapes* action and illusion show. The show starred Superman and would borrow elements from *Conan* and combine them with traditional magic tricks.

WARNER'S LOONEY TUNES LAND

WHAT WAS SURE TO BE ONE OF THE BIGGEST DRAWS would have been the land dedicated to the Looney Tunes characters. Bugs Bunny, Daffy Duck, and the rest of the gang certainly rivaled the Disney roster in familiarity and popularity. Phil Hettema and Dale Mason were responsible for the design and attractions. The irreverent tone of the Warner Bros. cartoon shorts fit perfectly with the Universal attitude.

It is not hard to imagine the possibilities for the Coyote Canyon roller coaster featuring Wile E. Coyote and the Roadrunner. Another concept working its way through the process was Duck Dodgers

Space Adventure, an indoor roller coaster like Space Mountain, starring Daffy Duck and Marvin Martin. *Prof. Bugs' Laws of Animation* was a 3-D film with in-theater special effects like the *Muppet-Vision 3-D* attraction at Disney-MGM.

One of Phil Hettema's favorite concepts was Yosemite Sam's Posse Ride. Inside of a Circle-Vision theater would be two-person motion simulators dressed like horses. The horses could pivot 180 degrees. At one point during the show, one of the characters would yell out, "They went that-away!" Suddenly, the movie would screech to a halt and another character would yell, "They went that-away!" and the horses would turn once again.[28]

Like Disneyland's Fantasyland, there would be plenty of dark rides. Harking back to the days of Walt Disney, guests would be transported to desirable locations by a variety of conveyance systems. Floating along in a flume, guests would encounter the Wabbit Season and watch Elmer Fudd and Bugs Bunny battling it out. Nearby would be a traditional dark ride that would wander through the Acme Factory. One ride that certainly would have long lines all day would have been Dale Mason's Ali Baba Bunny Magic Carpet Ride using an E.T.-like ride platform.

The multimedia spectacular Pepe Le Pew's Tunnel of Love would have provided live entertainment. For those wanting an overview of the land, there was the Sylvester and Tweety Skyway Ride. All of this would have been supported by a small area set aside for younger guests called the Tiny Toons playland. It would have a Star Jets–like ride called Plucky Ducks Plane Ride, the teacuplike Dizzy Devils Whirlwind, and the Jet Pack swing ride. Merchandise would be available at the ACME Outlet and the Broken Arms Hotel. If guests were getting hungry, they could stop in to Foghorn Leghorn's Barnyard Bar-B-Q or Speedy Gonzales Really Fast Food (Cantina) in the shape of a large sombrero. Reflecting on what they had designed, Hettema said, "The Warner's attraction concepts that are in the drawer are the best thing anybody has ever seen."

Cartoon World would be only a part of a much larger expansion. Following Disney's example, Stein wanted to build five hotels. The 400-room Portofino was chosen because it was the perfect scale and theme just as it exists on the Italian Mediterranean. Guests would have the option of staying in the hotel or on a yacht in the harbor. Built along the banks of a network of Venetian canals would be the 425-room Hotel Venezia. The 1,000-room Buccaneer Hotel would be the flagship hotel. The lobby would emulate the art direction from the movie *Hook* (1991). The 1,000-room Hotel Esplanade Del Rio would be organized around a river walk.

Bob Ward was working on an entertainment-shopping complex called College Hill that would compete with Pleasure Island and Church Street Station by not charging an admission. On the second and third floor would be the 150-room College Hill Hotel. At the southern edge of the property would be a golf-related timeshare to compete with Disney's 1991 entry into that market. A water taxi devised by Barry Upson would connect all of these destinations.

From the start, the plan was to match Disney land for land, then "provide an experience that will be equal or better than what is found in the Disney parks."[29] Why go on Space Mountain when you could race along with the Roadrunner being chased by Wile E. Coyote? Sure, Big Thunder is a nice roller coaster, but how could it compete with Batman? The design team was excited about a partnership with Warner Bros. Gary Goddard said MCA would "offer a unique attraction with drawing power that far outweighs that of Epcot or the MGM-Disney Studio Tour. Cartoon World offers something for everyone, young or old."[30]

However, the battle for Bugs Bunny and Batman would turn out to be a contest between Hollywood titans. In one corner were Lew Wasserman and Sidney Sheinberg at MCA. They were not terribly excited about opening another theme park in Florida until the current park got fixed, but they also knew they could not stand still. They decided if they could snag a good deal for the right intellectual properties, then maybe Stein's Florida resort could finally move forward.

In the other corner were Terry Semel and Bob Daly from Time Warner. They held the rights to DC Comics and Looney Tunes. MCA's first offer was a 6% royalty, while Warner countered with 10%. The negotiations dragged on for months. At one point, the two parties came within two points, with Warner down to 8% and MCA holding steady at 6%.

Jay Stein and his team had put in so much work on developing concepts based on the Warner characters that he was pressing his bosses to agree to the 8%. He argued that the cost to MCA would be approximately $70,000 more than their current offer. Stein considered calling Steven Spielberg, as he had done in the past, to get him to press Warner to come down to 7% so that his bosses could feel like they won. Stein figured that Warner Bros. loved Spielberg ever since he wrote *The Goonies* (1985). At the time, Spielberg was editing *Jurassic Park* while beginning principal photography for *Schindler's List*. Stein was warned about calling the director. Sheinberg killed the deal when he said to Terry Semel, "We don't need your [expletive] characters." As a result, the deal with Warner Bros. fell through.[31]

1 Harrison A. Price, Harrison Price Company, "Confessions of an Itinerant Consultant," speech to Universal Creative of Universal Studios Recreation Group, 24 June 1999, Series III, Box 60, Folder 116, Harrison "Buzz" Price Papers, Special Collections & University Archives Department, University of Central Florida Libraries, Orlando, FL.

2 Kathryn Harris, "MCA Keeps Up Its Tough Act," *The Los Angeles Times,* 18 Nov. 1984.

3 Bryan Burrough and Kim Masters, "The Mouse Trap," *Vanity Fair,* Dec. 1996.

4 Bob Gurr, *Design: Just for Fun* (Bloomington, CA: Ape Pen Publishing and Gurr Design, 2012).

5 Terry Winnick, interview with author, Las Vegas, NV, 25 Feb. 2014.

6 Susan G. Strother, "Universal Embraces Halloween," *Orlando Sentinel*, 21 Oct. 1993.

7 Ron Schneider, *From Dreamer to Dreamfinder* (Clearwater, FL: Bamboo Forest Publishing, 2012).

8 Ibid.

9 Ibid.

10 David Wharton, "Scaring Up Some Fun," *The Los Angeles Times,* 30 Oct. 1992.

11 Winnick, interview with author, 25 Feb. 2014.

12 Phil Hettema, interview with author, Pasadena, CA, 7 May 2014.

13 David J. Fox, "Universal Tours Fires Up Its Backdraft," *The Los Angeles Times,* 24 June, 1992.

14 Ibid.

15 Barry Upson, interview with author, Napa, CA, 10 Mar. 2014.

16 "Park's Dress Rehearsal Almost Over," *Orlando Sentinel*, 21 May 1999.

17 Peter Alexander, interview with author, South Palm Beach, FL, 21 Oct. 2013.

18 Gary Goddard, interview with author, North Hollywood, CA, 12 Jan. 2014.

19 Hettema, interview with author, 7 May 2014.

20 Hettema, interview with author, 16 Jan. 2014.

21 Sharon Bernstein, "MCA Takes on the Mouse," *The Los Angeles Times,* 3 June 1990.

22 Alexander Matzkeit, "The Days of 'Build It and They Shall Come' are Over: An Interview with Theme Park Veteran Barry Upson," *Real Virtuality,* June 2009, tinyurl.com /upsonrvinterview (accessed 23 Apr. 2013).

23 Upson, interview with author, 10 Mar. 2014.

24 Ibid.

25 Hettema, interview with author, 7 May 2014.

26 Goddard, interview with author, 12 Jan. 2014.

27 Dr. Hugh D. Greer, MD, Department of Neurology, Santa Barbara Medical Foundation Clinic, letter to Gary Goddard, 12 Aug. 1992.

28 Hettema, interview with author, 16 Jan. 2014.

29 Goddard, memorandum to Jay Stein, 7 Aug. 1992.

30 Ibid.

31 Goddard, interview with author, 12 Jan. 2014.

CHAPTER 9

SEAGRAM,
1995–2001

NOBODY ELSE *to* BLAME

WHEN MATSUSHITA ACQUIRED MCA, Lew Wasserman had great hopes. He insisted that the top management team remain in place for several years to implement their grand plans. He was hoping that the Japanese would be hands-off owners. He was wrong. Unfortunately, Matsushita was reluctant to expand. They lacked an understanding of show business, and the cultures of the two organizations did not mesh.

By 1995 the Japanese were not very happy with the entertainment moguls, either. At one point, some Matsushita executives suggested to Wasserman and Sheinberg that the way to succeed in the movie business was to make more hits and fewer duds. According to Joseph Osha, a stock analyst from Smith New Court Securities, the electronics firm complained that the aggressive nature from the Hollywood leadership was "wheeling and dealing, and they are not wheelers and dealers."[1] Both parties started to look for a way out.

Stepping in to exploit the situation was Hollywood super agent Michael Ovitz. He secretly convinced his old friend, Edgar M. Bronfman Jr. from the beverage giant Seagram Company Ltd., that the time was right to take over MCA. Just like the Japanese manufacturing firm, Seagram had no direct experience in show business. Seagram was started by Bronfman's grandfather in 1916 and was best known as the largest distiller of alcoholic beverages in the world. However, Bronfman was an ambitious chief executive who longed to be a major player in the entertainment industry. Earlier in his career, Bronfman produced the 1981 film *The Border* with Jack Nicholson and wrote a couple of songs including "Whispers in the Dark."

To finance the deal, Bronfman sold off 156 million shares of chemical and oil giant DuPont for $8.8 billion. At the time, the income from DuPont accounted for 70% of Seagram's earnings. Ovitz conceived of a plan in which he would make $250 million for putting the deal together and then replace Lew Wasserman. He achieved his first objective in April 1995 when Matsushita sold off 80% of MCA Inc. to Seagram Co. for $5.7 billion. What Bronfman got was a company that was last, or close to last, in all its businesses—television, publishing, music, and theme parks. Only the movie division was doing well, and that was soon to end because Steven Spielberg was leaving to start a new competitor, DreamWorks SKG.

During the negotiations between Matsushita and Seagram, Lew Wasserman and Sidney Sheinberg were kept in the dark. Both men felt betrayed by Ovitz and Bronfman, and they predicted that the new leadership would fail. Sheinberg said, "I think the ultimate 'fire-ee' will be Edgar. There comes a time when there's nobody else to blame."[2]

Just as Ovitz was ready to step up and run the company, Bronfman betrayed him when he put Ron Meyer, Ovitz's former partner at the powerful talent agency CAA, in charge. Ovitz went on to a very brief and controversial career at the Walt Disney Company.

On December 11, 1996, MCA Inc. changed its name to Universal Studios Inc. Universal chairman Frank Biondi, Jr. said the new name "reinforces Universal's association with the excitement of Hollywood and the best in entertainment."[3]

Sheinberg was disappointed. "The thing that hurts me the most is there is no MCA. I don't know where to find it. It doesn't exist. The culture that Jules Stein started, Lew Wasserman built, and I worked on has been replaced by I know not what." He added, "[Bronfman] destroyed our company. The most important thing he destroyed is the base of manpower, the sense of history and continuity."[4] Sidney Sheinberg and Lew Wasserman had enough. They both retired.

Bronfman wanted to quickly put his stamp on the parks. In Hollywood, the entrance was rebuilt. The new arch was modeled after the gateway at Paramount Pictures; the studio's signature globe was placed out front, resting on a mist fountain; and the studio tour entrance was moved from the lower lot back up the hill to make way for the Jurassic Park–themed ride.

As a demonstration of Seagram's commitment to Orlando, Bronfman announced in August 1995 that he planned to spend $2.6 billion to turn the theme park into a resort. Of that, $2 billion would go to a second theme park, and an additional $600 million would go to four new hotels.[5]

Despite all of the boardroom struggles, the show had to go on. Recognizing that Universal Studios Florida was still short on things for young children to do, they took a chance on a purple dinosaur. In 1992 *Barney and Friends* debuted on local PBS stations and was an instant hit. Universal wanted to test the waters for his theme park appeal and feature him in a parade that year. His presence gave youngsters in strollers hope that there might be something for them to do. Then in April 1993, he returned for a sing-along show. Sensing that they had a winner, a permanent facility was opened in July 1995 for a new show called *A Day in the Park with Barney.*

According to Tom Williams, "Our mission from day one was to make it the best toddler experience that's ever been done."[6] Visitors enter the theater through a quiet, circular courtyard, surrounded by trees, grassy areas, and flowers. Sounds of birds, crickets and frogs are piped in, and no neon lighting was allowed. Even the bathrooms are scaled down to meet the need of the guests with child-size toilets. Project director Craig McIntyre said, "We want people to find it as a little bit of an oasis in an otherwise hustle-bustle theme park."[7]

Inside the air-conditioned theater is a stage at the center. The host, a clown named Mr. or Mrs. Peek-a-boo, starts the 15-minute show that features Baby Bop, B.J., and Barney. The interactive, child-friendly show has plenty of opportunities for children to let off a bit of steam. After the show, the children can continue to play in Barney's Backyard, a large playroom with a water play area and musical color stones in the floor. There is also a holiday version of the show.

DRY LAND

UNIVERSAL STUDIOS INVENTED THE SUMMER BLOCKBUSTER in 1975 with *Jaws.* Twenty years later, *WaterWorld* was expected to go down in the history books. At least that was the plan. The post-apocalyptic science fiction film was set during a time when the polar ice caps had melted and the continents were covered by water. Among those people who remained, the myth of dry land persisted. The action was driven by the conflict between the evil Deacon (Dennis Hopper) and his band of "Smokers" and a mutant (Kevin Costner) who befriends a woman (Jeanne Tripplehorn) and a young girl with a tattoo of a map to the mythical dry land (Tina Majorino). The movie had action, drama, special effects, and big-name stars. Studio executives were confident they had a winner.

The studio was so confident of the film's success that, in late October 1994, Phil Hettema and Norm Kahn, vice president of entertainment, got a call from the producers of *WaterWorld* to come to Hawaii and check out the elaborate floating set they made of rusted corrugated metal. They immediately saw that the atoll and the atoll gates were perfect for the existing arena. The timing could not have been better. Ron Bension had determined that the *Miami Vice* stunt show had run its course, and he was searching for a replacement. He decided to debut the new stunt show the same day it opened in the movie theaters. That way, he could take advantage of what was sure to be a huge box office success. The live-action show was put on the development fast track.

There was a storm on the horizon. The film was plagued with problems. The director, Kevin Reynolds, walked off the picture two-thirds of the way through, and Kevin Costner was forced to finish directing the film. The picture's budget had ballooned to $235 million, making it the most expensive movie made up to that time. The prerelease buzz was negative, and when the film finally opened on July 28, 1995, it was critically panned and a box office disappointment. It never stood a chance.

For the theme park, it was too late. They were committed. After delays expected from the challenges of creating a breakthrough show, *WaterWorld—A Live Sea War Spectacular* opened in October 1995. The movie may have been a box office dud, but the live show would go on to become one of the most popular theme park stunt shows ever produced and a giant leap forward for the genre.

"Rather than try to tell a story, the script is formulated around the most repeatable stunts and gags from the movie," according to Norm Kahn. "We also identified the large pieces from the movie, like the atoll and the seaplane, that could serve as the main show action equipment."[8] A production budget of $15 million was set. Construction began in January 1995.

Visitors enter a 3,000-seat horseshoe-shape amphitheater through the 42-foot-tall Gregor's tower, named after the balloonist character in the film. His balloon and other props decorate the tower's interior.

The dominant feature of the set is the 30-foot-tall, 15,000-square-foot wall of rusted corrugated sheet metal. Each piece of steel was cut and welded on-site. The materials were specially treated to look old and withstand the aquatic environment. Unlike the temporary nature of the original film set, the park's backdrop had to be custom built and designed to last at least 10 years and be repeatedly blown up, rebuilt, and reset up to 15 times a day. The wall is dwarfed by the 52-foot main tower and the two 35-foot-tall atoll gate towers. The atoll gates are 10 feet wide, 30 feet high, and weigh 3 tons. An additional cyclorama (concave wall) was built behind the gate to prevent guests from seeing out of the facility, further immersing them in the *WaterWorld* experience.

The lagoon built for the *Miami Vice* show was widened, the bottom reshaped to accommodate the new stunts, and it was painted blue. The new lagoon holds 1.4 million gallons of recycled water. The deepest part is the dive pit, at 22 feet. Drums that move up and down were installed at the edges of the pool to create waves, which break up the surface of the water and disguise the true depth of the water.

By July 1995 the pool had been filled and three months of rehearsals began. At the start of the show's run, there were five casts of eight stunt people. The performers did not work for Universal; instead, they were professional stunt people working for another company. Universal was not going to have labor problems with this show like they did with the *A-Team*. Potential cast members were tested on their swimming abilities, watercraft knowledge, stunt abilities, fight coordination, and acting abilities. The pool is unheated and averages 52°F–54°F in winter and about 70°F during the summer. The performers wear wet suits, and a hot tub was placed backstage for them to warm up before and after a show.

Making sure the cast is safe and that the show can go on is a special effects technician who runs the show from the control booth, a sound-stage manager who controls the sound effects and microphones, and two stage managers. One is hidden in a booth built into the set, while the other one is located backstage. The actors step on pressure sensor pads or break infrared beams to enable many of the special effects, and one of the stage managers has to push a button agreeing that it is safe. To provide an additional level of safety, several underwater speakers and a surveillance camera system were installed to monitor the pool. Also, the show is not performed in the rain, and some of the special effects and pyro are not used during high winds.

As the 20-minute show begins, the heroine Helen has returned to the atoll with evidence of dry land. The happy moment is short-lived when a hole is blown through the wall and a villain on a Jet Ski is launched into the arena pulling a skier. Advanced Entertainment Technology of Monrovia fabricated the elaborate watercraft stunts. David McMurtry, president of the company, said, "The Jet Ski launch is one that has never done before—the Jet Skier and water-skier are propelled through a wall, thrown 30 feet through the air, and then land on the water surface."[9] The Mariner, the hero, enters the arena on a Jet Ski launched from a submerged catapult.

There are more than 20 flame effects and 50 pyro effects. Other special effects include a 40-foot rope lift for the Mariner to the top level of the tower. It uses a counterweight and a crane to suspend a stuntman over the Organo Pit by his ankles. The show features more than 50 stunts, a 45-foot-high fall, fires, explosions, and simulated bullet shots.

Possibly the most spectacular special effect closes the second act. "Universal suggested doing a big seaplane on a mechanical arm that would be laid out in the water," said John Richardson, who was responsible for the effect. "We came back to them and said, 'If you want to make it look realistic, let's throw it.' Their first reaction was, 'No way in hell. You're out of your minds.' But we proceeded to make it happen."[10] His firm developed the concept for the runaway seaplane, modeled it on a computer, and then built a dummy unit, which was test-launched in a pond for two weeks. The concept worked.

Installed backstage is a hidden 30-foot hydraulic catapult trolley system with a three-quarter-scale seaplane weighing 2,200 pounds mounted on top. The seaplane is made of a T6 aluminum skin stretched over a frame, then pop-riveted together and painted. The wings are cut shorter than an actual plane, with fixed control surfaces and reverse airfoils to spoil lift.

On cue, the seaplane is launched at a 40-degree angle through a breakaway wall. Untethered, the plane achieves free flight and lands 30 feet from the audience, exploding in a shower of pyrotechnics. Depending on the wind and the temperature, the seaplane can land within a 5- to 8-foot margin. Once the show is over, a crane is used to tow and lift the seaplane back onto the launcher.

Phil Hettema said of the show, "It convinced me of something I think I always believed in, but I certainly do now. The success of the movie is not what is important. It's the idea behind the movie and how much the public is able to capture the idea in their own minds. *WaterWorld* was so powerful in its concept that people thought, 'That would be a cool place to go.' Regardless of that, they don't know or care about the story—they are intrigued about going there and we pay off."[11]

An expanded version was built for Universal Studios Japanese theme park and became a fan favorite. Many of those improvements were brought back to Hollywood in a 2014 refurbishment. Though many visitors are not familiar with the source material, *WaterWorld* continues to delight audiences even today. The show has consistently ranked as the best in the park.

I'LL BE BACK

DIRECTOR JAMES CAMERON HAD BECOME WELL KNOWN for his use of cutting-edge technology in telling monumental stories. His low-budget science-fiction thriller *The Terminator* earned almost $79 million and was followed by an even bigger sequel, a Hollywood rarity. *Terminator 2: Judgment Day* debuted on July 3, 1991, and people could not believe how a computer-generated villain could seamlessly blend in with the live-action characters. The movie was a smash hit, earning more than $500 million worldwide.

Jay Stein was looking to replace the *Conan* show in the Castle Dracula Theater and thought the *Terminator* movies were the perfect edgy intellectual property. He learned that the first movie was tied up between James Cameron and his ex-wife Gale Anne Hurd, but the theme park rights for *Terminator 2: Judgment Day* were available. All he had to do was come up with a concept so compelling that James Cameron would sign over the rights. Stein turned to Gary Goddard of Landmark Entertainment in the fall of 1992 to develop some ideas.

For the first few weeks, the Landmark team struggled to find the right angle. Goddard went back to basics and broke the movie down. He realized that it was basically four chases. Goddard knew that one of the worst things you can do onstage was a chase scene. He said, "I am envisioning a guy in a tin-foil outfit and a lookalike Arnold taking swings and that is going to be awful, awful and I know we don't have the rights yet."[12]

To get beyond this creative block, Goddard tried a theatrical exercise created by Viola Spolin.[13] It was called "The Magic 'If'" game. When people get stuck coming up with ideas, the facilitator asks, "What if you were a spaceman, what would you do if. What if you were a fireman, what would you do if?" While mulling over this question, Goddard suddenly had the image of the T-1000 coming out of the screen. Then the image of the motorcycle following him out of the screen and entering the theater came next. From there, he furiously jotted down other ideas and called the attraction *T2:3-D* as a placeholder.

Goddard knew Stein would shoot him down unless he could tell him how these illusions could be achieved, so Goddard roughly figured out a way to use 3-D film technology and combine it with live in-theater effects and real actors. Stein was impressed and gave Goddard the green light for further development. By December, Goddard was ready to talk with James Cameron about their plans.

They met in the basement of the MCA Tower. In the room were Sidney Sheinberg, Jay Stein, Barry Upson, and Gary Goddard. On the wall were drawings of the show. Goddard made his pitch and sat down, and then there was an awkward silence. Goddard tried to speak, but Cameron stopped him and then stood up to take a closer look at the drawings. He said, "These are really good." He then told the group in the room, "You know, I have to say when I was driving over here I thought to myself, 'who the [expletive] are these guys who have developed a show based on my stuff. What the [expletive] are they going to show me, and I was prepared not to like it, but I have to say I am very impressed." He added, "Not that I couldn't make it better." What the group found in Cameron was a willing, excited, and engaged partner.

During 1993 and 1994, Landmark Entertainment and Universal Creative collaborated with Cameron's production company, Lightstorm Entertainment, and his special effects team, Digital Domain, to develop the technology for the show. Digital Domain was responsible for the digital composite imagery and had worked on films such as *Jurassic Park* and *Apollo 13*. The project was given the formal green light in March 1995.

Terminator 2: 3-D Battle Across Time was a breakthrough attraction. The show used state-of-the-art 3-D camera technology combined with a custom-built projection system, a specially outfitted theater, and computer technology to create an environment in which characters on the movie screen come to life and for the first time enter the theater as live actors. The result is a blurring of the line between what is real and what is movie magic. Everything is perfectly synchronized. Adding to the spectacle are audio-animatronics robot warriors and plenty of theater special effects.

The show is basically a mini-sequel to *Terminator 2: Judgment Day*. During the preshow, a live actor plays the head of the fictional Cyberdyne Corporation's public relations and media control department, Kimberley Duncan, who introduces the defense and technology company using a slickly produced video. The video is a sales pitch for a defense program called Skynet. Suddenly, two fugitives from history, Sarah Connor (Linda Hamilton) and John Connor (Edward Furlong) from the film *Terminator 2: Judgment Day*, interrupt the presentation. After some panic, Duncan gains back control and ushers the audience into the Miles Bennet Dyson Memorial Auditorium. Once seated, she introduces the T-70 warrior robot, a new product.

While the show was under development, the plan called for audio-animatronic T-800 Endoskeleton soldiers to surround the audience. Cameron corrected the team and reminded them that the T-800s were from the future (about 2029) and would not be appropriate for the show. So he designed a more primitive version called the T-70. The robots are 8 feet tall and more than 4 feet wide. They are made of a high-carbon steel substructure and covered with a fireproof polyresin/glass fiber. They are controlled by a sophisticated computer control system and are driven by a hydraulic plumbing system operating at more than 3,000-psi fluid pressure.

Once again, Sarah and John Connor, this time played by live actors rappelling from the ceiling, interrupt Kimberley Duncan. The actors are carefully choreographed to lip-synch with the audio tracks and to be in the right spot at the right time so that the special effects can be enabled.

For many, the most spectacular effect is when the Terminator rides his motorcycle off the movie screen and directly onto the stage. Production Resource Group was hired to create the in-theater effect that would allow for the characters to move from screen to stage and back again. The patented system was quite ingenious. When the Terminator character makes his entrance, he is on the screen riding a Harley-Davidson Fat Boy motorcycle. Suddenly, he turns toward the screen, and in a flash, a look-alike live actor enters the theater through the screen on the same motorcycle. To achieve this effect, a stage manager backstage, along with another stage manager in the production booth, enable the giant screen to lift in a fraction of a second, revealing a hidden door on the lower portion of the screen. The door is hidden from the audience using lighting effects and fog. The actor rides onstage via the replica motorcycle attached to a track. The motorcycle is launched at precisely the right moment through the door. Once safely through, the screen quickly lowers back into position. All of this action takes place in less than 3 seconds.

The patent document stated that the technology created the illusion of "a live-action show, actors, stage sets, and show action equipment [to] appear to interact with the three-dimensional film. The filmed set blends with the stage sets to give dimension and a feeling of depth to the viewing audience. The audience cannot easily distinguish between the real elements and filmed elements, ethereally intensifying the theater experience."[14]

To test the concept, a mock-up of the theater was built in a hangar at the old Hughes airport property in 1993. Three 60-foot screens were hung and the basic layout for the projectors were tested. Mark Eades, who worked on the project, said, "The theater, seats, and actors were blocked at this location, as well as shooting some tests to see if the three-screen 3D would work as desired." Then the project was put on hold in mid-1994 while Universal considered the final concept. The mock-up was destroyed and members of the project team went their separate ways to work on other projects.

The project was restarted in 1995. The Hughes hangar was unavailable, so a new mock-up of the project was built in a hangar at the Van Nuys Airport. It was determined to reduce the size of the building footprint, which meant reducing the width of the screens to 50 feet and restaging the actors' movements. Rehearsals began with the actors. Video footage of the rehearsals was used to synch up the live action with the films in postproduction.

Principal photography for the project began in May 1995 at a deserted steel mill in Desert Center, California. It took two weeks of all-night shooting to capture the action. The attraction involved getting together almost the entire original film crew, which was the first time in movie history that this had been done for a nontheatrical release. James Cameron was responsible for the overall production and directed the first section of the film. Once the Terminator and John Connor entered the parking structure and were pursued by the flying robots, effects specialist Stan Winston took over. Finally, when the two characters entered Skynet and all three screens were revealed, visual effects supervisor John Bruno was put in charge.

The 12-minute short was shot on 65-millimeter 3-D movie stock that ran at 30 frames per second instead of the conventional 24 frames per second to increase the resolution of the film image. At a reported cost of $24 million for the film and another $36 million for the venue, *Terminator 2: 3-D* was considered, frame for frame, the most expensive movie ever made. It took another six months after photography and 47 computer graphics artists and eight compositors working full time to integrate all of the digital imagery.

A custom projection system was designed for the show. To achieve the 180-degree field of vision, six fully automated Iwerks 70-millimeter projectors are aimed at three screens. Although the film was shot on 65-millimeter film, it was printed on 70-millimeter stock so that it could be fed through the projectors in the theater. The 23-foot-high by 50-foot-long screens were treated with a layer of ultra-high-gain material to produce a superior 3-D image. Dr. Ken Jones, a specialist from the Jet Propulsion Laboratory in Pasadena, California, was hired to perfect the interlocking of the three images.

The theaters were outfitted with the most sophisticated audio system ever installed in a theme park attraction at that time. The 45,620-watt audio system surrounded the audience with more than 159 speakers. Brad Fiedel composed a new musical score. Sound effects by Gary Rydstrom from the original *Terminator 2* film were reused.

The show opened at Universal Studios Florida on April 27, 1996, in an unmarked theater hidden behind an Art Deco facade in the Hollywood section. A Cyberdyne Systems logo and pillar sign were added later. Once inside the auditorium, six T-70 robots (instead of the four in Hollywood) confront visitors. Visitors exit through a gift shop behind a Kress Five & Dime facade.

In Hollywood, placing the show building was much more of a challenge. In 1993 Morris Architects was hired to design the structure. Unlike most theme park show buildings, *Terminator* would be prominently perched on top of a parking structure and seen from all sides. The 37,000-square-foot building was designed so that it could also be used as a large screening room. Architect Jim Pope said that Universal Creative's Mark Woodbury challenged the team "to rethink the guest's experience of an attraction from start to finish or 'curb to retail shop,' and from the perspective of the architect and guest who may not be familiar with the storyline."[15] The theater's exterior carried a pattern of pixels abstracted from the visuals used for the Terminator's computer screen visual field and was punctuated by biomorphic curves of Silvergray: Cyberdyne's "morphing liquid metal."

Before *Terminator 2: 3-D,* the project site was being used as an outdoor theater. To compensate for the added loads from both the new show building and the show's climax, where the audience's seats drop several inches, the parking structure had to be reinforced. Construction started on the Hollywood version on January 2, 1997.

On April 13, 1999, for the press grand opening, musician George Thorogood joined actor Arnold Schwarzenegger, while a stuntman rappelled from a helicopter. The show opened to the public on May 6, 1999. The Hollywood version was basically the same as the attraction in Florida, with two

unofficial **TIP**
The Hollywood version of *Terminator 2: 3-D* closed on December 31, 2012, to make way for a new, child-friendly ride based on the *Despicable Me* animated films.

fewer T-70 robots. Just like Florida, the show exited into a gift shop with arcade games. Just outside was a Harley-Davidson motorcycle like the one in the show, available for guest photos. The Cyber Grill, a fast food restaurant, was placed nearby.

STRAIGHT *from the* NOVEL

RELEASED IN 1990, MICHAEL CRICHTON'S *Jurassic Park* would become a publishing phenomenon. The best-selling science-fiction/fantasy novel was set in an imaginary tropical theme park filled with previously extinct dinosaurs re-created through their DNA. From the very beginning, Steven Spielberg was interested in bringing this story to the screen and to the theme parks. *Jurassic Park* was the perfect property for Jay Stein. It had a compelling story, a beautiful background, and Spielberg's support. Stein would have all the resources necessary to build something great.

For Lew Wasserman and Sidney Sheinberg, there was a standing rule. Be nice to Steven and let him do whatever he wants. They did not really have much choice. Spielberg's production firm Amblin grossed $548.7 million, or 60% of Universal's movie revenues in 1993. Even the shouting matches that routinely took place during meetings were quelled while the director was in the room.

unofficial **TIP**
To bring the book *Jurassic Park* to life in film, Steven Spielberg decided to forgo using stop motion to animate the dinosaurs and used computer-generated imagery to create the prehistoric beasts. The illusion would prove to be magical, and in 1993 the film became one of the biggest box office hits in Universal's history, grossing more than $400 million in its initial run.

All sorts of ride systems were considered. One that made it pretty far in the development process was Helicoptours, an aerial simulator ride that would take visitors over the island. A walking safari where visitors could get a close-up view of the beasts was also considered. Peter Alexander suggested a Jeep ride similar to the dramatic sequence in the film where a four-row truck creeps through a jungle filled with audio-animatronic dinosaurs. At one point, the windows would fog up, and when they cleared, there would be a hungry Tyrannosaurus Rex.

Gary Goddard from Landmark Entertainment was brought on board in early 1991 to develop concepts for a Jurassic Park ride for Florida. Goddard got permission to read the draft script that was locked away at Amblin. He only had 2 hours and could not take any notes. From what he learned, he went to Alexander and said, "Looks to me like [the jeep scene] is going to be a Steven Spielberg action spectacular, and we'll never be able to do that."[16]

Goddard dug deeper into the novel and found a story line where the heroes find themselves floating down a river filled with dinosaurs.

A boat ride! That was the answer. Stein told him all he had to do was convince Spielberg. Goddard was confident and told the director, "Think about this. It is a boat ride in Florida, which was desperately needed. It is going to be a great way to tell the story. And it is straight from the novel."[17] Spielberg loved the idea and gave it his blessing.

Goddard envisioned the rafts gently floating down a stream. As the jungle thickened, the music would swell while the trees and vines began to block the view. Without realizing it, the visitors would go under a giant sunroof. Goddard did not like the look of large-scale animated figures in daylight, and he felt they would become a maintenance nightmare in the harsh Florida weather. The sunroof would help cut down on the UV rays and give the skins that covered the dinosaur animatronics a longer life—and give him a way to control the lighting.

*un*official **TIP**
Many years later, *Jurassic Park III* (2001) would feature the heroes in a small boat floating down a river filled with dinosaurs.

Once they were deep into the jungle, the rafts would tilt forward and drop toward an Ultrasaurus towering over them at 30 feet, chewing on some vines. The gentle pace of the ride would continue, and the visitors would encounter an adorable baby Ultrasaurus, a couple of Psittacosauruses, a Triceratops, and a Stegosaurus with their babies.

The tour would continue, and the rafts would float in an area where the carnivores were safely caged. To demonstrate, a Deinonychus would try to jump at the steel fence of his enclosure and be repelled by an electrical charge. No harm done. The rafts would continue past another cage, but this time the cage would have been ripped open and would stand empty.

Enough of the carnivores. The next destination was the Hadrosaur Ravine, "where we'll meet some of the most charming dinosaurs," according to the script. Of course, nothing goes as planned on a Universal ride, and a startled Parasaurolophus would jump out of the water and turn the raft in the wrong direction 60 degrees toward a double set of doors. Beyond those doors, Goddard needed to find a way to take advantage of the visitors going backward and then turn them around for the ride's climax.

In one version, the doors were marked "Danger: Toxic Chemicals. Authorized Personnel Only." Once through the doors, the raft would travel through a tight corridor surrounded by the sounds of dinosaurs on the prowl. At the end of the hall was another set of doors where the raft would stop momentarily before being pushed backward by a dinosaur trying to break through. The backward journey continued through another confined space with spitting dinosaurs and entered a room with a very large Spinosaurus carcass rotting in the toxic water. At the end of this sequence, the boat would stop and turn around to face forward again.

Another concept was through the doors marked "Boat Maintenance—Empty Boats Only Past This Point." This time the boat would fall into the abandoned maintenance bay for the boats. While guests were floating backward through this cramped space, dinosaurs would pound at the doors, and one of them would push the raft around to face forward, almost taking a bite before the boat would move away.

Another innovative take on this segment involved a live actor. As the raft entered a cave, it would come to a stop. A performer dressed as an attraction worker would tell visitors they needed to run for their lives and would try to release the lap restraints. Unfortunately, the loud sound of a dinosaur would turn the boat around. The last thing guests would see was the tail of a dinosaur and blood in the water. Gary Goddard said, "Jay [Stein] loved this."[18] The illusion would have been achieved using an acoustically designed cave and a sophisticated audio system.

As the ride continued, there would be a quiet moment before Velociraptors, held back only by an electric fence, would suddenly attack the raft. One of the dinosaurs would bite a wire, and the raft would plunge into complete darkness while being pulled up a lift hill. At the top of the hill would be a Tyrannosaurus Rex, who would lunge at the raft but be blocked by water pipes.

As the raft would turn a corner and float forward, a huge waterfall blocking the exit would distract visitors. However, that would be the least of their worries when a giant animatronic Tyrannosaurus Rex would break through the falls and get perilously close to the raft. The only escape would be a 70-foot drop with a 30-foot splash.

To make sure that the animated Ultrasaurus had realistic movement, Goddard hired Professor Marc H. Raibert of MIT. This was the first dinosaur the visitor would see and it had to look right. The professor modeled the movement after a giraffe but a bit slower. To fabricate the mechanical systems and the skins for the dinosaurs, Goddard consulted with experienced companies, such as Arrow Dynamics and PVK Architects. The estimated cost for the ride was $52 million.

Then, in January 1993, Jay Stein was gone and so was Florida's first go at a Jurassic Park ride.

A **CHANGE** *in* **LEADERSHIP**

ON JANUARY 6, 1993, MCA QUIETLY ANNOUNCED that Jay Stein would be resigning as chief executive of the MCA Recreation Services Group and as vice president of MCA Inc. His longtime protégé Ron Bension would be taking over. The stated reason for Stein's departure was "personal and charitable pursuits." He was only 55 years old and had worked at the company since 1959. Stein had dedicated his life to building MCA's Recreation Services Group since he took over in 1967.

Bension was formerly president and chief operating officer of MCA's Recreation Services Group. Bension started in 1971 as sweeper while he was in high school and worked his way up the ladder. Stein had groomed him for the job. At 38, Bension would become responsible for all of the parks. He had his work cut out for him. "There was only one boss," Terry Winnick said. "Jay. It was tough to hand over the keys to Ron."[19]

Peter Alexander worked side by side with Stein for many years. He said, "The corporate politics was if you worked on the Universal staff long enough, your judgment was questioned." Stein had been running the division a long time, and he had changed. When Alexander left in June 1991, he signed a two-year consulting contract. "Jay wanted to be a creative guy," said Alexander. "As soon as I left, he grew his hair long with a ponytail, and that signified to him that he was a creative guy. He was a production executive at the studio before the tour and handled budgets. He was very good at it. He was a very good executive. He was actually good at motivating people to work for him. We all did the best work we ever did working for Jay Stein because he was so demanding. He was so difficult to work for, but he drove us."[20] Alexander decided to end his relationship with Universal six months later.

Gary Goddard admired Stein. He said, "Guys like me need guys like Jay for great things to happen."[21] Phil Hettema was blunt, "Jay was a true P.T. Barnum. He didn't have a lot of budget to add things to the tour, so he always designed things by making the commercial in his mind first. The additions often did not live up to the hype, but it pumped people through the gates."[22] He added, "I really do think Jay Stein, as colorful and as challenging of a guy, was a visionary. He wasn't just being competitive; it was that he really had a vision. The fact that this vision was so not of the traditional Disney mold is exactly what set Universal apart."[23]

Simply stated, Stein created the DNA for what the Universal Studios experience would be. That DNA is still in use today. Universal Studios Florida would not exist at all without him. Phil Hettema did make this observation about his old boss: "Interestingly enough, he wasted no time in being done. Some people retire and they come back. When he was done, he was done."[24]

Like his mercurial predecessor, Bension had big plans for the Universal parks. He decided to open Jurassic Park in Hollywood first and bring the *Terminator* show to Florida. He also had ideas for a second gate in Florida and wanted to line up his assets correctly.

With the dinosaurs in Florida gone, so was Gary Goddard. Although he had developed the concept for Jurassic Park, "when they decided to move it [to Hollywood] nobody consulted with me," said Goddard.[25] The Hollywood version of Jurassic Park would share some elements from the original design but would be something entirely its own. Landmark Entertainment shot the ride's preshow footage starring Richard Attenborough with a cameo appearance by Steven Spielberg. They also produced the sound track.

According to Phil Hettema, the drop for the Hollywood version was designed specifically to take advantage of the hillside. Then came a protected oak tree on the hillside. They had to spend millions to design around the tree. It was not long after the ride opened that the tree died.

The movie had not even opened in the theaters in February 1993 when Universal Studios Florida announced they were building the ride. The budget for the ride was an astronomical $70 million. That was twice the cost of producing the hit film. When the film opened on June 13, it became the biggest film of the year.

A 6-acre site was selected on the lower lot. The ride replaced the old studio costume shop and some of the office bungalows for the producers, including director Ron Howard. To create a lush tropical jungle along the barren hillside, Universal planted 353 palm trees representing 11 different species, including sago, king, queen, kentia, and Canary Island date palms. Three hundred bamboo plants of six varieties, as well as more than 900 trees, were planted, including flame, golden rain, orchid, Australian tree fern, giant bird of paradise, and dragon. The final touch was the more than 7,500 shrubs, plants, and flowers. More than 76 species were planted, including star jasmine, breath of heaven, rattlesnake grass, Tasmanian tree fern, shell ginger, mystery gardenia, sugar bush, bougainvillea, and giant Burmese honeysuckle.

unofficial **TIP**
On occasion, the Jurassic Park ride has been tweaked to provide a new incentive for repeat visits. Jumping on the bandwagon for the release of *Jurassic Park III* (2001), Universal created the Summer Splash by adding an additional 240,000 gallons of water to the 1.4-gallon waterway. Then in 2003, the final splashdown was made adjustable to enable the amount of splash depending on weather conditions. This was especially important for foreign visitors who do not wish to get wet, a significant Universal audience. Then in 2007, a new Wetter Than Ever experience was announced with 60-foot water geysers added to the ride. The addition became an annual event.

The ride opened on June 21, 1996. It took 18 months to build. Riders boarded the largest amusement ride watercraft ever built. Each of the 16 boats can hold 25 riders. On a very busy day, they can leave the dock every 30 seconds, which means that more than 3,000 visitors per hour can enjoy the attraction. There are very few rides at Disney that can satisfy that many guests so quickly.

Once on board their raft, the guests float through 12 scenes and past 16 animated dinosaurs.

Salt Lake City–based Sarcos built the dinosaur robots. Disney had hired them to develop the Wicked Witch of the West Audio-Animatronic in The Great Movie Ride. Gary Goddard predicted that the dinosaurs would be a maintenance nightmare and recommended a different company with more experience in a theme park environment. He was right. The skins that cover the mechanics did not last very long, and the mechanical systems needed constant repair.[26]

As the boats are lifted up the ramp into the 135-foot-tall building, dinosaurs jumping out in the dark terrify riders. At the top of the ramp, the boats approach a waterfall, and a divertor closes off the waterfall, creating an opening exposing an audio-animatronic Tyrannosaurus Rex. While the riders are focused on the T-Rex, the boats plunge down the 84-foot drop. At the bottom of the drop, along the shore, is the can of Barbasol shaving cream containing the DNA for more dinosaurs. A sequel? Most certainly.

The SIMULACRUM

FOR DECADES, LEW WASSERMAN and Albert Dorskind explored adding a shopping and entertainment center to Universal City. In 1989 they hired architect Jon Jerde to draft a master plan for the property. Jerde was well known for his simple, effective architectural elements at the 1984 Los Angeles Olympics and the urban infill Horton Plaza shopping center in the Gaslamp District of downtown San Diego. Jerde was hired by Disney in 1985 and designed Satellite City for EuroDisney. That development would have been a disc-shaped city, more than a mile in diameter, with 50 hotels, spas, a conference center, shopping, and recreation zones. Transportation would have been provided, in part, by a canal system. The project was never built. However, as always, having worked for Disney got you noticed at Universal.

The shopping mall project was driven by the need to create a dynamic path for people walking between the existing studio tour, cinemas, and the amphitheater. "I saw CityWalk as a venue for human intercourse," according to Jerde. "All America is now private [and only] New York and San Francisco held on to more foot driven aspects of human interaction, but most of the country has been given over to separateness and loneliness." He wanted to create something that was different. Jerde said, "Our enemies are artifice and the ersatz [with] fake this and that, like those theme restaurants. But people reject it. It's exceedingly difficult to make sure that what you do isn't exceedingly synthetic and contrived."[27]

CityWalk opened in May 1993. The result was a two-block-long "street" made up of eight separate structures with 27 individual building facades that connect the theme park's front gate to the parking structures required by this isolated, compact hilly site. Jerde said he wanted to capture the emotional impact of Tuscany or North Beach in San Francisco.

"CityWalk had to be appropriately built on the architectural language of L.A., as opposed to New York or Paris," Jerde said. "And the language of L.A. is that there is no language except stucco buildings and layers put upon them. So the thematic element is layering." Juxtaposed facades, historic neon signs, towers, and billboards framed the narrow street, which Jerde says created "a sequential plan of orchestrated events." The massing of the buildings came from computer-compiled traces of local architecture. No one building was replicated. Instead, you have a collage of images and traits of the city. Jerde wanted a space that was "self-consciously designed" yet tried to appear to have grown organically. The architect claimed that City-Walk was a simulacrum, a copy with no original.[28]

CityWalk does feel energetic, bordering on chaotic, as it tries to echo the visual disorder of a complete city within the space of a few yards. The street leads to a large central plaza capped by a steel-web canopy. In one corner is an interactive fountain by WET Design. Up above is a second level of nightclubs and restaurants dubbed CityLoft. More than a third of CityWalk's 540,000-square-foot building area is dedicated to offices and a satellite college campus.

Many critics disliked the design. Cultural critic Norman Klein wrote, CityWalk is "a Victorian-style separation of classes in our public life,"[29] while writer Lewis Lapham argued it served consumers who "had no intention of going to see the original city four miles to the south."[30] Cultural critic Mike Davis simply concluded, "It fulfills our worst prophecies."[31] Paola Giaconia wrote, "This hilltop shopping mall impersonating a city street was commissioned by MCA Development and garishly overdesigned for mass appeal by the Jerde Partnership." He added, "In designing this privatized social area for the privileged, the architects didn't make much of an attempt to connect it with the surrounding community and actually shielded it by a wall of parking garages."[32]

Jerde disagreed with the critics. He said, "These things are vast consumption machines, but we treat them as communal complexes that happen to have shopping in them. What we provide is urban glue." Jerde said he "doesn't aspire to the kind of social idealism and aesthetic purity that were the foundations of Modernism."[33] Professor David Sloane of USC also found something to like. "In one sense, people went there and found it to be a familiar place," he said. "The circus-like street reminded them of an old midway. On the other hand, it's different enough to be exciting."[34] Architectural historian David Gebhard said, "This is the cleaned-up retail strip as it should be. It is excellent stage-set architecture, lively and well carried out."[35]

CityWalk proved to be a perfect complement to the tour. The number of locals crossing over and visiting the Studio Tour had increased dramatically. The new mall changed the visitor mix at Universal City from 80% tourists to 50% tourists and 50% residents.[36]

It turned a struggling Cineplex into one of the most successful theaters in Los Angeles and helped boost theme park attendance. With almost 3 million new visitors, parking revenues boomed. Buzz Price said, "Universal City's hilltop operates as one big mega theme park made up of three paid gates all supported and reinforced by a free entry festival marketplace. It is in the same genre as Harborplace in Baltimore, which contains three paid gates (the aquarium, the science museum and IMAX, and the USS *Constitution*) operating in concert with a major festival marketplace. It is also in the same genre as Knott's theme park with its festival market outside the gate."[37] Lew Wasserman was so proud of CityWalk that he used to pull the tallies of the lunches and dinners served at the restaurants and show them off to visitors.[38]

The success of CityWalk was vital to the long-term sustainability of Universal City and became a catalyst for Universal Hollywood's transformation from an industrial tour to a full-fledged theme park.

When MCA commissioned a study in 1996, they found that demand for the center far outstripped capacity. Price said, "The demand for expansion is obviously there. It's a slam-dunk."[39] In fact, the study suggested Universal could double the size of CityWalk. Other recommendations included Universal taking over as many of the store leases as possible to cut out the middleman, as well as operating the themed restaurants as joint ventures to maximize profits. He also recommended adding an IMAX large-screen format theater, which would happen a few years later.[40] This was all Wasserman needed to hear. Planning for the expansion began immediately.

With this kind of success, it was only natural that Universal would try to build a sequel. The second phase of CityWalk opened in April 2000. The new addition became known as EastWalk. More than 93,000 square feet of retail and restaurant space was added to the existing 300,000. Thirty new shops, restaurants, and attractions were part of the mix. Twelve new retail stores included such diverse goods as vintage clothing, movie memorabilia, wind-up toys, and a Hollywood Harley-Davidson outlet. Dino Vindeni, general manager of the Harley store, said, "We've been so packed that we had to close our doors at some points. We're catering to a different crowd than a dealership would, so the hard-core Harley owner might be disappointed. But we've been getting great feedback so far."[41]

Entertainment venues included Jillian's Hi-Life Lanes with neon bowling balls, Howl at the Moon dueling piano bar, and Café Tu Tu Tango, a smaller version of a House of Blues. Universal's Larry Kurzweil said, "We were looking for choices and concepts that had a lot of attitude, fun and energy. The key concept is that this is an extension of Universal Studios Hollywood."[42] For a very brief time, an artists' loft was above one of the restaurants, and some of the profits went to struggling artists.

Lighting, as well as giant 80-foot billboards above the pedestrian walk, was used as the signature architectural component. *Los Angeles Times* critic Nicolai Ouroussoff suggested, "The new structures offer fewer architectural quotations, leaning toward a more abstract aesthetic" with "images distilled from Los Angeles' own peculiar landscape of fantasy." He wrote, "The effect is a 'Blade Runner'-like collage of commercial images, a tensely energetic mix of fantasy and reality." He also advised that the new addition was best experienced at night, when the lighting provided an eerie effect.[43]

There was another positive by-product to the success of City-Walk. This time it was internal. Buzz Price was an outsider with a keen eye for detail. He noticed, "The old battle between the tour people who thought that the Tour was the mother of all profits and the periphery development team was obsolete. It was one dynamic place, one of a kind."[44]

A BIGGER, BETTER HOLLYWOOD

THE BATTLES BETWEEN UNIVERSAL AND DISNEY were not limited to Florida. The Walt Disney Company was growing increasingly concerned that constant regional discounting and annual passes had started to turn Disneyland into a regional theme park rather than a world-class destination. They wanted to correct that perception and turn Anaheim into a multiday tourist resort like Walt Disney World.

On July 12, 1996, Disneyland officials met with local leaders in the Disneyland Opera House to unveil plans for the expansion of their Anaheim property.[45] As announced, the new Disneyland Resort would include Disney's California Adventure—a 55-acre theme park—the 750-room Disney's Grand Californian Hotel along the perimeter of the park, and the 200,000-square-foot Disneyland Center shopping and entertainment district.

Not to be outdone, Universal announced its own expansion plans on January 21, 1997, at a public hearing before the Los Angeles County Planning Commission. The meeting was held at the Universal Hilton Ballroom, and the studio provided free food. Recognizing that things were getting more complicated politically, a pro-development group called Universal City Tomorrow attended to balance out any neighborhood objections.

The 25-year plan was estimated to cost $2 billion and would create up to 13,000 permanent jobs. The plan outlined four development sites: the Studio District, the Business Center, the Entertainment district, and the Greenscape district. Overall, the project would create almost 5.9 million square feet of new development.

Not everybody was happy with the announcement. Gerald Silver from the Encino Home Owners Association told the public officials, "We don't want another Disneyland in our backyard. We don't want a large workforce of hot dog and hamburger salesmen [attracted by] a worldwide tourist attraction."[46] Another local resident, Wayne Brunette of Studio City, quipped, "You may recall the objections to O'Malley's Dodger Stadium. Universal is the Valley's benevolent rich uncle ready to take a giant cultural step forward, and providing jobs, that would receive a warm welcome in 49 other states." The quiet residential neighborhood of Toluca Lake adjacent to Universal City formed a residents association to combat the expansion plans. One of the early supporters of the organization was Roy E. Disney, who lived in the neighborhood.

By July 1997, pressure from the surrounding neighborhoods forced Universal to cut back its project by 44%. Under the new proposal, Universal was to focus on expanding the studio and not on the theme park. The development area was reduced to 3.3 million square feet of office and production space, hotels, and retail stores.

Even existing attractions were impacted. One requirement was to reduce the noise of the *WaterWorld* show or to eliminate it. Universal attorney George Millstone conceded, "Universal has worked very hard to listen. Listening is sometimes very hard and painful. We think this reduced project is appropriate." It was still not enough. Neighbor Patrick Garner said, "We don't want Universal to expand their theme park at all."[47]

Inside of the theme park was a new show that opened in 1997, bringing a bit of the Nickelodeon Network to Hollywood. *Totally Nickelodeon* opened in the Panasonic Theatre, replacing *The Flintstones Musical Revue*. The show was an interactive experience in which members of the audience played three different games inspired by the popular children's television channel. A press release promised, "Whether it's dumping a TV dinner on a couch potato, crossing an aerial bridge, collecting sweaty socks, rescuing Alex Mack or building the better Good Burger—*Totally Nickelodeon* is big fun and you're in control."

TWISTER

UNIVERSAL EXECUTIVES WERE ALWAYS on the hunt for intellectual properties or new technologies that they could exploit. Any film with a clear vision and extensive special effects was game. Amblin Entertainment's *Twister* (1996) seemed like a perfect fit. The special effects–loaded film was based on the adventures of scientists who chased after tornadoes. Bringing a tornado indoors and repeating the show dozens of times a day would be an impressive feat of engineering and showmanship. Just imagine what the commercial could look like.

Inspiration for a new ride can come from some of the strangest places. Artist Ned Kahn specialized in sculpting tornadoes and vortexes with installations in science centers around the world. Someone working for Phil Hettema saw one of Kahn's pieces that generated a vortex in San Francisco and realized that the illusion looked like a small tornado. What if they could create a reliable indoor tornado?

The team at Universal Creative began work on creating a larger vortex and hired wind-flow experts Cermak Peterka Petersen, Inc. The firm had worked on more than 2,000 projects, including the World Trade Towers in New York. Its goal was to build a twister that was approximately five stories tall and 12 feet wide. If successful, the firm would have built the largest indoor tornado ever created by man. They began by building a one-fourth-scale model of the vortex, which worked beautifully. Feeling confident, the model was scaled up to full size. That was when the problems started.

To generate the full-size effect, it was necessary to generate constant winds of 35 miles per hour. A studio was outfitted with 30 specially designed fans arranged in three tiers: ground level, mid-level, and high-level. Eighteen of those fans had blades 7 feet tall. "We invited our employees into the ride," said J. Michael Hightower, the project director. "It had a detrimental effect on the tornado. This special effect is the most difficult at Universal because we don't have direct control over it. For instance, if we want the Jaws shark to move faster, we just turn up the pressure."[48]

They hired a university professor to run calculations to figure out how to make a reliable tornado of the right size. One solution was to install a computerized weather tracking system that monitored the outside wind velocity, humidity, and barometric pressure to maximize the size and shape of the twister inside. They brought in 240 mannequins with clothes to tweak the effect. The result was a reliable tornado of the correct size that could move as much as 30 feet in any direction from its origin. The volume of air used could fill four full-size airborne blimps.

Twister: Ride It Out became a high-profile project. The film was a joint production between Warner Bros. and Universal. Instead of spending money on a ride system, the $16 million budget was spent on a spectacular, memorable show that represented a new level of sophistication in special effects demonstrations. The show opened on May 4, 1997.

Like *Backdraft*, the attraction is broken into three acts. The first act is a preshow that includes an audio-visual presentation. The second room resembles a tornado-damaged building. The two stars of the film, Bill Paxton and Helen Hunt, were filmed separately for their introductions on the same day and are shown on two separate screens in the preshow.

The final act takes place on a set that resembles an outdoor scene inside of a 25,000-square-foot soundstage. The show replaced the *Ghostbusters Spectacular* in the New York zone. Visitors stand on an elevated viewing platform and come face-to-face with more than 55 special effects. Hundreds of xenon strobes flash, simulating lightning. The sound of thunder is piped through 54 speakers powered by 42,000 watts, enough to power five average homes. The roar of the storm is made of a combination of sounds, including those of camels and lions, and backward human and animal screams. More than 65,000 gallons of recycled water feed the rainstorm and can be ready for the next show every 6 minutes. The 20 laser disc players, 300 speakers, and 60 video monitors are connected by 50 miles of electrical wire and controlled by 20 computers. One of the most memorable effects from both the movie and the show is a flying cow.

The grand opening was originally scheduled for April 1997, but it was delayed a month due to February 1997 tornados in Central Florida that killed 42 people. Universal donated $100,000 to aid the victims.

Along with the addition of *Twister* came a change to another of the original attractions at Universal Studios Florida. In the summer of 1997, the *Murder, She Wrote Mystery Production Theater* was transformed into *Hercules and Xena: Wizards of the Screen*. The half-hour demonstration was the latest version of the special effects show and was based on the popular syndicated live-action television shows *Xena* and *Hercules*. More than a dozen volunteers were selected from the audience to help produce the segments. The volunteers created sound effects, operated props, and saw their images morphed by computers with footage shot in New Zealand. At one point, visitors entered a "creature lab" where several volunteers were asked to operate a large creature while others played centaurs.

Another opening day attraction was repurposed. The MCA Recording Studio allowed guests to play with various sound and recording effects used during postproduction. In 1997 the space became Stage 54. Over the years, the showcase was used for displays of props from films including *How the Grinch Stole Christmas*, *The Mummy Returns*, and *The Fast and Furious*. The exhibit space lasted until 2003. Two more pieces of the past have gone away.

Bronfman's plans for Orlando were becoming grander and more ambitious. If he was going to beat Disney, he thought he needed more land. Land meant more theme parks, hotels, shops, and restaurants. On January 26, 1998, Universal entered negotiations to purchase 2,000 acres from Lockheed Martin. The site would allow for eastward expansion adjacent to the convention center.

The aerospace company had been using the site since the late 1950s to build missile

unofficial **TIP**
In mid-2013, Universal purchased the 50 acres of land under and around Wet 'n Wild Orlando for $30.9 million.

systems and components. On the site were six landfills. Molten metals, solvents, and other materials were dumped. Groundwater pollution was detected in the early 1980s, and a cleanup started in 1984. The estimated price for the land was $150 million.

To make the deal happen, Universal entered an agreement for a land swap with Orange County. The county wanted to double the exhibit space at the convention center, and it needed 230 acres. Universal would buy the land from Lockheed Martin and then sell a portion to the county. Universal would also be responsible for the environmental cleanup. In October Universal was forced to lower the price from $350,000 per acre to $300,000 per acre, saving the county $10 million. The deal closed in December for $69 million. Now Bronfman had enough land for anything.

Because Disney had a water park, Bronfman felt he needed one as well. In 1998 he purchased Wet 'n Wild Orlando, a popular water park.

1   James Bates, "Matsushita to Sell 80% of MCA to Seagram Co.," *The Los Angeles Times,* 7 Apr. 1995.
2   Ibid.
3   Ibid.
4   Ibid.
5   "Company Town Annex," *The Los Angeles Times,* 16 Aug. 1995.
6   Christine Shenot, "Barney the Dinosaur Gets a Home at Universal Studios," *Orlando Sentinel*, 7 July 1995.
7   Ibid.
8   Robert Cashill, "WaterWorld Live," *TCI,* 1 Apr. 1996.
9   Ibid.
10 Ibid.
11 Phil Hettema, interview with author, Pasadena, CA, 7 May 2014.
12 Gary Goddard, interview with author, North Hollywood, CA, 12 Jan. 2014.
13 Ibid.
14 Gary Goddard and Adam Bezark, Theater with multiple screen three dimensional film projection system, US Patent 5,964,064, filed 25 Apr. 1997 and issued 12 Oct. 1999.
15 Ellen Lampert-Great, "Morris Architects' Walter Geiger & Jim Pope," *Entertainment Design,* July 2001.
16 Goddard, interview with author, 12 Jan. 2014.
17 Ibid.
18 Ibid.
19 Terry Winnick, interview with author, Las Vegas, NV, 25 Feb. 2014.
20 Peter Alexander, interview with author, South Palm Beach, FL, 21 Oct. 2013.
21 Goddard, interview with author, 12 Jan. 2014.
22 Phil Hettema, interview with author, Pasadena, CA, 16 Jan. 2014.
23 Hettema, interview with author, 7 May 2014.
24 Ibid.
25 Goddard, interview with author, 12 Jan. 2014.
26 Ibid.
27 Ed Leibowitz, "Taking the Walk," *Los Angeles Times,* 9 Apr. 2000.

28 Ibid.

29 Norman Klein, *The Vatican to Vegas: A History of Special Effects* (New York: The New Press, 2004).

30 Virginia Postrel, "From Shopping Centers to Lifestyle Centers," *Los Angeles Times,* 10 Dec. 2006.

31 Ibid.

32 Paola Giaconia, "Universal City Walk Displacement of Hetrotopia," *Architettrua,* 29 Nov. 2002.

33 Nicolai Ouroussoff, "Fantasies of a City High on a Hill," *Los Angeles Times,* 9 Apr. 2000.

34 David Wharton, "CityWalk Ready to Launch Second Phase," *Los Angeles Times,* 8 Jan. 1996.

35 David Gebhard and Robert Winter, *An Architectural Guidebook to LA* (Salt Lake City, UT: Gibbs Smith, 2003).

36 Harrison "Buzz" Price, *Walt's Revolution by the Numbers* (Orlando, FL: Ripley's Entertainment, 2004).

37 Ibid.

38 Connie Bruck, *When Hollywood Had a King: The Reign of Lew Wasserman, Who Leveraged Talent into Power and Influence* (New York: Random House, 2003).

39 Price, *Walt's Revolution by the Numbers.*

40 Ibid.

41 Suzie St. John, "Hopes High for Bigger CityWalk," *Los Angeles Times,* 25 Apr. 2000.

42 Ibid.

43 Ouroussoff, "Fantasies of a City."

44 Price, *Walt's Revolution by the Numbers.*

45 Marla Jo Fisher, "Officials Glimpse Disney Plans," *Orange County Register,* 13 July 1996.

46 Barry Stavro and Martha Willman, "Studio Expansion Plan Receives Mixed Reviews," *The Los Angeles Times,* 22 Jan. 1997.

47 Barry Stavro, "Universal Cuts Expansion Plan by 44%," *The Los Angeles Times,* 3 July 1997.

48 Alan Byrd, "Riding High into the Future," *Orlando Business Journal,* 17 Aug. 1998.

CHAPTER 10

UNIVERSAL'S
ISLANDS *of*
ADVENTURE

 ## UNIQUELY DIFFERENT

RISING FROM THE ASHES OF CARTOON WORLD was Universal's Islands of Adventure. Starting in 1994, a new vision was starting to emerge. "Ron [Bension] was the stimulus behind Islands of Adventure," said Barry Upson. "He actually did a really rough little diagram on the back of an envelope. Literally did it while on an airplane. The fundamental notion of the islands environment was his." He added, "We stuck with the basic idea, and it matured very nicely. It was a park compatible with Universal Studios Florida but uniquely different."[1]

Once again, finding the right mix of intellectual properties to license would be critical to the park's success. After the negotiations for the Warner Bros. characters failed, Phil Hettema asked, "Well, we think we still have Seuss, really what else do we have?" Making Jurassic Park the centerpiece to the new park allowed the design team to rethink the entire concept. They already had the rights for the Dr. Seuss characters from Dr. Seuss Enterprises L.P. for Cartoon World. Replacing the DC Comics heroes was the stable of characters from the New York–based Marvel Comics. Marvel was struggling at the time, and Hettema said they were "very obtainable."[2] The agreement between Universal and Marvel was restricted to east of the Mississippi River. They also had permission from Jay Ward and King Features, a division of the Hearst Corporation of New York.

On May 6, 1997, the press learned new details about Universal's Islands of Adventure. The $1 billion, 110-acre park would benefit by the participation of Steven Spielberg as creative consultant. In addition to Jurassic Park, Seuss Landing, Marvel Super Hero Island, and Toon Lagoon would be the Port of Entry and The Lost Continent. The two new islands represented adventure, exploration, trading, myths, and legends.

Each of the six large "islands" would become complete immersive environments containing attractions, restaurants, and merchandise shops. The park would be part of a $2.6 billion expansion that would also include hotels, shopping, dining, and entertainment. Universal would finally compete head to head against Disney. "Now we were going to rob from Disney's market and do it in our own way with a much more team-focused mix and balance."[3]

The Hollywood property benefited by being part of an active movie studio. Universal Studios Florida started as a working studio, but it became a chance to let the visitor enjoy a stroll through a production studio back lot and get to "ride the movies." Islands of Adventure would focus on the themes of adventure based in books, cartoons, and literature. The material ranged from Greek classics to Dr. Seuss to the Sunday funnies.

Islands of Adventure opened with 11 rides, 15 restaurants, and an additional 20–25 food carts. The construction process was not without its problems. Universal gained a reputation for sending thousands of change orders to the construction companies, and some of them pushed back with lawsuits.[4]

Despite these issues, Islands of Adventure opened on May 28, 1999. Learning from the grand opening of Universal Studios Florida, every precaution was taken to make sure that everything worked. This was not going to be a repeat of 1990. Cathy Nichols, CEO of the Universal Studios Recreation Group noted, "A lot of key players were involved. That helps us to avoid it ever occurring again." Mark Woodbury said, "A lot of it lies in making sure the technology works. We've tackled the tough stuff early in the process." Lisa Girolami, producer for Seuss Landing joked, "The only surprises that will be here are the ones we create."[5]

Of the original 11 rides, 4 were roller coasters. These were the first new coasters since Boardwalk and Baseball closed Central Florida's only wooden coaster in 1990. Mark Woodbury suggested that Islands of Adventure is "for people who like to be scared. That like to be on the edge. That like to push themselves. We give them that opportunity."[6]

More than either of the existing Universal parks, the landscape design approached Disney levels of attention. The six highly themed lands were all designed with different plant and hardscape palettes. Port of Entry was designed to resemble the worn, interesting back streets found in the oldest port cities of the world. Seuss Landing used intense colors in paving and unusual formed/textured trees to reinforce the famous Seuss stories. Lost Continent used rockwork, evergreen oaks, and palms to re-create the Mediterranean images in the minds of visitors. Jurassic Park used abundant tropical plantings and simulated dirt for the paving. Toon Lagoon featured cartoon rocks and wood while allowing the landscape planting to fall into the background. Marvel Super Hero used trees clipped in tight forms, stainless steel rail systems, and terrazzo pavement to simulate the desired comic book imagery.

A DIRECT LINE
to OUR EMOTIONS

ANOTHER INNOVATION THAT MADE ISLANDS OF ADVENTURE stand out from the competition was the park's sound design. John Rust was hired in 1996 to produce a custom sound track for the park. He said, "Music is a direct line to our emotions—I can control the kind of emotion I want you to feel by the kind of music I play. We go to the effort of theming every other part of a theme park. We need to theme the music, too." He said for Islands of Adventure, "What we do is create immersion experiences. Music is a tremendous part of that."[7]

Instead of relying on existing music, Rust set out to create an entirely new sound track for the park. "Usually, music is the last thing everyone thinks of instead of the first," Rust said. "Music is usually badly underfunded." That would not be the case for Islands of Adventure.

The background music for the Lost Continent is an exotic, multicultural blend written primarily by William Kidd, a protégé of composer John Williams. Kidd also wrote the sound tracks for *Return to Lonesome Dove* and the theme song for the *Lois and Clark* television series. The Lost Continent and Port of Entry music was recorded in December 1997 at venues ranging from a state-of-the-art soundstage to a former monastery.

The other lands were recorded in December 1998. Chip Smith and Tony Humecke were responsible for the sound track for Seuss Landing and Toon Lagoon. The park used the iconic score by John Williams for Jurassic Park. Howard Drossin penned the music for Marvel Super Hero Island.

The park-wide music effort was considered the most ambitious yet in the industry. Islands of Adventure was the first theme park designed with a stereo sound track in mind. John Rust described the system. "There's a bed of music in each zone," he said. "Then, hidden in each zone are about 10 point-source speakers broadcasting specific effects—frogs croaking, a peacock call, people trading camels in Arabic. Any time there's a backstage wall, we put speakers behind it, implying there's another street down there."[8] Just as a movie sound track changes as the plot progresses, the background music changes as visitors move through the islands. For example, in Seuss Landing the separate elements on separate tracks are tied to different characters along the path. From one end to the other, visitors experience 14 different song vignettes.

There were special challenges with the sound track for Seuss Landing. Composers Chip Smith and Tony Humecke had to work with an existing inventory of imaginary instruments created by Theodor Geisel (Dr. Seuss) and to interpret what sounds that they might make. They wanted a sound track that's "played with a certain attitude, a little off center, a little naughty," according to Humecke.[9]

"We didn't know what an oom-pah or a boom-pah was, so we made one," said Chip Smith. Humecke said, "Part of the process is finding just the right kind of junk." While studying the books, they discovered that one group of Who musicians is "very serious and studious [while the other is] always just on the edge of chaos," according to Smith. "Anything that sounded too normal for Seuss land, we tweaked in digital land."[10]

For the Lost Continent, William Kidd combined a Javanese gamelan orchestra with ancient instruments from several cultures, including metal and percussive instruments from the Middle East, India, and Greece. "We wanted the music to be as important as the art direction," according to Rust. "We wanted to come up with an authentic sound of Old Baghdad. But the real thing isn't very pleasant to our Western ears, so we created a romantic, 1940s feature-film version. It's filled with authentic instruments—finger cymbals, gongs, and all kinds of local musical instruments." Rust described Kidd's Celtic-Style sound track for the Merlinwood section as "happy, but on a bed of uneasiness. There's something foreboding in it. As you come in from Jurassic Park, there's a drum track done with ancient rack drums, which evoke the Celtic time."[11]

PORT *of* ENTRY

RIGHT FROM THE START, IT WOULD BE OBVIOUS that Universal's Island of Adventure would be a different experience than the studio park next door. Marking the front gate is the iconic 130-foot-tall Pharos Lighthouse. The obelisk is named after the Pharos lighthouse of Alexandria. The original was built sometime between 284 and 246 BC and considered one of the Seven Wonders of the World. For centuries it was one of the tallest man-made structures in the world, before it fell during the 14th century. Oddly, its namesake at Islands of Adventure does not resemble the original at all.

Port of Entry is Universal's Islands of Adventure's first act. Show producer Phil Hettema said, "If the journey was visiting the five islands, then the Port of Entry was the stepping-off point. It was where guests gather supplies on the way in and a place to celebrate their adventures on the way out."[12]

The architecture is an eclectic blend of Mediterranean, Middle Eastern, and Asian influences. The signage reinforces that this is a land of adventure, exploration, and trading. Throughout the Port of Entry, the signs juxtapose crude and elaborate elements, incorporating ship and airplane relics, as well as other salvaged materials. Phil Hettema credits Norm Newberry and his team of art directors for the highly immersive experience.

As in any trading port, look hard enough and one can find evidence of the destinations beyond. For example, beneath the sign for the Trading Co. is a hint for every island in the park, as it sells Rare Wares, Fantastic Finds, Mesozoic Marvels, Seussian Supplies, and Notions & Potions. Inside of the lobby for the sit-down Confisco Grille are artifacts from each of the islands.

Along the narrow, meandering corridor are the usual guest services. Much care was taken to place them in settings that hinted at their true functions. Guest Services is located inside of the Open Arms Hotel, and the restrooms are in the Water Works Authority. Other shops include O Wau's World's Finest Jewelry, Croissant Moon Bakery, and a camera shop called DeFotos Expedition Photography. An elaborate fountain made of shells is overhead.

At one point, Universal toyed with the idea of a private club similar to Club 33 hidden away at Disneyland. On the second floor above the Confisco Grille was a space dedicated to the Navigator's Club. The idea of a paid membership club was shelved before the park opened, but a VIP space was still built.

Site gags, supported by audio enhancements, abound. Perched on a rock is a mini-monastery built into the stone with the sound of chanting monks emanating from it every few minutes. Guests find evidence of a prison break at the end of one alley, while the remains of the Fire Department after its facility burned down is at the end of another. Listen closely in front of the Lucky Monkey, and you can hear the sounds of gamblers. "We tried really hard to create a sense of leaving the world and then having larger-than-life adventures," said Hettema.[13]

As guests walk forward through the Port of Entry, they are unaware that they have actually been walking on a ramp with an elevation change of approximately 6 feet. The high point is a large stone bridge framing the cinematic reveal of the lagoon. Engraved on the bridge is the park's motto, "The Adventure Begins." The only attraction in the Port of Entry was the Island Skipper Tours. The boat ride connected the front of the park to Jurassic Park at the rear. The boats did not last very long.

Like Universal Studios Florida next door, the park is organized as a loop around a large lagoon with a single entrance. An early plan called for an island in the middle of the lagoon to avoid what Hettema called "the death march."[14] Goddard argued for the island. Dale Mason stuck with the loop because he felt it would help to organize where each island should be placed. They studied the site plans for parks around the world to find a solution. As a result, the island was removed, and the park became what Hettema describes as "the peninsulas of adventure with the water creating a point of transfer from one area to the next."[15]

Hettema said, "I am a huge believer in intuitive navigation of the parks. I think there are a lot of circulation patterns you can use, but it is really important that when the guests arrive, you have some kind of landmark so that they can intuitively know for the rest of their stay where they are at."[16] Therefore, they placed a visual "weenie" for each island. A weenie was a Walt Disney term for a visual terminus or iconic structure that draws guests forward by acting like a beckoning hand. "Human nature drags people to the right," according to Dale Mason. "The families are going to the right, so we put Dr. Seuss at the front in the right. The instinct of rebellious teenagers is to go in the opposite direction. So the thrill rides in Marvel Super Hero Island are being built on the left side of the entrance."[17]

The park was designed as a series of detailed environments that could stand alone but together created something truly special. According to Hettema, "In its own way, Dr. Seuss is a complete immersion in its own world of fanciful charms, Lost Continent was grand and at an impressive scale, Jurassic Park was dinosaurs that have their own scale. Toon Lagoon was the kid in everybody and just silly. The Marvel's superheroes was finding that within yourself."[18]

SEUSS LANDING

NO DOUBT ABOUT IT, BRINGING TO LIFE the multigenerational characters of Dr. Seuss was a once-in-a-lifetime opportunity for Universal. Theodor Geisel, better known as Dr. Seuss, told his wife, Audrey, "Never license my characters to anyone who would round the edges."[19] She said what made the Seuss books so special was, "He never let the school system have it to be a primer. He said, 'That will kill it. They have to read it after the throes of the school day.'"[20]

As the president of the Dr. Seuss Enterprises and the Dr. Seuss Foundation, Audrey Geisel resisted commercialization, and for many years she refused any merchandising deals. She only relented in 1991. She also refused to let the characters be used in any amusement park. "Mrs. Geisel would not talk to anybody," Phil Hettema said. "She would not take calls. They had everybody call her. They had Steven [Spielberg] call her and she wouldn't discuss it. We did a year's worth of spec design on Seuss alone."[21] Then they found a lifelong friend of hers that set up a meeting with her literary agent in New York. The agent liked what he saw and called her immediately.

The first meetings took place in 1993. Tony Sauber recalled, "We did a presentation of the concepts we had for the whole Seuss Landing [from Cartoon World], and she kept saying, 'Can you really do this?' and 'You can accomplish this?'" Hettema replied, "Yes we can."[22] Only then was she convinced and she insisted, and received, final approval for everything. A deal was announced in 1995.

Hettema said, "We really wanted to make sure we brought Seuss to life. It was a long and protracted path to get approvals to do that. Part of it was, could you do justice to this. It is a very unique visual world and nobody had ever done anything like this before." Hettema added, the goal for the island "was to make something that really appealed to the family and make this their home base and trying to create something that was delightful and had that sense of whimsy of his books."[23]

The island was organized around the Seuss story of the Zax. As the story goes, rising from the dirt and concrete of Universal Studios construction, the North-Going Zax and the South-Going Zax stand face-to-face, never moving "an inch to the west or an inch to the east" while the city is built around and over them. Such is the tale of two pigheaded Dr. Seuss characters that refused to change their direction and subsequently spent their lives standing in one place.

In keeping with the source material, no straight lines were allowed on the 11-acre island. Show producer Lisa Girolami said, "Everything we do is coming straight from the books. Ted [Geisel] drew freehand, so everything's curvy, wonky, sneeringly."[24] The structures were made out of Styrofoam and were carved into shape. Many of the palm trees were painted yellow and came from Homestead, Florida, where they were bent in half during Hurricane Andrew in 1992.

Seuss Landing contains a dark ride, a carousel, a children's play area, and a spinner ride. Cat In The Hat serves as the island's family-friendly dark ride. While sitting on a couch that spins, the guests ride through 18 scenes taken right from the book. Dale Mason created a delightful and straightforward retelling of the classic book.

Lisa Girolami designed the If I Ran the Zoo children's play area. The interactive park has 19 elements "that must be tinkered with to be seen or made active. It's interactive and not just technology."[25] This type of interactive is also part of the Caro-Seuss-El experience. Guests are not passive riders. By pushing and pulling, riders can animate the characters on which they ride.

The Dumbo-like One Fish, Two Fish, Red Fish, Blue Fish put a new spin on the traditional ride. As the poem is read aloud, elements that squirt hit riders who are not paying attention. The fish can rise up and down 15 feet.

One ride not ready for opening day was Sylvester McMonkey McBean's Very Unusual Driving Machines. Sylvester McMonkey McBean started out as a merchandise cart, but his name was so appropriate that a grander attraction was built around the character. Based on a character from *The Snitches and Other Stories,* the ride was a low-profile, low-volume one aimed at small children. The ride would have individual cars moving along an elevated track with tremendous views of the entire park. Riders would have some control over speed, so they could bump one another.

However, safety concerns delayed the opening. The lack of an adequate evacuation plan prevented the ride from opening to the public. A sign was put up saying the ride would open in 2000. Rumors for the delay suggested the ride system proved unworkable and too expensive to be worthwhile. By October, that sign was taken down, and park spokesperson Jim Canfield said, "We are not opening in 2001. There is no opening date at this time."[26] Until 2005, the Grinch would use the lobby space during the holidays.

The park tried to build a reputation with unique dining experiences. One of those can be found at The Green Eggs and Ham Café. Here, visitors can buy a Seuss sandwich with eggs mixed with parsley paste.

There were some Seuss-related rides that sat on the design table. For a long time, a proposed Grinch-themed wild mouse mini-coaster was considered. Riders would sit on the Grinch's sleds and roll down Mt. Crumpet. The ride was fully conceived and ready to be built. However, it was cut at the last moment due to the balance of the rides. This was common in building theme parks. "When you build a park the first time, you can get away with attractions that you would never build as an add-on because you can build the critical mass attractions that help to contribute to the environment," Hettema said. "But when you add something later, it has to have marketing draw on its own."[27]

Hettema was rightly proud of Seuss Landing. He said, "It turned out to be one of the jewels of the park. There was a lot of lavish attention paid to the details even down to the signage." More important, "[Seuss Landing] certainly showed that we were able to go take an IP, study it faithfully, know it forward and backward, and do something great."[28]

The LOST CONTINENT

THE LOST CONTINENT IS A NECESSARY BREAK for the cartoon-heavy park. Along with the Port of Entry, The Lost Continent has an exotic feel that balances out the park. It is the only island that has no direct tie-in to any films, books, or comic strips, a rarity in the modern-day theme park business.

"Throughout the whole park, the other thing we tried to do that was sort of Universal in character was to be larger than life, to be audacious," Phil Hettema said. "Audacious is a really good Universal word. We try to do something that nobody else had done. The thing we like about Lost Continent was an audacity to the scale and the mythic power of all of that big imagery like the trident and the big facades. In return, it formed the rest of the mythology in the park."[29]

According to producer Amelia Gordon, it was not easy. "When you do Spider-Man, you have a great deal of information about him," she said. "When you want to create some mythic story, you have many choices to make. That's a wonderful palette of freedom, from a designer's perspective, but it also means that many, many people can have opinions about what's going on and it makes the decision-making process more difficult."[30] The lack of an existing property made it difficult for the design team to make choices. Construction for the island began late. Gordon credits Tom Gibb for getting the project done. She said, "He made it OK for us to take risks; he insisted we think out of the box. He got everybody together every day and said, 'What do we need to do now?'"[31]

The island is divided into three realms. The Lost City is based on Greek mythology, Sindbad's Bazaar brings to life Middle Eastern tales, and Merlinwood re-creates the days of King Arthur.

The big attraction in The Lost City is *Poseidon's Fury*. Out front is an impressive set that appears to be that of a collapsed temple camouflaging the giant show building. At first, what was inside was a jumble of incredible special effects looking for a reason to be on display together. The $80 million show featured water screens, projections, fire effects, fountains, and much more. The show was an artistic disaster. Yet it cost so much to build that Universal certainly could not just tear it down.

Upon reflection, Phil Hettema said, "There is a certain point of time in the development of a project where if the concept is not in place and there is not a very clear vision of what you are trying to achieve, the team by nature grows so large that it becomes expedient that things have to move forward. Decisions start to get made. If the story had been able to come together and be so coherent and the effects were so much part of that story, then everybody would have been clear about why they were doing this." Ultimately, he said the show was a "kit of parts that was assembled but the sum was less than the parts. It was a huge amount of technology and effects put into an illusion that nobody got."[32]

Gary Goddard was hired in 2002 to try and fix the show. At first Goddard thought the target audience should be parents with small children, and he recommended putting a mine car ride inside the show building. He felt it would be a certain hit. He said, "It was drummed into me by [Disney Legends] Marc Davis, Bill Justice, Herb Ryman— if there is one thing that was an unwritten rule at Imagineering, it was that walk-through attractions don't work."[33] Unfortunately, the entire budget for the remake was only $2.8 million, and he had five months to complete the project. Universal did not want to throw any more money at it. Goddard said, "They just wanted to make sure it was no longer embarrassing." As a consultant, his agreement was such that any costs above the budget meant his money.

"You were supposed to believe that this 'temple' was ancient in every way, yet there were anachronisms everywhere," said Goddard. "The biggest violation was in the Grand Finale room, where, upon entering, guests could clearly see speakers above the audience area, wires and lighting instruments, the lighting grid above, bare walls behind (funding for theming must have run out) and so on."[34]

The original script included a live actor to guide the guests through a quest that led to a battle between the Greek gods Zeus and Poseidon. Goddard noticed that they always seemed to hire younger people in the role "so all of them wore fake beards and did typical caricatured 'old man' performances." The script was poorly written and included Goddard's pet peeve about theme park shows: "really bad puns and jokes that are not funny." He added, "In the finale, after supposedly going through this 'real' world of the Gods, an animated cartoon comes to life—with pretty bad CG animation—all in this giant room that we have already seen as we walked in, and which always looks like an unfinished room with no attempt to hide all the modern-day speakers, lights, and other show equipment."[35]

Goddard focused his limited resources where the audience could experience them and change little else. The story line was reconfigured as a "fish out of water" idea. "I would not try to make people think they were going back in time so much, but rather, they are visiting a mystical site where a current 'dig' is taking place as scientists and archaeologists are studying the place and this dig unearthed something dangerous." This meant the setting could be contemporary, and there was no longer a need for a college-age performer acting as an elderly person. Instead, the character would become Taylor, a young assistant to the professor/researcher in charge of the dig, who could only be heard over a radio. "This allowed the young actors to play in their own age range and to concentrate on connecting with the audience members during the initial scenes," according to Goddard.[36] There were four chambers, and Goddard planned to have one magical moment in each. He focused on the show's two existing strengths, the "magic room" and the water vortex tunnel.

The "magic room" was originally the ending for the show. It was "supposedly making you think you were in the same room that you had started your journey through, a fact most audience members did not get," according to Goddard. "And even those that did were confused when the exit path clearly did not match the way they entered."[37] The solution was to keep the water vortex and the magic room but reverse their order in the script.

In the limited space of the first chamber, the set was redressed as the base camp for the dig. Taylor uses a black light to highlight a message on the wall, telling the guests about the curse they are about to unleash. Goddard relied on the familiar story line of the young assistant who causes something bad to happen and must then work to correct it during the course of the show.

A new door was added that hid the water vortex. The water vortex is an 18-foot-by-30-foot tunnel of water through which visitors walk. Nozzles shoot water at a high rate of speed onto a curved surface up and around the semi-cylinder. The water layer remains against the curved surface through centrifugal force.

Once through the water vortex, the audience enters a small chamber. Suddenly, the small chamber vanishes, and they find themselves in a huge temple right in the middle of a battle between Poseidon and an evil god that he locked away centuries ago. Goddard swapped out the poor animation and replaced it with live footage that he filmed in one day. When the battle is over, the audience is suddenly back in the small chamber looking for the exit.

Goddard was proud of what he had done with such a small budget. He said, "What this did was to save the reveal of the giant chamber to a point where it would be revealed ONLY under theatrical lighting—so you would no longer see the speakers, projectors, fountains, overhead grid, etc.—a HUGE plus to the show. It created a major surprise for the audience through the 'reveal,' and by returning them to the smaller chamber at the room, provided a better conclusion as well." [38]

One of the most talked-about attractions in The Lost City was not a ride or a show but a restaurant. When Mythos opened, it was considered one of the best restaurants in any theme park. Dale Mason and Jordan Mosier designed a Grecian grotto with carved images of gods and goddesses. There is a long, narrow passage from the modest lobby that leads to a large main dining room with a wall of glass and the most amazing views of the park.

SINDBAD'S BAZAAR
and MERLINWOOD

THE NEXT AREA WITHIN THE LOST CONTINENT is Sindbad's Bazaar. The theming is straight out of a Hollywood version of the *1,001 Arabian Nights*. Within the land is *The Eighth Voyage of Sindbad,* the park's stunt show. Housed within a 1,700-seat covered amphitheater, the show emulates the style of the *Conan* and *Miami Vice* shows in Hollywood by throwing in virtually every special effect that can safely be carried out multiple times a day. The interior set is an elaborate grotto in "The Graveyard of Ships." The theater design took into account the Dueling Dragons roller coaster next door.

The plot involves Sindbad looking for the Sultan's Heart with his trusty sidekick Kabob and Princess Amoura. On their journey, they encounter the villain Miseria, and the special effects spectacle begins. The show features 50 pyrotechnic effects, a 10-foot-tall circle of flames, and an actor falling 22 feet while on fire.

On the way toward the *Sindbad* show is the Mystic Fountain. This interactive fountain mysteriously talks with guests, with comic results.

Leaving the mythical Middle East, guests entered the age of King Arthur: Merlinwood (later replaced by Hogsmeade). At the center of Merlinwood was the Enchanted Oak Tavern & Alchemy Bar, which appeared to have been carved out of an old tree stump that happened to be about 50 feet tall. On the other side of the main pathway were large sculptures of two fighting dragons, one made of red carnelian stone and the other blue cobalt. The pair represented the gateway to Dueling Dragons (later redesigned as the Dragon Challenge).

At the entrance to the queue was a small, round plaque in the ground, where the knowledgeable guest could stand and see all three near misses in action before joining the queue. Knowing that the ride was going to be in high demand, the operations people insisted that the creative team carve out a very long queue, one of the longest ever created for a theme park attraction. The result would become an attraction in itself.

Along the path were warning signs tacked up by the villagers. The festive music of the main path faded to drums, then fell silent as riders approached the broken doors of a derelict castle. An enchanted stained glass window (a rear projection video created by Pixel Factory) told the backstory of Blizzrock and Pyrock, two dragons battling for control of the kingdom. Visitors were sent on a mission to slay the dragons and win back the castle. The ride was inspired in part by the book *The Once and Future King*.

The queue was filled with eye candy. Hundreds of (fake) human skulls were embedded in the catacombs. In one large room was a knight frozen in place by one dragon, while in another room, a knight has been fried to a crisp by the other dragon's breath. When the time came to choose which coaster to ride, a sign warned "Choose Thy Fate To Freeze or Burn." Art director Catherynne Jean designed the memorable queue.

Bolliger and Mabillard built the inverted coasters. Unlike traditional dueling or racing coasters, which typically run side by side, Dueling Dragons separated and "attacked" at three different points. Dale Mason said, "We wanted the coasters to meet and actually duel and intertwine . . . the idea of showing courage by riding on the back of dragons and dueling in the air was really kind of the basic idea behind Dueling Dragons."[39] To achieve the three near misses, a patented controller system weighed each of the loaded trains and then generated a vehicle performance parameter that determined which vehicle to launch first; it also calculated the amount of delay between launching the vehicle on the first track and launching the vehicle on the second track. The analysis included factors such as the maintenance history and the weather conditions to better achieve simultaneous arrival at the near-miss points. Universal's Mark Woodbury said, "It's really something that hasn't been tried before."[40]

The top of the first lift was 125 feet; the trains would reach a maximum of 60 miles per hour, with Fire falling to the right with a drop of 115 feet and Ice falling to the left, dropping 95 feet. There was another difference. Ice featured a "walking up the wall" effect, where the train came within 18 inches of a 55-foot wall, built to minimize noise complaints from nearby neighbors. However, the near misses were the main attraction. Woodbury said, "You come at very high speeds within 12 inches of each other, and all this happens over water."[41] To complete the theming, the lake below the coaster was shaped like a dragon.

 # JURASSIC PARK

JURASSIC PARK IS THE CATALYST for the transformation of Cartoon World into Universal's Islands of Adventure. What story could be more perfect for a theme park than Jurassic Park? After all, the book was set in a fictional theme park on a beautiful remote tropical island called Isla Nublar, where a mastermind has brought back dinosaurs from extinction. Then something goes horribly wrong. Perfect for a Universal theme park.

Jurassic Park was given the most prominent location at the back of the park. The full-scale replica of the Discovery Center across the lagoon is the first thing guests see once they leave the Port of Entry. The structure acts like a beckoning hand, drawing people around the lagoon. Once they get there, they see a building that looks just like the one destroyed in the film. "We are the oasis," said show producer Bob Shreve. "By the time guests get to us, we figure they've done half the park, they're tired, they're hungry, and they need to refuel. It's subdued and comfortable—but we don't want you to get too relaxed." He added, "This is a place where we can mix relaxation and thrills in one easy, greasy motion."[42]

Inside of the Discovery Center is a two-story rotunda with two life-size dinosaur skeletons fighting it out. On the entrance level are the Burger Digs and the Dino Store. On the lower level are numerous interactive exhibits, such as a hatchery where visitors can analyze dinosaur eggs and witness a live birth. Younger guests have the chance to name the new dinosaur. Other activities include a quiz show called *You Bet Jurassic* and lenses that simulate the eyes of a dinosaur. For many guests, the greatest feature may be a roomy air-conditioned space. On the other side of the Discovery Center is a beautiful plaza along the lagoon with incredible views of the park. Even on the busiest days, the space remains mostly vacant. Phil Hettema said, "I think we made a mistake in not putting more programming out there even if it was a dining program."[43]

At 21 acres, Jurassic Park is the largest of the five islands. The art direction was based on *Jurassic Park* (1993) and *Jurassic Park: The Lost World* (1997). Shreve said, "I identified what the story was at each individual attraction to make for a cohesive guest experience, ensured that the design and engineering processes supported what we needed, and oversaw the installation to get the quality and value we were supposed to." He said, "This whole place was basically a swamp when we got here. We brought in and planted every stick."[44] It took more than 4,000 newly planted trees and 65,000 shrubs and bushes to create the lush jungle. In the evening, this is the only island to be bathed entirely in its own stylized theatrical wash, a moonlight blue.

Just beyond the Discovery Center is Camp Jurassic. Dale Mason was responsible for the design of the children's interactive play. At the center is a smoldering caldera. Hettema said, "The geotechnical backbone to the entire island is centered on the caldera at the middle of Camp Jurassic. The ground twists around the caldera, and this twisting extends all the way out to the drop of the raft ride. The evidence is different shifts of rock."[45] Children can view the caldera and romp through the caves and quarries of a lava pit and amber mine. Sound gags are everywhere, including dinosaur footprints that trigger dinosaur growls embedded in thematically paved paths.

Circling above Camp Jurassic is the Pteranodon Flyers. The child-friendly ride is meant to be a gentle introduction to the world of roller coasters. Two riders sit under a Pteranodon with a 10-foot wingspan and go on a slow, circular path 60 feet above the play area. Because the "birds" can only seat two guests, and only three "birds" can be on the track at the same time, the ride's capacity is extremely limited. So Universal placed a height limit of 56 inches and one adult. At one point, Bob Shreve said, "Universal is considering ways to cut down on what is certain to be a long wait. It may mean a complete redesign of the vehicles to increase their capacity."[46] The redesign never happened.

Overall, the Florida Jurassic Park River Adventure is similar to the version in Hollywood. The 85-foot plunge at a 55-degree angle is the longest drop for a water ride in Central Florida. Journey to Atlantis at SeaWorld is 60 feet, while Splash Mountain at the Magic Kingdom is only 52 feet.

Set within a lush, tropical environment was another cutting-edge attraction. The Triceratops Encounter was a walk-through attraction that led to a paddock holding an audio-animatronic adult triceratops. Universal hired Toronto-based Spar Aerospace to build the robots. The firm had built the robotic cargo arms for NASA's space shuttles and the dinosaurs in Hollywood. The 23-foot-long and 10-foot-tall audio-animatronic interactive characters had 34 articulated joints animating their heads, tails, and musculature.

Actors portrayed veterinary assistants and tested the beasts for signs of a cold. The dinosaur breathed deeply, blinked, grunted, flinched, sneezed, and even urinated. Universal took care to add a dinosaur "scent" for added believability. They were painted reddish brown for a "classically reptilian look," according to Shreve. There were three holding paddocks, and the dinosaurs were named Cera, Topper, and Chris.

Upon reflection, Phil Hettema was disappointed with the attraction. "In spite of much effort, it never really sparked with people," he said. "I couldn't tell you to this day if it was a fault of the figure. It wasn't dynamic enough or flexible enough in its programming? Or it just didn't appeal to people. I still understand the appeal of dinosaurs. If we had been able to give kids a chance to get up close and personal with the dinosaur and they felt like they were doing that, it should have been a slam-dunk."[47] He also suggested it was difficult to maintain.

 # TOON LAGOON

FOR MORE THAN 100 YEARS, the Sunday funnies brought families together once a week to share a laugh or learn a lesson. A stroll along King's Row in Toon Lagoon was designed to bring back memories and give visitors a chance to become a part of their favorite comic strip, if just for a photo. Show producer Chris Stapleton said, "One thing that's great is that our demographics are the forgotten ones—grandparents and little kids. We need to attend to a lot of people who can't do rides."[48]

Toon Lagoon is built on more than 150 characters from 80 comic strips licensed from King Feature Syndicate. The entire history of the format is represented. Characters range from *The Yellow Kid*, the first Sunday supplement comic strip (1895–1898), to the underground favorite *Zippy the Pinhead* (1971). Popular favorites, such as Betty Boop, Blondie, Beetle Bailey, Hagar the Horrible, and Popeye, can also be found. The island is also a tribute to attorney Tony Sauber, who was responsible for securing the theme park rights for all of the characters.

The island is divided into two areas, King's Row and Sweethaven. King's Row is the primary pathway, and Sweethaven is along the waterfront. King's Row was shaped like a dogleg. Stapleton said he wanted "comic strips exploding all around you and immersing you in the diverse world of comic strips. We wanted people to be the comic strip character, be in their world. From the music to the special effects, we wanted you to feel like you're in the melodrama."[49]

Phil Hettema said, "The retail area was probably one of the hardest pieces of design in the whole park." He recalled, "It was hard to get all those disparate elements to feel like they had some shape and form and place." One weekend, Hettema gathered a small group and "attacked it with foam core and kind of built up several of the main pieces until we thought, 'OK, this is starting to work.'"[50]

What they came up with were larger-than-life panels from the comics surrounding the visitors and providing guests with opportunities to insert themselves into the action by posing under the illuminated voice bubbles. The landscape became a 3-D collage made up of snippets from the Sunday funnies. Tying it all together is splashing water. In some spots, the water squirts up from the sidewalks; in other areas, the fountains are integrated into the architecture and signage. The quantity of sight gags and one-liners staggers the mind.

Water rides are the main attractions in Toon Lagoon. Dudley Do-Right's Ripsaw Falls is along King's Row, and Popeye &

unofficial **TIP**

In March 2000 Dudley Do-Right's Ripsaw Falls was closed because passengers complained the ride was too rough. The track layout was adjusted, and lap bars were added.

Bluto's Bilge-Rat Barges is in Sweethaven. The story lines for both rides are similar. The villain kidnaps the heroine, and the hero must rescue her. Both rides are sure to cool off the warmest Florida visitor.

The Jay Ward–style of limited animation was perfect for Dudley Do-Right's Ripsaw Falls. Dale Mason and Phil Hettema were huge Jay Ward fans. In tribute, the drop is hidden by a snowcapped mountain with a Mount Rushmore–like exterior with the faces of Dudley, Nell, Inspector Fenwick, and Dudley's horse. Spread out along the flume are two dozen vignettes of Dudley trying to save Nell from Snidely Whiplash. Instead of a traditional free-floating log, the ride is an aqua-coaster: half flume and half roller coaster. The ride system allowed the design team to create a unique experience for the climax.

At the top of the 75-foot final drop, all things seem normal. The drop is impressive at a 55-degree angle, sending the logs down at speeds of 50 miles per hour. What riders don't see is the extra drop. Just when the riders think they hit the bottom, they are surprised by a 15-foot camel hump hidden inside of a "TNT" shack. From the outside, the shack appears to explode. This was a first, a flume ride that creates the illusion that guests are going below the water's surface and deep into the 400,000-gallon lagoon.

During the planning for Cartoon World, Popeye and Bluto both had their own rides. For Toon Lagoon, the hero and the villain are brought together in Popeye & Bluto's Bilge-Rat Barges. Once again, it is up to Popeye to save Olive Oyl from Bluto. The rafts pass through all sorts of obstacles, including a boat wash and the Octopus Grotto with an 18-foot-tall, 14-foot-wide creature that sprays riders from his 10-foot tentacles. "Bluto's Bilge-Rat Barges is integrated into the whole area development," said Pat Gallegos, lighting designer. "It's a show for the people riding it and for people watching it as well. The challenge is to create an environment that works for both groups."[51]

Part of that integrated environment is Me Ship, *The Olive*. The three-story-tall children's play area is rigged with water cannons, a two-story slide, a crawling net, and a seesaw pump. It features little details, such as a hole in the ship's hull where guests can spot a shark swimming below and a piano that reacts when someone plays the notes correctly. On the upper level are water muskets to douse Bilge-Rat riders.

A short-lived attraction in Toon Lagoon was the *Pandemonium Cartoon Circus*. The circus-themed live show took place in a small stadium and used song and dance to entertain the little ones. The show featured familiar circus acts performed by Dudley Do-Right, Nell, Betty Boop, Popeye, and Olive Oyl. Other characters included Bullwinkle, Rocky the Squirrel, Bluto, Woody Woodpecker, Broom Hilda, Dagwood, Blondie, and many more.

MARVEL SUPER HERO ISLAND

WHAT DOES THE MARVEL UNIVERSE LOOK LIKE? People did not buy comic books for the backgrounds. "We spent a lot of time looking at comic books and studying how the artists portrayed the backgrounds," said show producer Scott Trowbridge. "The comic books are about doing and action. That really demands a personal experience that sort of fits into that milieu."[52] He revealed, "The concept development for Super Hero Island was a tricky one to pull off because there really isn't one look to Marvel. There's a multitude of looks, and each artist has his or her own style. Gene Nollman, the art director of the island, spent a significant amount of time looking at things like color palette, scale, the interplay between things like the supergraphics, the larger characters, and the building signage, to try and represent three-dimensionally what had always been represented two-dimensionally in the background of pages in a comic book."[53] Thierry Coup and Eric Parr were responsible for the island.

The island is organized around a sculpture of a meteorite that supposedly slammed into a plaza next to the lagoon. The trees were "blasted" to a slant by the meteorite's impact, and the ground decorations clearly mark the epicenter of the impact. Adding energy to the island is the powerful, rocking background music.

Seven separate buildings totaling 146,656 square feet create a Main Street with generic signage, such as Bank, Store, and Five and Dime. The urban space has curbs and gutters, regularly spaced trees, mailboxes, crosswalks, and fire hydrants, with facades every 10 feet. Some of the buildings were painted with Chrom-Illusion paint, which appears to change colors depending on visitors' viewpoints. Adorning the building facades are a number of aluminum-backed 3M Scotchprint graphics of the Marvel characters, painted by comic book artist Adam Kubert.

Interactive elements are scattered around the island. Telephones and call boxes are tempting targets for the curious. The shops and restaurants also echo the theme. At the exit of Doctor Doom is the Kingpin's Arcade. American comfort food, such as hamburgers and hot dogs, can be found at the Captain America Diner or Cafe 4. For comic book collectors, The Comic Book Shop has one of the largest collections of Marvel books found anywhere.

Nevertheless, guests are most interested in the rides. For many, the first destination (at least before Harry Potter was built) was The Incredible Hulk Coaster. Visible from outside the park, its signature sound is the principle draw. As you exit the Port of Entry, you hear it before you see it. The coaster track was tuned to be as loud as possible.

The Incredible Hulk Coaster acts as the gateway to Marvel Super Hero Island. The primary pathway into the island is a bridge that passes through the coaster's tallest loop. "[The coaster] plays a role as an icon in the park, but we never wanted it to dominate the park," according to Trowbridge. "We didn't want it to become The Islands of Hulk Coaster."[54]

Riders entering the queue learn that Dr. Bruce Banner is trying to resynthesize himself, put his two halves together, and rid himself of the beast once and for all. The riders have been invited to help in the experiment. The queue is light on backstory but very heavy on mood. "The Hulk is a great icon of Marvel, and he's a great character. So we thought, what is the Hulk all about? He's about raw emotion, he's about driving energy, [and] he's about these primeval feelings. We wanted to deliver on that idea, as opposed to more linear narrative storytelling, so we decided to do a roller coaster, because it fits with the park, it delivers on the Hulk myth, and there's nothing intellectual about it."[55]

Phil Hettema said, "It was a natural for an accelerated moment." Hettema and Dale Mason worked on creating a signature first move. They wanted to launch the coaster at high speed up a ramp and through a series of inversions. "We knew scientifically what the body could handle safely, but we weren't comfortable just building the thing without really understanding what that felt like," Hettema said. "So we welded two or three cargo containers together and put a track down the middle of them. We built a steel structure that would pick it up and put it at the angle that we thought was appropriate. We put a pulley at the top and ran a cable over the top with two or three iron railroad wheels as weights. Then we ran the cable down and rigged a go-kart to run on the track and put another pulley at the bottom so that we could literally pull this thing down and cock it. Then there was a simple ratchet to lock it. We could literally vary the weight, and we could adjust and predict what the acceleration load would be. To test it, you put on a helmet and strap yourself into the go-kart, and somebody would pull the pin on the cable, and you would go zooming up. We ended up putting a big target at the end. You had to trust that the weights would hit the straw bales on the ground so that you wouldn't keep going. My back twinges when I think about it."[56]

The eight-car trains sit four across and are slowly lifted up the 30-degree hill like a traditional coaster until *something goes horribly wrong*. Suddenly, the trains are launched through a 150-foot tunnel from 0 to 40 miles per hour in 2 seconds, the same force as a U.S. Air Force F-16 attack jet. The tire-propelled launch system developed by MTS Systems Corporation sends riders immediately into a weightless zero g heart-line roll, turning them upside down more than 110 feet above the ground. Then the trains dive at 60 miles per hour before skimming the waves of the lagoon. The next element is a 109-foot loop that plunges below the bridge of the main pathway.

The computerized safety system used on the Hulk was truly a breakthrough. Due to the launch system, the eight-car trains had to be weighed and, within a split second, either get launched or stop. If the acceleration was miscalculated, the trains would fail to make it through the first three inversions. Hettema said, "At the time nobody had done a launch coaster where the coaster really goes to the launch off the top and into an inverted spin. You have to reach a terminal velocity, and if you don't reach it, you don't go. The weighing of the vehicle is only a matter of feet."[57] After a mere 2 minutes and 15 seconds, riders experience seven inversions. Bolliger & Mabillard designed and built the coaster.

Another one of the Marvel Super Hero Island attractions visible from outside the park is the 199-foot tower for Doctor Doom's Fearfall. Originally, Universal considered installing an Intaman Freefall, popular at amusement parks around the world. During a free fall ride, four riders are pushed over a cliff onto an L-shaped track. As they fall, the positive g-forces are concentrated on their backs, which can be intense and uncomfortable. Instead, Universal chose to use S&S's newer Space Shot technology. A Space Shot is a drop tower attraction that uses compressed air to rapidly propel riders 150 feet up the tower and then gently lower them on a series of air-cushioned bounces back to the loading platform.

Doctor Doom's Fearfall is located on a side street called Yancy Street, also known as Villains' Alley. Instead of the vibrant colors found elsewhere on Marvel Super Hero Island, Villains' Alley was painted in muted tones to make the area feel forboding. In Villains' Alley, exoskeletons were added to the flat facades, with the implication that the villains had done it themselves. "We tried to create some tension with those issues," said lighting designer John Martin. "We threw up some lights all strung together very strangely, without any particular thought, as if the villains were in a hurry. The heroes all had time to think about their ideas, but the villains were always in a mad rush."[58]

The ride was based on Doctor Doom, the arch foe of the Fantastic Four. Visitors enter the Latveria Embassy, where Doctor Doom extracts Fear Fuel to power his secret weapon, the Trans-thermal Fusion Dynamo. Once guests are strapped in, they are shrouded in fog and blasted toward the sky. Along with the momentary weightlessness, the views of the park and the surrounding area are outstanding.

The **DAILY BUGLE**

CONSIDERING THE HUNDREDS OF MEMORABLE CHARACTERS created by comic book legend Stan Lee, he has reserved a special place in his heart for Spider-Man. "Spidey is the most human, empathetic and believable super hero because he's got the most problems," he said. "I modeled him after me. He has super powers but he still has to worry about dating, in-grown toenails, dandruff, acne and cavities in his teeth."[59]

When Universal was unable to get the rights to use the DC Comics characters, several of the rides were converted to reflect the Marvel theme. Gary Goddard worked on the first version. Phil Hettema suggested, "Nobody knows that universe better than he did."[60] Goddard had just finished with *T2:3-D* and wanted to take the 3-D technology, expand on it, and use it in a ride setting. The ride was going to be called The Amazing Spider-Man: A Web-Slinging 3-D Ride. He delivered a first treatment in July 1994.

To get the audience to focus on what he wanted them to see, Goddard recommended using an Omnimover, similar to the ride vehicles used in The Haunted Mansion at the Disney parks. An Omnimover is a moving chain of vehicles linked together to form a continuous loop and guided and supported by a continuous track. The advantage was a high-capacity ride and a way to manipulate the audience the same way he would with a camera if he were making a film.

In his version, guests would enter *The Daily Bugle* newspaper building to sign up as volunteers for a special Citizen Nightwatch program. J. Jonah Jameson, publisher of *The Daily Bugle,* sponsored the program. According to Goddard's script, each rider would be equipped with "night-vision goggles" to assist in scanning the dark streets of New York City.

It would not take long before guests encountered some of Spider-Man's most fearsome villains, such as Doctor Octopus, Venom, The Lizard, Electro, The Vulture, and the Green Goblin. The ride would attack almost all of the senses with 3-D films, water, wind, sparks, scents, and the heat from live fire. One by one, Spider-Man would take on the Sinister Six right in front of the riders.

One of the creepiest elements would be thousands of rats projected on the walls of a tunnel from a direct, front-on point of view. The same effect would be used later in the same ride during a high-speed chase with the Green Goblin. The ride's climax would involve a battle between Spider-Man and all six villains at the Statue of Liberty. The Omnimover vehicles would move in a semicircle through a domed screen, creating the illusion of flight. At the end of the ride, guests could purchase a copy of *The Daily Bugle* with their photos on the cover.

Goddard promised a ride that met the "in-your-face" test Universal had become famous for—without having to invest much in the way of research and development. The concept was designed with low cost, low risk, and reliable engineering in mind. This ride could use existing projection technologies and dark-ride technologies.

Then came Indiana Jones and the Temple of Doom at Disneyland. This was Disney's first attempt at creating an in-your-face adventure in the mold of the rides at Universal. It was Disney's attempt to out-Universal, and it worked. The ride opened in 1995 and drew record crowds.

At the heart of the ride was the troop transport. Bill Wolf and Ed Fritz at Walt Disney Imagineering engineered the patented Enhanced Motion System. Basically, the vehicle was a motion simulator similar to Star Tours but on a moving platform. The chassis supported the hydraulic motion passenger carriage on top. The Imagineers wanted to create a vehicle that would feel like a four-wheel truck capable of going anywhere. The ride was meticulously themed and was a reminder of what Disney Imagineers were capable of when they put their minds to it.

Over at Universal, Ron Bension decided to up the ante. Instead of slowly riding in an Omnimover, it was decided to develop a brand-new ride vehicle. Phil Hettema acknowledged that they really had no choice. On Spider-Man, "If you're going to be a superhero, you've got to really deliver something over the top," he said. "Because to do a superhero dark ride that's not really superhero is pretty lame."[61]

Universal's solution was to create a proprietary state-of-the-art motion vehicle. The patented SCOOP ride vehicles were a remarkable achievement. Hettema said, "What the vehicle became was very much reverse-engineered by what we wanted the vehicle to do, because nobody had done a vehicle like this before. How it opens up and all that stuff came late in the game." He figured that, if they could build this thing, then "we could really screw with you."

Each car sits 12 guests and is equipped with three computers that trigger all the actions. The vehicle chassis rolls on caster wheels. Pinch-drive wheels, driven by onboard electric motors, engage a guide rail and propel the vehicle along a track. A motion base is positioned on top of the vehicle chassis, allowing the passenger cabin to spin on the motion base. The motion bases provide pitch and roll movements, as well as heave, slip, and surge movements.[62]

The story line is simple. J. Jonah Jameson, editor for *The Daily Bugle,* has instructed the riders to look for crime stories. As they set off in the SCOOP from the newspaper's loading dock, Spider-Man jumps on the hood of the car to warn them to be careful. Despite the warning, they stumble on a group of otherworldly henchmen called the Sinister Syndicate as they try to steal the Statue of Liberty. That is when the chase begins.

At one point, the guests are zapped by Doctor Octopus's antigravity gun and sent plunging from the top of a skyscraper 400 feet to the streets below. The illusion is created by projections on the walls at the outer edge of riders' point of view. The drop is actually about 10 inches. "The big breakthrough was the lifting sequence, where it was not just the media that you are looking at, but we are literally moving scenery one direction and moving media in another," according to Hettema. "I defy anybody to go through that ride and still believe that they're constantly at the same height as they were before the sequence. I know exactly how it works, and it still fools my brain every single time. You cannot help but believe that you are high up in the air. To me that is the seminal moment of the whole ride and everything else is gravy."[63]

Like many projects, production started as a scale model based on artist sketches and a storyboard. Scott Trowbridge said, "We started with a small tabletop model, around 4 inches by 8 inches, that allowed us to look at not only ideas of space and spatial dynamics, but also helped us figure out how we were going to put all this technology into a building."[64]

The next step for the "virtual" Spider-Man ride was to use a larger, highly detailed scale model. Scaled at 1 inch to 1 foot, the model was huge, measuring 20 feet by 26 feet. It was placed on stilts, and the pathway for the vehicle was cut out. Trowbridge explained, "You could sit on these little stools we had and stick your head in the model, with your eye at the proper height in scale with the environment." According to Trowbridge, the low-tech, room-size scale model was the starting point for design elements in the attraction. He said, "A lot of the ideas germinated as designers, seated on chairs, rolled themselves through the model to visualize the riders' perspective."[65] The model was packed up and shipped to Orlando for reference during construction. When the project was completed, the design team had a barbecue and then destroyed the development model by bulldozer.

The Amazing Adventures of Spider-Man blends the motion-base ride system with large-format stereoscopic 3-D generated imagery, theatrically lit sets, and powerful special effects. The ride is housed inside a 200-foot-by-260-foot building. A quarter-mile track passes by 13 screens blended with 1.5 acres of Hollywood-style sets.

"The film had to be started very early on so we'd know every frame and every piece of action, and could then develop the rest of the ride," said production designer Thierry Coup. "To be able to compensate for the constant shift of perspective in the 3-D film—which we ended up calling 'squinching'—you had to determine exactly where the camera would be, because that was going to be your point of view later on. To do that, all the camera paths had to be established in the computer and locked. It's hard to plan that far ahead, but once it's done, you have a really strong argument against any changes anyone else wants to make down the road."[66] In a regular 3-D movie, where two projectors run two films and images seem to jump off the screen with the help of polarizing glasses, viewers have to sit or stand in one place to get the full effect. The system used in Spider-Man constantly adjusts to the location of the vehicle on the ride. If one were to stand in one place and watch the video, they would find it greatly distorted.

unofficial **TIP**
In 2012 The Amazing Adventures of Spider-Man was upgraded with all-new 4k high-definition resolution digital animation.

Universal paired 24 projectors with the world's first 3-D rear-screen projection system to create the experience. "We always try to make things a little higher, a little faster, a little bit more dynamic, so we have something to market technologically," ride engineering manager Ben Lovelace said. "Universal pushes the envelope."[67]

A ride on Spider-Man is not a passive experience. In the Universal tradition, the riders do not just witness the carnage but get to feel it. When Hydro-Man tosses pipes at them, they get wet. When the Hobgoblin hurls a flaming pumpkin, they feel the heat from the explosion. When Electro plugs in a high-voltage cable to the front of the car, the riders' behinds tingle as six Aura seat shakers buzz away. Trowbridge said, "We did not want this to become something you watched or looked at; we wanted it to be something you did. We wanted it to at least feel participatory and not voyeuristic, as you would in a theater seat watching a proscenium stage or film projector."[68]

As a cost-saving measure, many of the backgrounds in the ride were rendered images from the films printed out on canvas. "Canvas gave it just the right texture for this project," Thierry Coup said. "We got that first sample back, which was a facade for Scene One, and in a dark ride environment, with the right lighting, it was perfect. Having a scenic painter paint all the bricks and finishes in the style we wanted would have cost a fortune. The sets were built in the computer, with the same lighting, so we had a perfect blend. It was basically wallpaper that matched the texture on screen."[69] The Universal team called these "scan-a-murals."

To avoid the opening-day mechanical problems that plagued Universal Studios Florida, testing started in late 1996 in a warehouse in Buffalo, New York. After running the machinery through several thousand cycles, Mark Woodbury proudly proclaimed, "We ran the heck out of it back there." Trowbridge said, "All the systems had to be very reliable and very accurately synchronized to make it work. If you feel the bang a second after you hear the bang, it sort of spoils the illusion."[70] Lovelace added, "Part of the goal was making the technology as reliable as a Caterpillar tractor. You're playing with large sums of money. If it doesn't work out, there's hell to pay."[71]

The critics loved the ride. Jerry Hirsch of *The Los Angeles Times* said, "The Amazing Adventures of Spider-Man attraction at Islands of Adventure may be the best theme park ride in the world, melding story and technology in a way that surpasses Disney's top efforts." Mark Woodbury was very proud of the ride and called it, "A defining moment in theme park attractions."[72]

UNIVERSAL STUDIOS ESCAPE

UNIVERSAL DID NOT WANT TO REPEAT the opening-day problems of the studios' park. That project was rushed from the beginning. This time, Universal Creative would take all the time they needed to tinker. "We started the rides first, so we wouldn't be in a box," Tom Williams said. "The hardware you're seeing out there was in a warehouse in Orlando a year ago. We've already run vehicles in the Spider-Man ride."[73]

Starting in March 1999, limited numbers of guests were invited to preview the park. The preview period was extended two weeks because some of the rides were not quite done. Tom Williams said of the delay, "I want to have a polished jewel. Until I feel that I do, I have no reason to jump the gun."[74] When the park formally opened on May 28, 1999, it had to open the gates early due to the hundreds of guests lined up early in the morning. Those guests found a park filled with things to do. The *Eighth Voyage of Sindbad, Poseidon's Fury,* and Dudley Do-Right's Ripsaw Falls suffered minor problems throughout the day, but the very complex Amazing Adventures of Spider-Man held up with lines less than 40 minutes all day.

At the grand opening ceremony, Steven Spielberg said, "We want people to be dazzled, entertained, and to come back again and again and again."[75] The general public agreed. Local resident Julie Tchividjian said, "It tops Disney. I think people have been waiting for a roller coaster park in Orlando for a while so they don't have to go to Busch Gardens."[76] Jan Kiser of the Roller Coaster Enthusiast club said, "Florida has been short on coaster rides. Tampa has really had the Florida roller coaster market, and Orlando hasn't had much at all."[77] Gary Slade of *Amusement Today* said, "I think Disney's got to counter. Universal has built one incredible theme park."[78]

Buzz Price also praised the new park. He said, "The result is a family of parks that come close, if not equal to, the legendary Disney quality in storytelling, thematic perfection, and service."[79] Even Sidney Sheinberg weighed in. He said, "When I left, if there was any part of MCA I missed, it was being part of this theme park. I've always taken a great deal of pride in taking on Disney, a formidable opponent, and being successful."[80]

The design team dared to challenge Disney directly by building a fantasy park, and they nearly succeeded. Phil Hettema said, "Disney is always going to be at their own level because they had a head start, but Universal elevated itself as a major player and made Disney take notice."[81]

From a design perspective, author Salvador Anton Clave said, "In a far-smaller urban space, Universal has developed the concept of an urban entertainment center. Development on Disney property is extensive and the different elements it incorporates are carefully located. Universal in Orlando is far denser." He noticed that "there is a predominance of open spaces and a clear linearity between the recreational equipment [at Disney]," but "Universal is far-less natural." At Universal, "Its landscape is more urban, metallic in the material used and angular in its forms."[82] Another benefit of the compact 840-acre resort was access. Disney's sprawling 27,000-acre resort required a fleet of buses to move guests around. At Universal, guests could use walking paths, water taxis, or park in structures only 12 minutes away from the front gates.

Universal's Islands of Adventure may have been a creative success, but it was a marketing disaster. From a marketing perspective, the only thing Universal did was confuse the consumer. When the Florida project was first announced, it was known as Universal City Florida. Then in November 1997, that name was shortened to Universal Florida. To launch the newly expanded resort, Edgar Bronfman Jr. came up with the name Universal Studios Escape. Starting March 26, 1998, Universal Florida was no longer. The name was part of a much bigger plan to establish Universal as a brand equal to Disney. He said, "We're a little edgier. What is Disney? Disney is family, it's fun, it's warm, it's safe. We're not." Bronfman said Universal was "based on energy, exhilaration, excitement. And that means we're going to skew to a slightly older audience. North of 8, north of 9—that's who we're going after, plus parents." He believed Universal could "be leveraged into a brand if you can identify what it means and then take that meaning and generate revenue across new businesses."[83]

Bronfman felt that many would want to escape from Disney's family-friendly resort for something a bit more edgy. The plan was to focus advertising dollars on the Florida market with the hope that people who were visiting Walt Disney World would stay an extra day or two. A $60 million advertising plan was launched, and another $100 million of advertising was spent in conjunction with Universal marketing partners, such as Coca-Cola and Dodge. Marketing executives were especially proud of the purchase of five years' worth of pull-out ads in the in-flight magazine of Delta Air Lines, the official airline of Walt Disney World.

Edgar Bronfman Jr. hired Elaine Garafolo to market the expansion. Conventional wisdom would suggest that Universal should have been talking about a brand-new theme park with cutting-edge rides, immersive theming, and popular characters. Instead, she focused on trying to sell the entire resort, as her boss wanted. The result was confusion. Hettema said, "People could not differentiate Islands of Adventure from Disney because of the lack of marketing. People would be going to Disney looking for Spider-Man."[84] The park got lost.

A perplexed Michael Eisner said of Universal's marketing approach, "So far, their strategy—and I'm not giving away a strategy that's a secret—they don't spend a dollar marketing outside of Orlando, they're only going to cannibalize their own park."[85] Eisner was right. Universal's marketing plan was flawed, and the park got off to a very slow start. First-year attendance was only 3.4 million, which was well below expectations. Ron Meyer tried to put a positive spin on it and said, "We just want them for two days instead of one. The good news for us is that we don't need a big piece of Disney. We just need a shave."[86]

To make matters worse, Universal was struggling under Bronfman. He had bet heavily on music with the $10.4 billion purchase of PolyGram and the theme parks with the Florida expansion. At the same time, the movie studio was floundering after two years of box office duds.

By August 1999 most of the marketing team was laid off. In February 2000 the resort was renamed Universal Orlando. Jim Canfield said, "It's simply another option to use in the marketing and communication process. We think the alternative will give us greater flexibility and clarity."[87]

The poor start fueled rumors that Seagram wanted to sell off Universal. If that were the case, there were not many options. The Walt Disney Company was too far in debt, Anheuser-Busch had a reputation of being too cheap, and Cedar Fair and Premier Parks (the Six Flags chain) did not need a movie studio. Other contenders included the USA Network, Dreamworks SKG, and Viacom, which once owned the Paramount parks.

On January 2, 2000, Disney CEO Michael Eisner was spotted visiting Islands of Adventure. The *Orlando Sentinel* reported he was dressed casually and was part of a group of about 20 people, including security. "Eisner's group started its morning about 9 at Spider-Man, then headed to The Incredible Hulk Coaster," according to the newspaper. "All other tourists were blocked from that ride until the Disney entourage had a chance to ride. Eisner did not ride the Hulk or Dueling Dragons due to heart condition warnings."[88] All together, Eisner and his party spent about 5 hours at the Universal Park. When they rode the water rides, they all donned Mickey Mouse ponchos. When asked about his reactions, Eisner said, "While there is cannibalization, it's still slightly less than we expected. We're OK."[89]

Bronfman would not be deterred. Universal began the entitlement process in October 1999 for a third theme park to open after 2007 on the land they purchased from Lockheed. Along with the new park would be an additional 10,000 hotel rooms, 700 time-share units, two 18-hole golf courses, and 2 million square feet of retail space.[90]

 The **UNIVERSE** *and* **YOU**

ALTHOUGH MOST OF THE FOCUS was on the opening of Islands of Adventure, Bronfman was also showing some love for Universal Studios Florida in 1999. The park needed to add child-friendly shows and rides to help balance out a park best known for its thrill rides. The only offerings were Fievel's Playland and *Barney*.

Opening that year was the Woody Woodpecker KidZone. The new 8-acre area brought together a number of elements that were targeted to children 5–12 years old. New attractions included the Woody Woodpecker's Nuthouse Coaster, Curious George Goes to Town play area, a water play fountain, a themed restaurant, and new retail.

Woody Woodpecker's Nuthouse Coaster was Universal Studios Florida's first roller coaster and was engineered to be safe enough for a 3-year-old. Located on the former site of the Bates Motel facade used in *Psycho IV: The Beginning,* the coaster is designed to look as if Woody Woodpecker built it himself out of various gears and gadgets. Riders sit in cars that look like nut crates. The 30-second ride has a 28-foot drop and an 800-foot track.

The *Psycho* house was removed from its perch on a hill behind Barney's park and replaced with a children's play area based on *Curious George Goes to Town* by H.A. Rey. Like Camp Jurassic at Islands of Adventure, the play area was an opportunity to allow little ones to burn off some energy and give their parents a rest. Out front was a mock zoo, where the mischievous monkey has let the animals out of their cages. Children can use the tire swings in the monkey cage or slide into the polar bear den. Behind the zoo is a replica of a town with two different play areas. In one section, children can fire water guns or play in other water-related activities. The area is serviced with 15,000 gallons of continuously recycled water. The other play area is a toy factory with 12,500 foam balls and dozens of ways of firing them at others.

Bronfman's vision for Universal Studios Florida was not limited to adding kiddie rides. While Islands of Adventure was under development, Universal planners were concerned with what the new park would do to the existing park's attendance. Would people increase the length of their stay, or would they just skip the old park? In 1996 work began on the Universal Orlando Millennium Project. Different rides were considered, including one based on Ron Howard's *Apollo 13* (1995) and a dark ride featuring scenes from Stephen King stories. Neither of these attractions was built.

The Apollo 13 indoor roller coaster was to be housed in a giant show building that resembled the Kennedy Space Center's Vehicle Assembly Building. Riders would walk across a gangplank toward their Apollo-style capsule. The coaster would have simulated a trip around the moon and back.

The Stephen King dark ride would be a far cry from anything that Disney had attempted. Not only would the ride feature scenes from *The Shining* and *It, Theme Park Insider* editor Robert Niles reported that the ride would also have had a false ending. "Riders would approach an unload platform and hear a spiel, then the lights would flicker, and a river of blood would pour from the doors at the 'unload' platform (à la *The Shining*)," Niles reported. If that was not enough, Pennywise, the Dancing Clown, would "emerge from the control booth to attack the riders, who would narrowly escape as their vehicle lunged forward."[91]

One concept that came a little bit later and did get built was based on the distinctive techno-futuristic *Men in Black* (1997). When a motion picture grosses more than $250 million and Steven Spielberg is involved, it does not take long for Universal Creative to become inspired. "*Men in Black* is one of those movies that has everything. This is what makes it a perfect marriage between a movie and an interactive ride," said creative director David Cobb.[92]

Men in Black: Alien Attack was designed to be the sequel to the hit motion picture. It features Will Smith (Agent Jay) and Rip Torn (MIB Director Zed) reprising their roles from the film. The ride opened on April 14, 2000, at an estimated cost of $70 million.

From the entrance, the ride appears to be a fair pavilion called The Universe and You. Inside is supposed to be an optimistic world's fair–type attraction about our singular place within the galaxy. The 80-foot-tall show building is camouflaged as part of a retro-modern-style plaza that is a combination of a midcentury modern world's fair pavilion, Dodger Stadium, and the St. Louis Arch. Out front are the iconic towers from the State of New York pavilion at the 1964 New York World's Fair that were featured prominently in the movie. The ride was such a big deal that the Expo Center area became the World Expo area to better reflect the theme.

This is a participatory ride. After a brief, peppy, and optimistic introduction, the preshow suddenly stops, and the pretense that guests are about to go on a boring ride is quickly shattered. Visitors are quickly ushered out of the preshow area and snuck into MIB head-quarters. While in queue, the "recruits" learn that they are about to be tested to see if they have what it takes to join the organization.

Continuing down the queue, guests encounter the memorable wormlike aliens from the movie taking a coffee break and occasionally shouting out rude comments, such as "What are you looking at?" or "This is a groovy planet; aliens come in convenient snack sizes." In an interview, Phil Hettema pointed out this was his favorite gag.

At the loading platform, the recruits are divided into two teams of six. Each team boards its vehicle from the two-sided platform. The 44 cars can take up to 2,200 guests per hour through the training session inside the 76,000-square-foot show building. Once the vehicles have left the platform, the training is suddenly interrupted because a bunch of aliens have escaped from a crashed transport ship.

Armed with laser guns, riders compete against each other while roaming the streets of New York, earning points by shooting the aliens. Each of the 120 targets come to life, with varying degrees of animation, when hit. Being true to the source material, the aliens shoot back. When they hit the vehicle, it violently spins.

Craig Hanna came up with the idea for a dual-track shooting ride. "The notion of having spinning vehicles is a very cool one," according to Hettema. "The notion of being able to shoot at other vehicles and cause them to spin and interact is another cool one." After a scan reveals that the competition are also aliens, the riders can shoot at them and cause their vehicle to spin. David Cobb said, "It's just like a video game; you won't figure it all out the first time you ride."[93]

To escape, guests have to blast their way past the largest audio-animatronic in the world, a 30-foot-tall "Really Big Bug" with 8-foot teeth and 20-foot claws. At the end, the individual scores are tallied and averaged with the others in the same vehicle. The score is compared to the opposing team, and Will Smith renders a verdict on the performances. Up to 36 different endings are possible.

The innovative ride system was both a blessing and a curse. Hettema said, "When you start putting the idea against the technical requirements, such as the envelope of each vehicle as well as the reach envelope, all of a sudden you end up with a ride path that is a freeway. I would have loved to have more intimacy and make it much more closed in."[94] A few days before the grand opening, a father and his child fell out of the ride during one of the spins and suffered minor injuries. The lap bars were insufficient to keep them in. Seat belts were quickly installed.

There were other small changes to the parks in 2000. Islands of Adventure got two new low-cost, minor rides to round out its offerings and to add more capacity. In Marvel Super Hero Island, Storm Force Accelatron is a lightly themed classic eggbeater carnival ride. It opened in May and was themed to Storm, one of the X-Men who had the ability to manipulate the weather. Over at The Lost Continent was a new child-friendly roller coaster called The Flying Unicorn (later redesigned as Flight of the Hippogriff).

In Hollywood, another change came to the Panasonic Theater on June 9, 2000. Out went *Totally Nickelodeon*, the audience participation show, and in its place was an attempt to compete with Disney with a Las Vegas–style stage show. *The Rugrats Magic Adventure* was based on the "Angelica the Magnificent" episode of the television show. The 20-minute show used magic illusions designed by the same illusionists who created world-renowned marvels for David Copperfield, Siegfried and Roy, Lance Burton, and the late Doug Henning.

Also for children was a maze themed to DreamWorks/Aardman's stop-motion animated hit *Chicken Run* (2000). The maze was set up as a kid-size simulation of the pie machine's insides, where visitors crawled on their knees, bumped into 5-foot rubber vegetables hanging from wires, and then walked across a ramp while circular blades rotated around them. On display in the Chicken Run Museum were actual models from the film, including the chicken's endoskeletons and the inside of a few of the coops. Also on display was a model of the entire outside of the pie machine.

The biggest draw had always been the Studio Tour. From the beginning, the stars of the tour were the tour guides. Their knowledge and ability to weave a tale using whatever was in front of them was the reason the tour prospered. They were central to the experience. That was then.

In 2000 the trams were outfitted with video monitors. The video system allowed the tour guides to supplement their spiel with clips. Now guests could view scenes from films while traveling through the sets where they were shot. Stars and directors responsible for the productions could add their thoughts in interviews. Over the years, various hosts have worked with the guides, including Ron Howard, Whoopi Goldberg, and Jimmy Fallon. The video system provided a more consistent show at the cost of spontaneity on the part of the guide. The prerecorded material dominates today's tour, and the guide's role has been diminished considerably.

1   Barry Upson, note to author, 17 Mar. 2014.
2   Phil Hettema, interview with author, Pasadena, CA, 7 May 2014.
3   Ibid.
4   Alex Finkelstein, "Universal Can't Escape Lawsuits," *Orlando Business Journal,* 19 Apr. 1999.
5   Tim Barker, "Universal Says It's Time to Let Real Adventure Begin," *Orlando Sentinel,* 24 May 1999.
6   Ibid.
7   Jill Jorden-Spitz, "Music Has Starring Role in Theme Park," *The Los Angeles Times,* 18 Sept. 2002.
8   David Barbour, "Where Universal Tries Its Hand at Bringing Myths, Magic, and Legends to Life," *Entertainment Design,* 1 Nov. 1999.
9   Laurie Schenden, "Family: Tuning In to Dr. Seuss," *The Los Angeles Times,* 12 Feb. 1998.
10   Ibid.
11   Barbour, "Where Universal Tries Its Hand."
12   Phil Hettema, interview with author, Pasadena, CA, 16 Jan. 2014.
13   Ibid.
14   Ibid.
15   Ibid.
16   Ibid.
17   Mike Schneider, "The Making of Islands of Adventure at Universal Orlando," Associated Press, 5 July 1998.
18   Hettema, interview with author, 16 Jan. 2014.
19   Schenden, "Tuning In to Dr. Seuss."
20   Susan G. Strother, "Park Restaurants Aim to Dish up Dining Adventure," *Orlando Sentinel,* 7 May 1997.
21   Hettema, interview with author, 16 Jan. 2014.
22   "Park's Dress Rehearsal Almost Over," *Orlando Sentinel,* 21 May 1999.
23   Hettema, interview with author, 16 Jan. 2014.
24   "Park's Dress Rehearsal."
25   Ibid.
26   Tim Barker, "Promises Run Out on Kiddie Ride," *Orlando Sentinel,* 20 Jan. 2001.
27   Hettema, interview with author, 7 May 2014.
28   Ibid.
29   Ibid.
30   Barbour, "Where Universal Tries Its Hand."
31   Ibid.
32   Hettema, interview with author, 7 May 2014.
33   Gary Goddard, note to author, 9 Apr. 2014.

34 Ibid.
35 Goddard, interview with author, North Hollywood, CA, 12 Jan. 2014.
36 Goddard, note to author, 9 Apr. 2014.
37 Ibid.
38 Ibid.
39 Josh Mercer, "Dueling Dragons," *Parkpedia,* parkpedia.cc/article/dueling-dragons (accessed 21 Mar. 2013).
40 Christine Shenot, "Dueling Dragons Will Take Universal Visitors for a Thrill Ride," *Orlando Sentinel,* 7 Apr. 1997.
41 Ibid.
42 Barbour, "Where Universal Tries Its Hand."
43 Hettema, interview with author, 7 May 2014.
44 Barbour, "Where Universal Tries Its Hand."
45 Hettema, interview with author, 7 May 2014.
46 Barbour, "Where Universal Tries Its Hand."
47 Hettema, interview with author, 7 May 2014.
48 Barbour, "Where Universal Tries Its Hand."
49 Ibid.
50 Hettema, interview with author, 7 May 2014.
51 Ibid.
52 Tim Barker, "Marvel Super Hero Island," *Orlando Sentinel,* 28 May 1999.
53 Barbour, "Where Universal Tries Its Hand."
54 Ibid.
55 Ibid.
56 Hettema, interview with author, 7 May 2014.
57 Hettema, interview with author, 16 Jan. 2014.
58 Barbour, "Where Universal Tries Its Hand."
59 Strother, "Park Restaurants Aim to Dish Up Dining Adventure."
60 Hettema, interview with author, 7 May 2014.
61 Ibid.
62 Philip D. Hettema, William D. Mason, and Gary Goddard, Amusement ride vehicle, US Patent 6,095,926, filed 1 May 1998 and issued 1 Aug. 2000.
63 Hettema, interview with author, 7 May 2014.
64 Barbour, "Where Universal Tries Its Hand."
65 Ibid.
66 Ibid.
67 Ibid.
68 Ibid.
69 Ibid.
70 James Bernstein, "A Theme Park for WHEEEEE!," *The Los Angeles Times,* 23 May 1999.
71 Barbour, "Where Universal Tries Its Hand."
72 Catherine Hinman, "New Spin on Virtual Reality," *Orlando Sentinel,,* 23 May 1999.
73 Cory Lancaster, "Universal's Transforming Adventure," *Orlando Sentinel,* 11 May 1998.
74 Tim Barker, "Islands Opening Delayed," *Orlando Sentinel,* 6 May 1999.
75 Bernstein, "A Theme Park for WHEEEEE!"
76 Schneider, "Making of Islands of Adventure."
77 Ibid.

78 Bernstein, "A Theme Park for WHEEEEE!"

79 Harrison "Buzz" Price, *Walt's Revolution by the Numbers* (Orlando, FL: Ripley's Entertainment, 2004).

80 Scott Reckard, "Move Over, Mickey: Universal Studios is betting $2.6 billion," *The Los Angeles Times,* 14 Mar. 1999.

81 Hettema, interview with author, 16 Jan. 2014.

82   Salvador Anton Clavé, *The Global Theme Park Industry* (Cambridge, MA: CABI Publishing, 2007).

83 Frank Rose, "Edgar Bronfman Actually Has a Strategy—With a Twist," *Fortune,* Vol. 139, Issue 4, 1 Mar. 1999, 112.

84 Hettema, interview with author, 16 Jan. 2014.

85 Michael D. Eisner with Tony Schwartz, *Work in Progress* (New York: Hyperion, 1998).

86 Reckard, "Move Over, Mickey."

87 Tim Barker, "Universal Tinkers with its Name—Again," *Orlando Sentinel*, 1 Feb. 2000.

88 Leslie Doolittle, "Eisner's Orlando Adventure Takes Him Out of His World," *Orlando Sentinel,* 2 Jan. 2000.

89 Ibid.

90 Tim Barker, "Universal's Plans for Lockheed Land Include 3rd Park," *Orlando Sentinel,* 25 Oct. 1999.

91 Robert Niles, "Theme Park History: the Millennium Project at Universal Studios Florida," *Theme Park Insider,* 11 Dec. 2013.

92 "Men In Black: Alien Attack Opens," *Orlando Sentinel,* 14 Apr. 2000.

93 Ibid.

94 Hettema, interview with author, 7 May 2014.

CHAPTER 11

VIVENDI,
2001–2004

VIVENDI

THE UNIVERSAL THEME PARKS just could not get a break. After the successes of the 1970s and 1980s, MCA sold out to the Japanese. Then came a Canadian liquor baron that fashioned himself as an entertainment mogul. Bronfman may have had ambitions and pumped a lot of money into the theme parks, but he was a very poor businessman. Who would believe that next to come to the rescue would be a 148-year-old French water and sewer utility? On June 21, 2001, Vivendi acquired Universal from Seagram for $31 billion.

Vivendi was founded by the Rothschild family and the half-brother of Napoleon III. Over the years, it became the world's largest water and sewer company, serving 100 million customers in 100 countries. Vivendi's CEO, Jean-Marie Messier, believed the future of entertainment rested with the cell phone. Vivendi had built a wireless business in Europe and bought European film and television holdings. By merging with Universal, Messier hoped his company could dominate the digital and wireless age.

How the theme parks fit into this picture was a question on many people's minds. Pierre Lescure, Vivendi co-chief operating officer, tried to reassure investors and said, "The parks are part of the game, part of the intimacy with the studio itself."[1] Phil Hettema said, "As long as the cash flow was there, upper management left it to the theme parks."[2]

This confidence would not last very long. In less than a year, Messier put on the brakes at the theme parks. Virtually all funding for new projects dried up. Ron Meyer told the press that Universal would continue to add new attractions, "but they would be appropriately priced for us. We can find ways to give good experiences to our customers."[3] Phil Hettema said, "Frankly, when Vivendi was there, there was not a great appetite for doing anything with the theme parks. It was sort of been there, done that. It was obvious we were not going to build a third gate anytime soon."[4] The policy was to do more and more with less and less. The days of an attraction like the $75 million Amazing Adventures of Spider-Man were over. The focus would be on revenue-producing projects like hotels or an expansion of the shopping malls.

This concerned Mark Woodbury, chief creative officer at the Recreation Group. He said, "We are in a very competitive world and consumer expectations have grown exponentially since people first put robotic figures in dark rides."[5] To save money, the 30-member creative staff for the Universal parks was moved to Florida in July 2001. It did not help. The bleeding continued, and Vivendi lost $11.8 billion in 2001.

Vivendi was looking for any way that it could to raise money. Because there were no plans to expand the Florida parks, selling off land seemed like a solid strategy. In June 2001 hotelier Harris Rosen purchased 230 acres for $30 million. The property was adjacent to the convention center. Rosen planned to build a 1,500-room resort.

With hindsight, a much more painful cut was made in December 2003. Vivendi sold 1,780 of the 2,280 acres MCA purchased from Lockheed Martin in 1998. Thomas Enterprises, Inc. of Georgia paid $70 million and became responsible for any environmental remediation that would be required to make the land usable. There were some restrictions. Thomas could not turn around and sell or lease the property to another entertainment concern. In the meantime, the company planned to use the property as a cattle ranch. Even more property was sliced off for quick cash in June 2004 when Canadian developer Introits purchased 29.5 acres. Even tougher times would be ahead.

For families with young children, Universal Studios Hollywood was never meant to be a full-day park. That audience was driving to Disneyland. Unfortunately, many visitors came to Universal after visiting "the happiest place on Earth," and they had young children anxious to do something. E.T. Adventure was not enough. Even Knott's Berry Farm and Six Flags Magic Mountain were friendlier territory for those under 8 years old.

To capitalize on this opportunity, Universal opened the Nickelodeon Blast Zone in April 2001. To make room for the new attraction, the War Lord Tower, a landmark on the upper lot since 1965, was removed. Removing part of the parking lot created additional room.

The 30,000-square-foot interactive children's play center was divided into wet and dry activities. The Nickelodeon Splash! Zone used popular off-the-shelf water activities that could be found at any water park in the United States. However, those parks did not have permission to dress up the area with characters from *Sponge Bob Square Pants, Angry Beavers,* and *Rocket Power.* The kids could get drenched from a 30-foot-tall orange Nickelodeon rocket, two

500-gallon water buckets, a bank of 20 water pop jets, or from their peers using water cannons on a catwalk 25 feet above the ground.

For those trying to avoid getting wet, the Wild Thornberry's Adventure Temple was the destination of choice. Inside of a "thatched jungle house" adorned with Asian rain forest motifs were more than 25,000 lava-colored foam balls and various devices to propel them toward other family members. Occasionally, an enormous and mysterious orangutan statue would hurl exploding balls in all directions.

For the youngest guests, under the age of 6, there was the Nick Jr. Backyard. Like the corner tot lot, there were a variety of slides, cargo nets, and a slide-for-life pole. Featured Nickelodeon characters included *Blue's Clues, Little Bear,* and *Dora the Explorer.* There was even a 20-minute stage performance called the *Rugrats Magic Adventure!* Nearby, *The River Princess* riverboat restaurant was redressed as a Flintstones-themed barbecue joint. The smokestacks were hidden in giant horns.

With all of the new child attractions, the child-friendly Chicken Run maze was replaced with The Mummy Returns Chamber of Doom. The new maze was built to promote Universal's *The Mummy Returns.* Out front was the Duesenberg used in the

unofficial **TIP**
The Nickelodeon Blast Zone and the Flintstones restaurant were removed in 2013 as part of the Harry Potter expansion.

film; inside were actual props and set pieces used in the *Mummy* movies. While in line, visitors could terrorize others already in the maze by pushing buttons that would activate a skeleton to pop up or blast them with air or water. The maze lasted until 2004.

Aiming for maximum synergy, the Glacier Ice Tunnel was rethemed and renamed The Curse of the Mummy's Tomb. As the trams approached the tunnel, it looked as if the film crew had vanished. A coffin filled with scarab beetles outside provided a warning of the terror about to come. Inside, it was the same special effect, except for the Warrior Mummies painted in ultraviolet paint on the moving walls. By 2013 the tunnel was removed entirely.

Another victim of downsizing was the Western stunt show. Once upon a time, Westerns were the staple of movies and television. By the new millennium, they had become a rarity. The genre started to fade into the sunset. Universal officials have historically not been a nostalgic group, and when a theme was no longer relevant, they generally would not hesitate to change things. Change came on January 6, 2002, at Universal Studios Hollywood when the cowboys put down their arms for the last time. Since the very first days of the tour, there were cowboys fighting it out. Over the years, they performed in five different venues. The Wild West Theater was closed, remained vacant for many years, and was then removed to create a central performance space.

SELF-INFLICTED WOUNDS

BY 2003 THE UNITED STATES' HOSPITALITY INDUSTRY was slowly starting to emerge from the sharp drop-off in travel after the 2001 terrorist attacks. However, the domestic theme park industry was still in trouble. Although economists predicted 2003 would see an uptick in traffic, they also suggested that the American theme park was at a saturation point. About 315 million people were visiting theme parks each year in the United States. That is an average of more than one visit per person, compared to Europe's average of only one in three people visiting a theme park each year.

The American theme park industry was also facing a demographic shift that was having a profound impact on the business. The prime audience for theme parks was the 25- to 44-year-old segment. That group was expected to decline 2.4% over the next five years. Jim Cammisa, publisher of *Travel Industry Indicators,* said, "The growth rate is not going to be what it was in the past because the theme park market is shrinking in size."[6] In general, the population was getting older, and for a park like Universal, which was becoming increasingly dependent upon thrill rides, this was not a good trend.

Not only was Universal hurting, but things over at Disney were also stagnating. Reinvestment had all but stopped at Walt Disney World. During a speech to shareholders, Michael Eisner focused on cost-cutting measures. He said, "From 1994 to 1999, our attractions division was a net consumer of cash, totaling about $750 million. By contrast, between 2002 and 2003, we anticipate that attractions will deliver more than $2 billion in after-tax free cash flow." That was due to the lack of reinvestment.[7]

Ron Bension was blunt: "I don't think the industry's woes are 100% 9/11 and the economy. Fifty% of it is self-inflicted wounds."[8] Bension convinced Vivendi to pull the trigger and reinvest. Maybe something fresh and new at Universal could get people through the gates?

The Jimmy Neutron and Shrek rides came first in 2003. Universal invested $60 million for the pair of rides. Then in 2004, they spent $40 million each for a Revenge of the Mummy roller coaster on each coast. The Universal press machine was in full force. Tom Williams said, "We have huge confidence in the business, and we're long-term players. We believe the timing of this is going to work out perfectly."[9] Wyman Roberts, marketing officer at Universal said, "We continue to push on staying relevant and fresh. This isn't the time to take anything for granted."[10]

The first piece of this strategy began on April 11, 2003, when the familiar friendly cartoon characters from Hanna-Barbera exited stage right, and the animated cast from *Jimmy Neutron* and characters from the Nickelodeon network took their place. With Hanna-Barbera went another piece of the original Universal Studios Florida.

For Universal Creative, the benefit of switching out the intellectual properties made financial sense. With very little done to the show building, Jimmy Neutron's Nicktoon Blast was a relativity cheap update to an existing ride system with characters that were relevant to a new generation. It did not matter if the adults knew what was going on. The children got it.

The working title for the simulator ride was The Nicktoon Blast. When it became apparent that Jimmy Neutron was going to become a star because of the hit 2001 movie *Jimmy Neutron: Boy Genius* and his television series, the name was changed. "We wanted to create an attraction that was fun," said Scott Trowbridge. "We really wanted to make this one of a kind—unique in attitude and tone."[11] The show was a two-year collaboration between Universal Creative and Steve Oedekerk, producer of the animated series. Nickelodeon Animation Studios produced the film.

The change from Hanna-Barbera to Jimmy Neutron was rocket fast. It took only five months and two weeks to complete the project. The preshow area was left relatively intact. The show also used the same soundstage, motion vehicles, and 70-millimeter projection system as its predecessor.

In the story, Jimmy Neutron had invented a new flying machine called the Mark IV. Aliens from the planet Yolkus had come to Earth to steal his invention. After the theft, Jimmy would try to follow them in one of his older models and tell the audience to follow. That was when the audience would learn that they were sitting in an even older version of Neutron's flying machines.

The show would take the audience on a wild ride through the Nicktoon Studios world, with flybys past *Rocco's Modern Life, Ren & Stimpy, SpongeBob SquarePants,* and *The Wild Thornberrys.* The film was loaded with inside jokes for the sharp-eyed Nickelodeon fan. In-theater effects, including smoke coming out from under the screen and bubbles drifting from the ceiling, added to the chaos. The postshow was a visit to the Nicktoon Control Room with familiar Nickelodeon props, such as the pipe from *Double Dare 2000* and a sign from *All That.*

Next up was a partnership made in heaven. DreamWorks's animated hit *Shrek* (2001) was an in-your-face parody of the fairy tales that were the lifeblood over at Disney. Founding partner Jeffrey Katzenberg used to work at Disney and held a grudge. He took the challenge of adapting his prize set of characters to a theme park ride very seriously. Katzenberg said, "I love the challenge of trying to tell a good story in a virtual world, which is what a theme park is."[12]

Shrek 4-D opened on both coasts in 2003—in Hollywood on May 23 and in Florida on June 12. The show would become a franchise with versions at Universal Studios Japan, Warner Bros. Movie World in Australia, Movie Park Germany, and Universal Studios Singapore.

The sarcasm starts to drip as soon as the guests enter the queue. Humorous posters advertising fake theme-park-like attractions in the mythical Kingdom of Duloc are plastered along the walls. The pre-show area is dressed like a dungeon, and the 3-D glasses are called "OgreVision" goggles. After multiple warnings to run away by the likes of Pinocchio, Gingy, the Magic Mirror, and the Three Little Pigs, the rest of the show takes place in an adjacent theater.

The film's story line begins where the Academy Award–winning *Shrek* ended. Shrek and Princess Fiona, his new bride, are on their way to their honeymoon when the ghost of Lord Farquaad kidnaps Fiona, and the comedy begins.

Production on the ride started in 2001. "They came in with a menu of ideas and we laid out a story idea for them, which they liked very much," said Katzenberg. Once the story outline was agreed upon, Katzenberg asked, "How can we embellish it, how do we 'ride' this movie?" The use of 3-D appealed to Katzenberg. "When you make a CG movie like *Shrek*," he said, "it exists in a digital file so you can replicate images and move them around and adjust the cinematography to accentuate dimension at the push of a button in a way that is much more compelling than what you could do in live action."[13]

Scott Trowbridge agreed. He said, "Shrek's kind of an in-your-face kind of guy, and 3D is an in-your-face kind of technology. We pretty quickly got into the mindset that 3D was the way to re-create the style of imagery that would also allow us to bring back the voices and the acting that everybody loved."[14]

PDI/DreamWorks produced the 13-minute digital film. They were responsible for the original animation. Universal also scored a win with all of the original voice actors returning for the film, including Eddie Murphy, Mike Myers, Cameron Diaz, and John Lithgow, who voiced Donkey, Shrek, Princess Fiona, and Lord Farquaad, respectively.

The show buildings may have been lightly rethemed, but the film and projection technology used was state of the art. Universal used a proprietary system that projected an image that is "crisp, clear, rock-steady and bright," according to Trowbridge.[15]

Along with the 3-D film are in-theater effects, such as movable seats that are coordinated with the action on-screen, water splashing the guests, and special lighting. Scott Trowbridge said, "3D can bring the action off the screen, but then we came up with this idea of adding lots of special effects to create a fourth D, so the movie basically lands in your lap."[16]

The MUSEUM *of* ANTIQUITIES

THE LAST HURRAH FOR VIVENDI was the Revenge of the Mummy—The Ride. The ride opened on both coasts in 2004. The "psychological thrill ride" was based on director/writer Stephen Sommers

The Mummy (1999) and *The Mummy Returns* (2001). The two films grossed more than $1 billion, and the characters and setting seemed like the perfect fit for Universal. "Making the movies and ride were very similar experiences," said Sommers. "Both are very big, elaborate, complicated, and take years."[17]

The ride is one part dark ride and one part roller coaster. Scott Trowbridge was put in charge of the project and said, "We wanted to create a theme park experience that felt like a third movie in the franchise, and to embody many of the attributes of the *Mummy* movies: to be exciting and fun, with a lot of surprises, action, and adventure thrown in." The goal was sensory overload. "We wanted an immersive dark ride that turns into a thrill ride, and tried to find a way to make that work," according to Trowbridge.[18]

The Florida version opened on May 21, 2004. The elaborate queue provided the designers the opportunity to reveal the ride's story line. The story is revealed in a mock documentary about the making of the film. Visitors learn from Reggie, a bumbling production assistant, that they are entering the hot set of the next *Mummy* movie inside the Museum of Antiquities. They also learn that every time someone mentions Imhotep, the mummy, by name, something bad happens.

The queue winds around a burial chamber and an archaeological dig. Throughout the queue are activities to keep guests busy. For example, when two guests simultaneously place their hands on a sarcophagus, it triggers an animated light show on the ceiling. Another effect is a hologram of a treasure that blasts air at anyone who tries to grab it. Theme park critic Mike Thomas said, "I fear Universal went cheap with Mummy. There is evidence of an ongoing archaeological dig. It's not bad but there is a huge flaw. The set is way too neat and tidy. The wood looks fresh from Home Depot. There is no dust, and not one spider web. It's like we have entered the tomb of Felix Unger."[19]

During the roller coaster segment, Revenge of the Mummy— The Ride is the only indoor coaster to use forward and backward motion. The 16-seat ride vehicles are themed as mine cars used for removing artifacts from the mummy's tomb. The trains are powered by an electromagnetic propulsion system with linear induction motors around the track. As the vehicles start on their journey, they are weighed, so a computer can determine the amount of force necessary to launch the coaster.

Along the way, riders encounter Imhotep, Universal's most sophisticated audio-animatronic figure. The mummy stands 6 foot, 10 inches tall and is voiced by Arnold Vosloo, who also played the character in the movies. Production manager Mike Hightower said, "He's got 40 functions to make him look very, very lifelike—his neck turns, his neck bends, his eyes blink, all his fingers move. We did not invent a new technology, but took the engineering to a new level of application. He's very realistic, very close to you, very dynamic."[20] Hightower suggested that hydraulically powered Imhotep could bench press 10,000 pounds.

The audio system is a big part of the experience. Throughout the ride are 200 strategically placed speakers powered by an 18,000-watt sound system. Each ride vehicle has 22 speakers. The onboard MP3 audio system is powered by ultracapacitors that are recharged every time the vehicles stop at the loading platform.

One of the most spectacular special effects is the false ending, with real flames known as "Brain Fire" overhead. As the coaster stops, the silhouette of a ride attendant in the booth gets vaporized, and the ceiling catches on fire. When they first discussed the effect, Bob Shreve said, "Your reaction is, 'Oh, you can't do that!' Then, the second reaction is, 'Oh, you can't afford to do that,' and once you've worked all that out, you go, 'Oh, how can we pull that off?'" During a test, they suspended three pans, each larger than an SUV—upside down from the ceiling. The shallow sides trapped natural gas beneath the pans and created the effect. At the end of the ride, actor Brendan Fraser congratulates the riders on surviving, before the Mummy attacks him and the video suddenly cuts off.

The Hollywood version opened on June 25. The biggest difference between California and Florida was the need to stuff the ride inside of the existing E.T. soundstage building. Although E.T. was a beloved character from director Steven Spielberg and one of the few child-friendly rides at Universal Studios Hollywood, space was at a premium and its time had come. Barry Upson said, "An attraction keeps its appeal by remaining relevant to its market and to the primary entertainment mission of the park. It becomes 'obsolete' when the original film or TV base drops from sight (for example, *E.T.*), when the technology becomes passé or when we find that the site or facility is better used for a new attraction."[21]

The Mummy was not the first tenant considered for the sound-stage. Another ride was planned, but the theme was quickly switched to take advantage of a bicoastal coaster publicity campaign. John Murdy said, "I started with the track layout and worked backward, designed the ride around the track, which is really unusual. You normally want the ride track to serve the story, but in this case there wasn't time for that."[22]

Due to this constraint, the entire preshow is different. Instead of the story line that the riders are extras on a movie set, in Hollywood they simply enter a plunder tomb. The lack of room forced the technical team to utilize Slow Linear Induction Motors (SLIM) to move vehicles at a variety of speeds for the very first time. In the dark ride section, mummy hands reach down from the ceiling. Just before the launch, four mummy warriors drop 20 feet straight down and stop 6 feet from the riders. Each figure weighs 5,000 pounds and uses magnetic brakes to enhance the free fall illusion. There is no need to decelerate. In Florida, the launch is on an incline. In Hollywood, the launch is flat and much of the coaster portion is backward. As a result, the ride is more intense.

After riding, Bob Sipchen of *The Los Angeles Times* said, "The Revenge of the Mummy ride at Universal Studios Hollywood is what the Pirates of the Caribbean at Disneyland would be if hijacked by a band of hyperactive genius teen pranksters who'd spent way too much time playing dark-themed fantasy games and watching movies about cloth-wrapped corpses come to life."[23] He also complained that in the coaster segment "the embellishments are incongruously cartoonish, undermining any suspension of disbelief."[24]

Now that Universal Hollywood had a proper Mummy ride, the Chamber of Doom maze was rethemed to Stephen Sommers's film *Van Helsing* (2004). Set pieces from the film were blended with historic artifacts from *Dracula, Frankenstein,* and *The Wolf Man.* A room with a spinning wall was added, along with a 50-foot bridge overlooking an expanded Frankenstein laboratory. Even some of the walls and floors would vibrate, adding to the terror. This version of the maze would last until November 4, 2006.

1 Jerry Hirsch, "Universal Puts Growth of New Parks on Hold," *The Los Angeles Times,* 7 May 2001.
2 Phil Hettema, interview with author, Pasadena, CA, 16 Jan. 2014.
3 Hirsch, "Growth of New Parks on Hold."
4 Phil Hettema, interview with author, Pasadena, CA, 7 May 2014.
5 Hirsch, "Growth of New Parks on Hold."
6 Richard Verrier, "Slumping Parks Try New Lures," *The Los Angeles Times,* 7 Oct. 2003.
7 Alan Byrd, "Men in Black Promises Dark Fun and Rip Torn, Too," *Orlando Business Journal,* 6 Mar. 2000.
8 Verrier, "Slumping Parks Try New Lures."
9 Richard Verrier, "Mummy Bound for New Ride," *The Los Angeles Times,* 17 May 2003.
10 Verrier, "Slumping Parks Try New Lures."
11 Rebecca Swain Vadnie, "Jimmy's Wild Ride," *Orlando Sentinel,* 11 Apr. 2003.
12 Hugh Hart, "New Dimension: A Jolt of Technology Breathes Life into Shrek 4D," *The Los Angeles Times,* 22 May 2003.
13 Ibid.
14 Ibid.
15 Ibid.
16 Ibid.
17 John Calhoun, "Mummy Dearest," *Entertainment Design,* Aug. 2004.
18 Ibid.
19 Mike Thomas, "That's a Wrap: Verdict is in on Mummy Ride," *Orlando Sentinel,* 23 May 2004.
20 John Calhoun, "Mummy Dearest."

21 Alexander Matzkeit, "The Days of 'Build It and They Shall Come' are Over: An Interview with Theme Park Veteran Barry Upson," *Real Virtuality,* June 2009, tinyurl.com /upsonrvinterview (accessed 10 Aug. 2013).

22 Jon Primrose and Christian Beana, "Interview with John Murdy," *thestudiotour.com,* 15 Apr. 2006, thestudiotour.com/ush/attractions/interview_johnmurdy.php (accessed 29 July 2013).

23 Bob Sipchen, "The Alternatives Theme Park Ride Review," *The Los Angeles Times,* 24 June 2004.

24 Ibid.

CHAPTER 12

GENERAL ELECTRIC,
2004–2009

WHAT ARE YOU
GUYS RUNNING?

ON MAY 12, 2004, GENERAL ELECTRIC (GE) became the fourth corporation to own the Universal theme parks. That made four different owners in just 13 years. The lack of constant commitment was beginning to show. The $14 billion deal for Vivendi's entertainment properties created a media company so vast it could compete with Time Warner Inc., Viacom Inc., and the Walt Disney Company. GE purchased 80% of Universal with an option to purchase Vivendi's remaining 20% after two years.

The new NBC Universal was meant to create a seamless production and distribution by combining the television and motion picture production owned by Universal with a long list of cable television channels owned by NBC. As part of the deal, GE also bought interests in five theme parks: Universal Studios Hollywood; the two parks in Florida; Universal PortAventura (1998) near Barcelona, Spain; and Universal Studios Japan in Osaka (2001).

The park in Spain had yet to earn a profit. Universal Studios Japan had been suffering from a two-year attendance slump due to the restaurants allegedly being caught selling food past the expiration date and the drinking fountains serving unsanitary water. Things were not much better stateside. The two theme parks in Orlando had lost $52.2 million in 2003. The resort was in debt to the tune of $1.17 billion. Even the Hollywood park was suffering from a 12% dip in attendance.

GE was a giant corporation with a reputation for avoiding high-cost, low-profit businesses. Finding support at GE for the theme parks was an uphill battle. When a group of Universal park executives met with the new owners, General Electric NBC Universal Chief Bob

Wright asked, "What are you guys running, a 501 (c)(3)?" in reference to nonprofit groups. Wright's only interest in the theme parks was the constant cash flow and the opportunity to promote and extend NBC and their other brands to more than 30 million visitors worldwide.

Universal Parks & Resorts Chairman and CEO Tom Williams tried to put the best face forward. He claimed that GE was still fully committed to the theme parks and pointed to the spring 2004 opening of the Revenge of the Mummy roller coasters. Unfortunately, theme park industry observers recognized that those rides were just leftovers from the last regime.

In May 2004, the team at Universal Creative was cut back from 100 people to fewer than three dozen. All major rides in development were put on hold. The cost cutting that began during the Vivendi era was not only going to continue, but it also looked like the parks were going to starve even further under GE.

OVERCOMING YOUR FEARS

WITH CORPORATE SYNERGY THE PRIMARY GOAL, the first theme park attraction to benefit was *Fear Factor Live*. "We've always looked at *Fear Factor* as kind of a theme park ride on television," according to NBC Universal Television Group President Jeff Zucker. "It made sense to extend that brand into the theme parks." The show represented the first time that a reality television show was transformed into a theme park experience. Tom Williams said, "Creating an extreme experience such as *Fear Factor Live* is perfect for us, and a perfect way to fit our brand within the NBC brand." GE wanted to copy the Disney model of promoting ABC shows in the theme parks. Zucker joked, "If this one works, maybe someone will be saying, 'You're fired!' at a theme park," referring to the Donald Trump show *The Apprentice*.[1]

The 20-minute show opened in 2005 on both coasts. It debuted in the Castle Theatre at Universal Studios Hollywood and the arena formerly used for the *Wild Wild Wild West Stunt Show* in Florida. The show involves three controlled-risk stunts with two audience member volunteers being eliminated after each stunt: an endurance test, a team-based challenge, and a final head-to-head competition between the two finalists. The stunts are designed to test the physical and emotional limits of each contestant. In between the three main stunts, audience members are invited to spin the Wheel of Fear and participate in challenges, such as drinking a horrifying smoothy or having scorpions placed on their heads. Their reward is a T-shirt and $10 credit in Universal script.

The show was meant to go beyond any of the many audience participation shows that came before. Scott Trowbridge warned, "When you think *Fear Factor*, everyone expects sticky, ooey and gross, and we will not disappoint." However, Trowbridge did suggest, "It isn't about victimizing. It's about overcoming your fears."[2]

The park runs five to eight shows a day. Volunteers audition to be part of the show, and the selection process is rigorous. Executive producer Matt Kunitz joked, "The odds are more in your favor for getting into Harvard than being chosen to appear on *Fear Factor*." In Hollywood, the show lasted until 2009 and closed during the economic slump, but the show goes on at Universal Studios Florida.

For the next few years, GE did little to enhance its theme parks. The big new thing for 2005 was a leftover set from a major motion picture. Steven Spielberg spent millions re-creating a neighborhood devastated by a 747 jetliner crash for the film *War of the Worlds* (2005). The set was tucked up against the residential area adjacent to the back lot and covered Falls Lake. A real Boeing 747 was trucked in to the back lot. The tail was so large that it had to be airlifted and planted in front of the Discovery Center used in Jurassic Park. A devastated residential neighborhood was built around the prop. Filming took place January 5–7, 2005, and the set appeared in the movie for less than 3 minutes. The set was so dramatic (and already paid for) that it was decided to leave it in place for the studio tour. Some of the fake houses were moved to create a roadway for the trams. Otherwise, the set was left intact.

Another way to raise cash was to sell the naming rights to the Universal Amphitheater. On April 8, 2005, the historic music venue became known as the Gibson Amphitheater as part of a 10-year agreement with the legendary Gibson Guitar Corporation.

Things were not getting much better in 2006. The big news was that Universal's House of Horrors replaced Van Helsing: Fortress Dracula. Inside the maze were more than 20 infamous Universal horror film characters spread out in themed areas that included Count Dracula, Nosferatu, The Wolf Man, The Mummy, Frankenstein's Monster, the Bride of Frankenstein, the Phantom of the Opera, and the zombies

*un*official **TIP**
The Botanicus figure (E.T.'s teacher) from E.T. Adventure is still in storage at Universal Studios Hollywood.

of *Dawn of the Dead* (2004) and *Land of the Dead* (2005). The displays in the lobby included the original corduroy blazer worn by Anthony Perkins in *Psycho*, the Hannibal Lecter mask from *Red Dragon,* the police uniform worn by Roy Schneider in *Jaws*, and the original Chucky doll.

Many of the props were repurposed from movies and rides. For example, the huge electrical transformer was used in Dr. Frankenstein's lab in *Van Helsing* (2004). After four years in storage, the fake trees and plants from the E.T. Adventure queue were recycled for the Wolf Man's forest, and an audio-animatronic police officer became the Phantom of the Opera figure.

Adding to the sensory overload were the nine different smell generators pumping out scents, such as formaldehyde, machine oil, pine forest, and rot. Tucked inside was a toy monkey placed by Universal creative director John Murdy, a tradition for virtually every ride or show on which he worked.[3]

A few new tweaks came to the studio tour in 2006. The Fast and the Furious: Extreme Close-Up opened on June 15 and was based on *The Fast and the Furious: Tokyo Drift,* the third film in the series. The demonstration was designed to show how stunt directors use a process called previsualization to define and refine complicated action sequences. The trams pulled into the 10,000-square-foot Stage 55 where two Volkswagen Golf vehicles were parked. The car bodies were made of carbon fiber and weighed only 500 pounds instead of the typical 3,300 pounds. Then they were each mounted on a KUKA robotic arm.

As the show would begin, an unseen director would call out for action. The loud sound of a helicopter filled the arena and then machine gun fire could be heard. As the shots hit the set, water was sent high in the air and then some barrels were hit, which would set off an explosion with a 25-foot plume of fire and smoke. Reminiscent of the Runaway Train of years past, the cars were sent hurtling toward the tram, but they would stop just short. In a comedic finale that demonstrated the revolutionary motion control system, the two cars named Carnage and Carma would begin to dance to "Gasolina" by Daddy Yankee. The show lasted until 2013.

For 2007, the big new attraction was a museum. New on the lower lot in Hollywood was the *Universal Experience: Behind the Scenes of Universal Pictures,* which opened on May 22. The exhibit space was divided into two main sections. The "On Screen" section focused on items that were used in the physical production of a movie (that is, props, costumes, and so on). The "Behind The Scenes" section looked at the elements that go into moviemaking, such as models, miniatures, artwork, and special effects. Some of the items that have been on display include the communicator prop from *E.T.* (1982), Gregory Peck's briefcase and glasses from *To Kill a Mockingbird* (1962), the Best Picture Academy award for *The Sting* (1973), and the DeLorean from *Back to the Future* (1985). Visitors could learn more about the displays using interactive kiosks with scenes and other information. The Studio Commissary was converted into a Panda Express.

A HOLOGRAPHIC EFFECT

THINGS IN FLORIDA WERE ONLY SLIGHTLY BETTER than in Hollywood. Broadway stars Blue Man Group brought their unique blend of humor and music to CityWalk. Their show borrows from Blue

Man Group shows in New York, Boston, Chicago, and Las Vegas, with a few new gags exclusively for Orlando. A specially built 1,000-seat theater was installed in Sound Stage 18, which had been formerly used by Nickelodeon.

With the disaster movie *Earthquake!* far from the memories of most audiences and Universal Orlando trying to do anything possible to keep the park fresh without actually spending much money, park management decided to close *Earthquake: The Big One* in November 2007 and quickly retool the show. After one month and three weeks, the fastest turnaround time for a new attraction in Universal Orlando history, the ride reopened as *Disaster: A Major Motion Picture Ride . . . Starring You!* The official grand opening was January 17, 2008.

The new story line revolves around the casting for *Mutha Nature,* a new film by the fictional Disaster Studios director Frank Kincaid. Just like before, volunteers are selected to play roles in Kincaid's latest film. Only this time there is a new twist. Everybody gets into the act.

New to the attraction is a screening room featuring actor Christopher Walken playing the role of director Kincaid. Using a remarkable high-tech illusion called Musion technology, Walken appears to be standing on the stage interacting with a live actor. Musion is a modern take on the Pepper's ghost illusion used by magicians. Musion Systems Ltd. used specially designed cameras and high-definition video projectors to achieve the same effect. Instead of using glass, Musion used a sheet of micro-thin, transparent foil. While many viewers believe the effect is a hologram, "technically, it's not accurate," according to James Rock of Musion. "What you're looking at is always a two-dimensional projection. . . . We call it a 'holographic effect.'"[4] This was the first use of the technology in a theme park and the largest permanent installation anywhere.

After the introduction in the screening room, visitors move to a soundstage where the selected volunteers record their stunts in front of a blue screen just like before. As the segment ends, visitors are instructed that they are now extras in the making of *Mutha Nature* and they are being called on to the set. The train pulls back to the subway station set as before, and the special effects show remains relatively the same. However, in this version, visitors are told when and how to react. As the train pulls back to the loading platform, an over-the-top 90-second video trailer for the film starring actor Dwayne "The Rock" Johnson is shown that includes the elements shot with the volunteers and the riders on the train. The show had shifted away from how movies were made and toward a postmodern look at why movies are made.

Time waits for no one, and the future had come close to catching up to the present. When Back to the Future: The Ride opened in 1991, it redefined what was possible in a theme park ride. However, part of the ride was also set in 2015, and by 2007 that was too close for comfort. To avoid looking dated, Marty McFly and the flying DeLorean were retired that year and replaced by The Simpsons in 2008. The Florida version opened first on May 15, and the Hollywood version opened May 19.

Development of the ride took two years with a budget of $30 million for each coast. *Florida Today* tried to assess how much Universal had paid Twentieth Century Fox for the rights to use *The Simpsons,* but could only find that a large amount of money was set aside for "intellectual property rights" in an SEC filing.

Universal Creative worked with *The Simpsons* creators James L. Brooks and Matt Groening. Groening said, "The ride is designed to duplicate *The Simpsons* home-viewing experience, only at high speed and with lots of screaming."[5] Once guests walk through the mouth of a 33-foot-wide Krusty the Clown head sculpture, they learn that Sideshow Bob is loose in Krustyland and wants to kill the Simpsons. After two different videos expand on the backstory, the riders sit in a Krustyland-themed vehicle. Twenty-four of the cartoon's characters make an appearance, all voiced by their original actors. Changes to the ride system were minimal to keep down the cost. The ride vehicles were retrofitted with a new hydraulic system, and a new digital projection system was installed. Changes to the building's exteriors were also modest.

Blur Studio and Reel FX Creative Studios produced the 6-minute CGI-animated film. The digital film runs at 60 frames per second instead of the typical 24, for added clarity and brightness. The film is filled with in-jokes lampooning the theme park industry. The ride starts on a rickety roller coaster and then parodies Shamu, Walt Disney World with Capt. Dinosaur's Pirate Ripoff Ride, and Universal itself with the *Wet and Smoky* stunt show. More important, the nearby gift shops were rethemed as Kwik-E-Marts, and sales of *Simpsons* items shot through the roof.

From **BAD** *to* **WORSE**

A MUSICAL BASED ON THE *Creature from the Black Lagoon,* Universal's 1954 3-D horror film? Yes. "We are interested in our teen and young adult and adult audiences," according to Chip Largman, Universal Creative vice president. "Our interest was to take advantage of the library of characters that were available in the horror genre and find an opportunity to come up with something that was different and fun and ambitious for us." Largman was chiefly responsible for one of the worst shows ever produced at Universal Studios.

Breck Eisner, son of Disney mogul Michael Eisner, was working on an updated version of the classic movie for Universal. The original story revolved around a geology expedition to the Amazon that discovers a mysterious amphibious "gill-man," who falls in love with the beautiful girlfriend of one of the scientists.

The 25-minute show opened on June 2, 2009, in the Castle Theater. The show was staged by Tony-nominated director and choreographer Lynne Taylor-Corbett and produced by Tony Award–winner Marc Routh. Fred Barton composed the music and said of the challenge, "People are not coming to the lobby of the theater knowing what they are going to see, which means the opening number has to tell them." The show featured a 23.5-foot-tall "gill-man" whose reach was 32 feet wide from fingertip to fingertip. In a nod toward corporate synergy, *Today Show* hosts Matt Lauer and Meredith Vieira appeared in an introduction video.

Taylor-Corbett said of the effort, "You try to find an essence. In this case it is a very tongue-in-cheek work. It may not be Proust or *Hamlet* . . . but we are always trying to give the public our best shot." However, their best shot was not good enough. The show closed after only three months.

Things were not much better in Florida. The initial idea must have looked good on paper. Walt Disney World had Rock 'n' Roller Coaster Starring Aerosmith, an indoor roller coaster featuring a sound track by aging rock stars Aerosmith. Universal would offer a more-intense coaster where the guests could choose from a long list of current and classic songs and create a customized sound track for their ride. The ride would combine the repeatability of a roller coaster with a dash of hip, edgy music. Such a ride would surely attract young thrill seekers, right?

After a long delay, the $45 million Hollywood Rip Ride Rockit opened on August 19, 2009. The ride was built by Maurer Söhne and was considered the largest X-Car coaster in the world. An X-Car coaster allows riders to enjoy inversions without the need for over-the-shoulder restraints. They appear to flip from side to side along the rail. At times, riders are shifted onto their sides while in motion, but on this ride they are never completely upside down. Each train holds 12 passengers—six staggered rows of two across. The second row sits a little higher than the first, but the front row definitely still has the least-obstructed, most-exhilarating view. Creative director Louis Alfieri said, "You're staggered in height. The intent was that you could get a sense of looking before you are going all through the maneuvers."[6]

In the center of the lap bar is a touch-screen console for each person to lock in song selections. First, the rider touches the desired genre, which then reveals six songs available in that category. The technology was an outgrowth of a system used at Universal Studios Japan's Hollywood Dream: The Ride.

The speakers are built into the seat, near the ears for most folks. The music is played back "at such a volume right up against your ear that you can't hear the other people's music," according to Alfieri. The track and columns were filled with sand and pea gravel to dampen the amount of ambient noise generated by the coaster.[7]

Alfieri said, "This is a completely innovative experience for the music industry and how we're presenting the music and how we're synchronizing it and how we're promoting it on the Internet. I think once people have the opportunity to see what we've done here and see how the guests react to it, I think a lot of other artists are going to want to participate." Because the ride lasts only 1 minute and 39 seconds, Alfieri said, "the artists gave me the liberty to choose where the songs started and stopped that would be the best experience on the roller coaster."[8] There is even a social media element to the ride. Each seat is equipped with an onboard digital video camera, and videos can be purchased and uploaded to YouTube.

The trains are capable of a vertical ascent. The first lift hill is 167 feet tall at a 90-degree angle, with the trains traveling at 11 feet per second. At the top, they tilt forward before racing through the rest of the track at speeds of up to 65 miles per hour. The coaster was the tallest one in the Orlando area.

Another benefit to the X-Car is the ability to fit in very tight spaces. The 3,800 feet of orange steel track winds between the soundstages in Production Central. There was no attempt to theme or hide the coaster. At one point, the trains pass only 33 feet above the guests below.

One of the signature elements of the ride is the Double Take, a 103-foot-diameter circle in which cars flip from inside the loop to outside of it. This element is situated behind the park's concert stage. Another element is the Treble Clef, which forms the musical symbol as seen from above. It bursts through the building facades in the New York area of the park. The idea was first sketched on a napkin. Then there is the Jump Cut, which was designed to give the effect of a cork-screw maneuver without actually going upside down.

Each of the five trains, as well as each section of the track, was built with colorful lights. The result is a kinetic light show especially visible to visitors at CityWalk across the lagoon. From the beginning, the coaster was problematic and a maintenance nightmare. By 2013 all of the trains had been replaced with new equipment.

Theme park analyst Ray Braun of Economics Research Associates said, "Rule Number One in the theme park industry is 'Thou Shalt Reinvest!'"[9] GE was guilty of violating that rule. It began to show at the box office. All of the Universal parks were in an attendance death spiral at the end of the decade. Universal Studios Hollywood was matching attendance records from 20 years before. Universal Studios Florida only reached 5.5 million visitors in 2009, compared to 1998, when attendance was 8.9 million. Only Islands of Adventure had gained an audience since it opened. The inherent quality and beauty of the theme park and its roster of state-of-the-art rides kept the turnstiles turning.

1 Sean Mussenden, "Never Fear—Creepy-crawly Fun Is On Way," *Orlando Sentinel*, 17 Jan. 2005.
2 Ibid.
3 John Murdy, note to author, 6 Jan. 2014.
4 Scott Powers, "Attraction at Universal Studios Weds Modern Technology with Old Magician's Trick," *Orlando Sentinel*, 1 Jan. 2008.
5 Josef Adalian, "Theme Park Attraction to Open Spring 2008," *Variety*, 23 Apr. 2007.
6 Dewayne Bevil, "Universal Shares Rip Ride Rockit Coaster Details," *Orlando Sentinel*, 17 June 2009.
7 Ibid.
8 Ibid.
9 Judith Rubin, "2006 Theme Park Attendance Numbers Demonstrate the Benefits of Reinvestment," *2006 TEA/ERA Theme Park Attendance Report* (Burbank, CA: *InPark Magazine* and *Park World*, 2007), 1.

CHAPTER 13

COMCAST,
2009–Present

A **VERY ABLE EXECUTIVE**

RALPH J. ROBERTS WAS A BELT MAKER who had the vision to see that polyester pants were going to put him out of business. In 1963 he and partners Daniel Aaron and Julian A. Brodsky bought American Cable Systems, a small regional cable television company in Tupelo, Mississippi, with 1,200 subscribers. They changed the name to Comcast in 1969. By 1990 the company was being run by Brian L. Roberts, son of the founder, and under his leadership the subscriber base grew from 2 million subscribers to an astronomical 21 million subscribers in 2002, becoming the largest cable company in the United States. Comcast also entered the cellular telecommunications market with the purchase of American Cellular Network Corporation in 1988.

In 1998 Comcast hired a very capable young executive from Disney named Steve Burke. Burke was on the fast track from the beginning at The Walt Disney Company. He joined the company in 1986 and developed The Disney Stores concept just in time for the animation studio's renaissance. He was sent to France in 1992 to stabilize the troubled Euro Disney resort, and his reward was to become the president of ABC Broadcasting. "Stephen Burke is a very able executive," said Disney corporate board member Stanley Gold. [1]

When Michael Eisner wanted to find a new leader for the Theme Park and Resorts division, instead of promoting Burke, he chose Paul Pressler. Pressler was generally considered a thoughtful and hard-working executive, but his lack of theme park operational experience became quickly apparent. He brought a retail-oriented approach to the parks, and soon his staff was exploring the revenue generated by nearly every square foot of the parks, instead of focusing on putting on the best show possible. As a result, Disney's impeccable record of service and quality would be tarnished.

Burke left for Comcast. Gold said, "When he left, the company began to fall on bad times. Steve is the kind of guy that Disney ought to be populating all its divisions with."[2] Burke said that all of the problems at Disney could be traced back to Michael Eisner, Bob Iger, who replaced Eisner, and executives Tom Staggs and Paul Pressler.

Roberts was ready to take Comcast to a whole new level. He wanted to follow the business model developed by Rupert Murdoch at NewsCorp. Murdoch built a media empire with a satellite distribution system and content from Fox. Time Warner was another example, with interests in cable distribution, film, television, and the Internet with AOL. Roberts had the distribution system. By 2004 he decided he needed a content provider. Burke and Roberts had considered buying Universal when Vivendi put it up for sale. However, when General Electric became interested, the price skyrocketed and Comcast backed off.

Instead, it decided to buy Walt Disney Productions. Roberts and Burke smelled blood in the water. Walt Disney Productions was under attack from within. Comcast was a family-controlled company, and Brian Roberts, aided by Burke, could see that Disney chairman and CEO Michael Eisner was struggling. Disney's feature animation division could not deliver a hit. By January 2004, Eisner had alienated Steve Jobs and Pixar, the wildly successful animation studio that was propping up Disney. Jobs was ready to leave and was talking with other studios. The Disney theme parks were still reeling from the effects of the terrorist attacks on September 11, 2001. Disney's California Adventure, a new theme park that opened in the parking lot of Disneyland, was considered a creative and financial flop.

Roy E. Disney and Stanley Gold, two highly visible Disney board members, resigned and began a public campaign to oust Eisner. It did not go unnoticed by the business press that the two men were responsible for bringing Eisner to Disney as its savior in September 1984 and now they were trying to get rid of him. Things change in 20 years.

On February 11, 2004, Comcast proposed to merge with the Walt Disney Company. Comcast offered 0.78 a share of Comcast Class A voting common stock for each share of Disney and was prepared to spend more if necessary. The proposal was valued at $66 billion. Brian L. Roberts declared, "This is a unique opportunity for all shareholders of Comcast and Disney to create a new leader of the entertainment and communications industry."[3] Burke said he wanted to revitalize the animation business and to improve on the ABC network's performance. Disney had lost money on the television network ever since it acquired it in 1995.

If the merger was successful, the new company would become the world's largest vertically integrated entertainment company, with a market capitalization of more than $120 billion.[4] Stock analysts recognized that Disney stock was undervalued while Comcast was overvalued.

Why would Comcast be interested in Disney? First, with 21 million subscribers, it had a large enough audience to start its own cable networks. It had dabbled in content, beginning with a founding investment in the QVC Network in 1986. Over the years, Comcast invested in The Golf Channel, G4, Outdoor Life Network, and E! Entertainment. Second, its leadership really wanted ESPN. Disney kept raising fees for the popular sports network.

Comcast had a reputation for being successful with large mergers, as demonstrated in 2003 with the $29 billion purchase of AT&T Broadband, a company twice the size of Comcast. Wall Street was excited by the deal. Roberts argued, "This is a combination that we believe would restore the Disney brand. There is no doubt that these two companies can achieve things together that they would not be able to do alone."[5]

Burke did not underestimate his competitor. He said, "Michael Eisner, one of the entertainment world's great survivors, will no doubt try to fight to the death."[6] Comcast's strategy was to avoid Eisner and take the offer directly to the Disney board. Stanley Gold called it a "serious offer" and he hoped the board "would begin to handle this with the best interest of shareholders, and not the best interest of Michael Eisner, in mind."[7]

Eisner did oppose the deal. "I don't think content and distribution belong in the same company," Eisner told television personality Charlie Rose. "Content is evergreen . . . distribution is replaced by better technology." In an aside aimed directly at Burke, he added, "Content people come from a different planet. They don't get along well."[8] With regards to the theme parks, Eisner suggested that Comcast did not care about those assets and would sell them off to the highest bidder. Longtime Disney ally and hotelier Harris Rosen said Comcast "would chew up the parks and spit them out."[9]

By April 28, 2004, the deal was off. On that day, Comcast withdrew its bid to merge with The Walt Disney Company. Brian Roberts said, "It has become clear that there is no interest on the part of Disney's management and Board in putting Comcast and Disney together."[10] He added, "We have always been disciplined in our approach to acquisitions. Being disciplined means knowing when it is time to walk away. That time is now."[11]

Eisner may have won the battle in 2004, but it would not be long before Comcast found a new partner who just happened to have many of the same types of assets as Disney, including theme parks—Universal Studios.

Over the decades, Universal Studios had been tossed around from owner to owner like a cursed diamond. Laemmle lost control in the late 1930s, and it was not until MCA purchased the property and the Studio in the late 1950s and early 1960s that stability reigned. That all changed in 1990, when MCA went from Matsushita (electronics) to Seagram's (liquor) to Vivendi (water and sewers) to General Electric (pretty much everything), and then Comcast in 2009.

General Electric was looking for the exit and found a willing partner in Comcast. In December 2009 a new partnership was formed to control NBC Universal. In a deal valued at $30 billion, Comcast would own 51% of the company and General Electric would own the remaining 49%. The transaction was not simple. First, General Electric needed to buy out Vivendi's 20% share for $5.8 billion. Then the deal needed to pass muster with federal regulators, which it did.

In February 2013 Comcast bought the remaining shares from General Electric.

KING KONG: 360 3-D

ALTHOUGH THERE WAS ALWAYS THE THREAT of competition, one very real threat to the studio would periodically remind the management of how fragile things were: fire. Since MCA purchased the Hollywood property, there had been five major fires. The first came on May 15, 1967, torching 12 acres near Little Europe and Laramie Street. On September 4, 1987, arson caused a fire that burned down Spartacus Square. Another case of arson was to blame for a fire on November 6, 1990. A security guard with a cigarette lighter started a blaze, with damages estimated at $50 million. Fueled by gale-force winds, the fire was considered one of the largest in Los Angeles history and required 400 firefighters from 86 companies to extinguish. Over a fifth of the standing sets were destroyed, including New York Street, the Ben Hur set, and Courthouse Square. Then on September 6, 1997, a fire started in a chemical storage area adjacent to Courthouse Square.

Around 3 a.m. on June 1, 2008, a workman's blowtorch started a three-alarm fire that would destroy the New York Street sets, half of Courthouse Square, the video vaults, and the King Kong attraction. It took 17 hours before the fire was extinguished. Fortunately for Universal, duplicate prints were stored at another location, but the giant ape was not so lucky. He was cremated inside his burned-out show building.

Market research showed that fans missed King Kong. "When the park first started in '64, all there was was the tram ride; that was the whole experience," said Universal vice president Eliot Sekuler. "You took a ride through the backlot of Universal, which until that time had been closed to the public. . . . So that was how it began. It's our roots. Then Kong came along in the '80s, and it sort of changed things. It was the first big major investment they made in creating an attraction specifically for the guests to see. So when we lost it in June of 2008, it was always, 'We gotta find some way of bringing it back.'"[12] Park president Larry Kurzweil agreed: "After the 2008 fire, we knew we had to bring him back to the back lot studio tour, but in a way that has never been experienced before."[13]

The seeds for the 3-D Kong attraction were planted well before the fire. Shortly after Peter Jackson's Universal film *King Kong* (2005) was completed, some of the technicians from his special effects company, Weta Digital Ltd., transferred some of the footage into the 3-D format. The results were stunning. Visual effects supervisor Joe Letteri said, "We saw it and we said we wish we had done the whole movie in a 3D visual format."[14] This technology was then used in James Cameron's groundbreaking film *Avatar* (2009).

When the decision was made to bring back the character, park management decided to do something different. Director Peter Jackson and his crew were recruited to re-create Skull Island from the movie. The feeling was that the audio-animatronic King Kong was an impressive figure, but he was only on one side of the tram. Sometimes guests would lose out. With a movie screen on each side of the tram, nobody would have a bad seat. Plus, the technology for 3-D films was advancing at a much more rapid pace than audio-animatronics.

Universal rented the same 281,000-square-foot hangar in Playa Vista that Howard Hughes used to build the 200-ton Hercules transport plane (also known as *Spruce Goose*) to develop the show. "It's a modern hybrid of the movie technology we've been developing for shows like *Avatar*—in that it's 3-D and entirely digital, but still naturalistic and photo-real—and combining that with the ride aspect," said Matt Aiken of Weta. "There's the thrill of it and the fact that, you know, it's quite a compressed canvas that we had to work on because of running time. That was a particular challenge as we worked with Peter on the animation, so it told the story he wanted to tell but still worked within the constraints of the running and physical space that the work will be screened in."[15]

Matt Aiken said, "What we've done is used all the technology that we had at our disposal and some very highly tuned specifications to make the experience a very compelling one; we're working with very high-resolution images so the images have an enormous amount of detail in them. We're working at a very high frame range—60 frames per second—so a lot of the [adverse things] associated with a typical movie experience at 24 frames per second—motion blur and flicker— those go completely out the window. The audience is getting delivered a huge amount of visual information at a very high rate."[16] The amount of data necessary to pull off the animation was enormous. The 3-minute film used approximately 90,000 frames, which is equal to half the size of a feature film.

Adding to the experience is the "tram-mover" system. The trams sit atop massive air bags that lift, shake, and drop them. During the 2.5-minute show, in-theater effects, such as fans, sprayers, and scents, add to the sense of reality. During the experience, visitors may find themselves unsure where to look and wanting to spend more time in the virtual world that surrounds them. The hope was to create a repeatable experience.

The show was placed in an ordinary soundstage next to the Collapsing Bridge. The entrance was decorated to appear as Skull Island from the film. Inside a darkened cave, Peter Jackson appears on the tram's video monitors and instructs the guests to put on their 3-D glasses. Cocooned between two curved screens measuring 187 feet by 40 feet, the riders are immersed in a jungle filled with exotic life. It does not take long before riders are attacked by a flock of Venatosauruses and a trio of Vastatosaurus Rex, lunged at by horse-size spiders, hurtled off the edge of a cliff, and then rescued by the three-story-tall silverback gorilla.

King Kong: 360 3-D made its debut on the Studio Tour on July 1, 2010. The project took approximately one and a half years from start to finish. It was well worth it. Attendance in 2010 topped 5 million visitors in Hollywood, a jump of 26% over the previous year. At the Disneyland resort, things were not so good. Despite the addition of the *World of Color* fountain show, Disney California Adventure only grew by 3%, while Disneyland's visitor count actually declined by 0.5%.

The WIZARDING WORLD *of* HARRY POTTER

UNIVERSAL'S RELATIONSHIP WITH HARRY POTTER goes back to 2000. J. K. Rowling's epic tale of a boy wizard and his friends had become a publishing phenomenon. Three books had been released, and Warner Bros. was about to begin production for the first motion picture. Phil Hettema was looking for something new for the Castle Dracula Theater and drafted a script for a Harry Potter–themed special effects spectacular along the lines of the *Conan* show. He built a mock-up of the set on a soundstage, including an illusion featuring the white owls in the books, for J.K. Rowling's consideration. No deal was struck. Harry Potter was not ready for the world of theme parks just yet. However, the seeds were planted.

Years later, both Disney and Universal were bidding on the boy wizard. Industry insiders and Internet bloggers were claiming that Disney had won the rights as early as 2003. "I've talked to Disney people that believed they had it and it was a slam dunk for them," according to Phil Hettema, who had left Universal before the bidding had begun. "It was a big competition." Industry watcher Jim Hill said Disney would be opening the first attractions just after all of the books had been published.[17] To the surprise of many, Universal won the theme park rights.

Hettema said, "That was another gift that Universal got because Warner had control, [J.K. Rowling] was so powerful, and the strength of the intellectual property was so strong. They had no choice when Rowling insisted (and Warner backed her up) on using art director [Stuart Craig] from the movie." Even though GE was not looking to invest any serious money in the theme parks, they knew they could not turn down the deal due to the strength of the franchise. Plus, it was thought it would only enhance the sale price of parks.

The Wizarding World of Harry Potter was a game changer for Universal and the theme park industry in setting a new standard of design. Just as Walt Disney relied on art directors who knew their way around a production studio, Rowling insisted that Stuart Craig be in charge of the design. He had worked on all eight of the Potter films and was responsible for the distinctive look of the series. Hettema understood why it was smart to rely on Craig. "[The Wizarding World of Harry Potter] absolutely would not have been executed at that level if Universal had done their version of it. It would never have happened. She didn't need to do it and was not motivated by the money. Warner Bros. was highly motivated to do it."[18] Through Universal, Warner Bros. was able to leverage the property at no risk, and it paid off.

After weeks of rehearsals, the new 20-acre island opened on June 18, 2010. The meandering and almost claustrophobic corridor forced guests to take in the entire experience slowly. By removing all visual contradictions, Universal created an environment that could withstand the most critical fan's eyes.

When guests take the time to look, they discover that window-shopping in Hogsmeade village is an attraction all its own. Many of the faux windows represent storefronts that are familiar to fans of the books and films. A mandrake plant with an almost human face can be seen shaking and screaming in one window, while Hermione Granger's Yule Ball dress is floating in another window. Throughout the village are all sorts of animated gems, such as an upright quill magically writing out messages unassisted, a music shop with instruments playing on their own, and a quidditch set missing the Golden Snitch, which can be seen occasionally fluttering about in the background.

The shops break every retail rule. Guests have to open doors that are too small. There is no air-conditioning blasting guests as they enter. The result is the highest per capita spending in the industry. The licensing agreement allowed J. K. Rowling to have final approval for everything, which meant the story took precedence over the standard operating procedures.

The dining also supports the overall theme. Because Coca-Cola products are not mentioned in the books, they are not sold within Hogsmeade. Instead, guests are offered Butterbeer, Pumpkin Juice, and Hog's Head Ale. Other beverages referred to in the books— including Knotgras Mead, Daisyroot Draught, Ocky Rot, and Fire Whiskey— are stocked on the shelves for display only. In an interesting twist, the Three Broomsticks restaurant and Hog's Head pub were used as the inspiration for the sets in the latter Harry Potter films.

A walk into the restrooms can be an unsettling experience, with the sounds of Moaning Myrtle filling the space. The Owl Post is both a shady place of refuge and home to numerous "living" owls among the supports overhead. Among the packages and letters waiting to be mailed by the owls is an open box with a Howler inside. To add a touch of authenticity, guests may get mail postmarked from Hogsmeade. Instead of stroller parking, guests use pram parking.

Taking the concept of the dark ride to an entire new level is Harry Potter and the Forbidden Journey. The ride would become a Harry Potter highlight reel, quickly going from character to character and from place to place.

Visitors cannot miss the entrance to the ride. If they are coming from The Lost Continent, they walk through the narrow corridor of Hogsmeade Village, make a slight turn around a bend, and then see Hogwarts Castle high atop a rocky cliff. The scale model uses force perspective to act like a beckoning hand and make it appear much larger and higher than it really is. Many of the familiar landmarks from the films, such as the Grand Staircase Tower, the Astronomy Tower, and the Great Hall, are included. The cliffs are (partially) hiding the giant show building.

Walking past the hog statues on top of stone pillars, the riders enter one of the most amazing queues for any attraction in any theme park. The first room beyond the lockers is the Dungeon. This is a sorting area for those wanting to ride, those wanting to take the walking tour of the castle, and those using the single-rider option. Along a hallway is the Mirror of Erised, the One-Eyed Witch, and the door to the Potions Classroom, where the teacher can be heard lecturing. Riders exit the hallway and return outside for a series of switchbacks in the Greenhouse before reentering and walking through the Oxford Corridor. A large statue of the Hogwarts Architect greets the riders, while an hourglass display shows that Gryffindor is ahead in points. At the end of the hallway is the golden griffin statue that guards Dumbledore's office.

What first appears as static paintings on the wall come to life using a patented illusion in the next two rooms, Tracery Hall and the Portrait Gallery. In Tracery Hall is Professor Swoopstick describing the finer points of quidditch, while another painting features a box of spectators watching a match. Occasionally, the Professor will walk from one painting to the other. The Portrait Gallery is a very tall room filled with dozens of paintings. For the first time, all four of Hogwarts's founders were featured in the animated paintings.

Turning a corner, the riders enter Dumbledore's office. On one side of the room is Dumbledore's desk, and high on a balcony is the master wizard greeting the riders and telling them to enjoy the history lecture they are about to attend. The illusion uses the same Musion technology used in *Disaster!* where a film is projected on a sheet of glass. When Dumbledore is done, he directs the riders toward the Defense Against the Dark Arts Classroom.

Above them is the skeleton of a dragon and in front of them is a staircase leading to the door of the Defense of the Dark Arts teacher's office. While the riders wait below, the door opens and Harry Potter, Ron Weasley, and Hermione Granger reveal themselves as they remove an invisibility cloak. Once again, the illusion is created with the Musion system. The trio encourage riders to skip the lecture and join them at a quidditch match instead. Another narrow corridor leads to the Gryffindor Common Room. Along the way, riders pass by animated paintings of quidditch fans offering their advice.

Invisible to the rider but right at the heart of the experience is the innovative ride vehicle. Universal had an exclusive contract to use the Robocoaster robotic arm manufactured by KUKA Robotics. Typically, the robotic arms are used in manufacturing applications such as automobiles. In Forbidden Journey, the arms are mounted on a moving platform that travels along a track at a constant speed, much like an old-fashioned dark ride. The sweeping motion of the arms creates all of the sensations the riders feel. Mounted on top of each arm is a four-person "enchanted bench." Riders board their "enchanted bench" in the Room of Requirement using a moving walkway. After a safety check, Hermione shouts "over here," and the bench seems to levitate.

Unlike Spider-Man, which blends three-dimensional sets with 3-D films, Forbidden Journey cleverly transitions between three-dimensional set and films. This called for dimensional sets within the ride, including the Observatory, a covered bridge, the Forbidden Forest, and the Chamber of Secrets. Riders confront all sorts of animatronic characters, such as the Sorting Hat in the queue or the Whomping Willow. Some of the characters sport in-theater effects, such as a massive dragon that breathes steamy breath, spiders and acromantulas that spit, and Dementors that try to suck out the souls of the riders. One Dementor gets close enough to perform the "Kiss," and riders see an image of their faces peeled away until Harry casts a spell.

Another benefit to the KUKA robotic arm is the ability to keep riders in front of a movie screen for an extended time. At Spider-Man, riders are in front of the screens for only a fraction of a minute before moving on to the next scene. In Forbidden Journey, there are three points where the arm places the riders within a 180-degree dome, and then the dome rotates on a carousel at the same speed as the riders, providing up to 30 seconds of film time. Like many cutting-edge ride systems, "Potter was struggling to work up until two months prior to opening," according to Phil Hettema.[19] The 4-minute-and-6-second ride can entertain the masses with a theoretical capacity of 2,880 riders per hour. Filch's Emporium of Confiscated Goods is at the exit.

Along with the Forbidden Journey ride, two existing roller coasters were rethemed. The child-friendly Flying Unicorn was transformed into the child-friendly Flight of the Hippogriff. Dueling Dragons became Dragon Challenge. The lengthy queue was sustainably rethemed, and the coasters no longer are allowed to pass each other, after two accidents in the summer of 2011. Flying cell phones were cited as the culprit in both accidents.

The business impact of the Wizarding World of Harry Potter was unprecedented. Attendance at Islands of Adventure jumped from 5,949,000 visitors in 2010 to 7,674,000 in 2011. In what was a very tough year for the industry, the additional 1.725 million new visitors to Islands of Adventure accounted for about one-half of all new theme park visitors nationally that year. John Robinett, senior vice president of economics for AECOM, said, "North America is a mature market that's slowly recovering from a recession. All that would reasonably dampen expectations; nevertheless Universal opened a major new 'land' and it paid off with tremendous returns." He added, "It takes guts to invest in the teeth of a recession, and it's these bold management moves that have led to the success of our leaders this year."[20]

TRANSFORMERS

STEVE BURKE WANTED COMPLETE CONTROL of the theme parks in Florida, and Comcast bought out Blackstone Group's $1.025 billion stake in the company in July 2011. At the time, the parks were valued at $3.17 billion. If Comcast had not made the purchase at the time it did, Blackstone Group had the right to seek out another buyer. However, most of the resort's key intellectual property licenses, including the deal for Harry Potter, would be revoked if a new owner purchased Universal. "The acquisition consolidates our ownership and confirms our long-term commitment to Universal Orlando and the theme park business," Steve Burke said. "Universal Orlando is a consistent and significant driver of operating and free cash flow and is performing extremely well."[21] In the 10 years that Blackstone was a partner with Universal, it tripled its investment. Blackstone would remain a player in Florida with the purchase of SeaWorld in 2009 from Anheuser-Busch/InBev for $2.5 billion.

In Southern California, the summer of 2012 was shaping up to be a colossal head-to-head battle between the Disneyland Resort and Universal Studios Hollywood. Disney was about to launch the final pieces of its ambitious five-year, $1.2 billion makeover of Disney California

Adventure, and Universal was ready to launch one of the most-sophisticated thrill rides on the West Coast.

Over at Disney California Adventure, the failed "walk-through postcard" entry was replaced by Buena Vista Street, an inviting re-creation of a mythical Hollywood street around the time that Walt Disney moved to Los Angeles. The big attraction was Cars Land. A 12-acre parcel that used to be a parking lot was transformed into Radiators Springs from the merchandise-friendly *Cars* animated films from Pixar. The new land opened on June 15 with three brand-new attractions, a restaurant, and three shops.

To take a bit of wind out of Disney's sails, Universal came to fight early on May 24 with its weapon, Transformers: The Ride—3-D. The Hasbro Transformer toys were introduced in 1984 and captured the imagination of (mostly) boys and girls worldwide. The toys would spawn an entire industry, including comic books, television shows, and feature films. Back in 1985, a short-lived Universal Studios Hollywood display called the Transformers Base Camp was built on the site of the Roman Courtyard on the upper lot. A small stage was set up where visitors could meet Jazz, Grimlock, and Starscream.

The new ride is set in Chicago, which is invaded by the evil Decepticons. Transformers are the good guys, and they need the help of the visitors to protect the All-Spark. The All-Spark is a piece of robotic technology that can make any piece of machinery it comes into contact with become a Transformer or Decepticon. Director Michael Bay became creative consultant after he said he did not like the original story line. The revised script includes 15 Transformer characters, including Optimus Prime, Bumblebee, Ironhide, Sideswipe, Ratchet, Wheelie, Megatron, Grindor, Starscream, Ravage, Skorponok, Devastator, Sideways, and Bonecrusher. The original film actors returned to provide their voices.

The backstory is explained in the lengthy queue, which is themed as the top-secret NEST military bunker. While in the queue, riders pass by an All-Spark containment chamber that houses the glowing module that is the life source for all Transformers. The queue is filled with buttons and switches that do nothing but entertain riders while they wait.

Twelve riders board EVAC, a new Transformer designed just for the ride that suspiciously looks and feels like the motion simulator vehicle used at The Amazing Adventures of Spider-Man at Universal's Islands of Adventure. The benefit to using the ride vehicle is the ability to control the audience's perspective like a director uses a camera, by turning the car in different directions to make cuts or jump to a new scene. Each motion simulator ride vehicle weighs 12,000 pounds and is capable of pivoting, pitching, undulating, vibrating, and rotating 360 degrees. Of course, the proven and reliable ride system also allowed Universal Creative to reduce the development costs considerably, while still providing a blockbuster attraction.

The vehicles travel 2,000 feet past high-definition 3-D images projected either from the front or the back on 14 screens. Industrial Light & Magic (ILM) was hired to create the films. Universal used the largest collection of 3-D screens ever assembled in a single theme park ride. For the backgrounds, ILM used a specially devised high-resolution, sphere-shaped still camera, shooting 360 degrees of panoramic imagery that captured 75 images every 50 feet within a designated square mile area of a major metropolitan city. The images are wrapped around a three-dimensional wire-frame to produce the photo-realistic films. "When you put photo realistic images on the screen, people immediately start to believe they're actually there," said Richard Bluff of ILM.

There are 34 projectors, and some of the screens are more than 60 feet tall. ILM had to produce a 3-D image that could shift one point of view to another as the ride vehicle moves along the track. To avoid the inevitable picture degradation and dimming of 3-D, the resolution for the images was rendered at four times the standard. Also playing a role are the glasses handed to each rider. They were designed with blinders built into the sides to limit what the rider can see. As a result, the screen disappears and the characters move seamlessly between the environment and back into the media. Comparing the ride to Spider-Man, Thierry Coup said, "Transformers is a much more photorealistic world than the comic book world of Spider-Man. You really feel like you are inside a city with Transformers, and when you are face to face with the characters, the experience is incredible."[22] Not only are the images impressive, so is the audio, with 5,000 watts driving a 14-channel audio system.

The limited amount of space in Hollywood was a major challenge. Universal only had one choice. Thierry Coup said, "We built the attraction on two levels and developed a 60,000-square-foot experience on a 30,000-square-foot space."[23] At one point, a lift takes the ride vehicle up one level, although the riders never feel like they are moving vertically due to the video in front of them, the wind behind them, and the wobble of the vehicle. Another lift, combined with the special effects, creates the illusion that the vehicles are falling hundreds of feet.

On May 24, 2012, in a flashy grand opening ceremony, the $100 million Transformers: The Ride—3-D formally opened to the public. Even more remarkable was a demonstration of incredible project management and sheer willpower a year later. On June 20, 2013, Universal Studios Florida opened its version of Transformers: The Ride. Coup said of the process, "It's definitely one of the most-ambitious [construction periods] ever done in the theme park world. It's a one-year turnaround. We've designed this twice before, we have the same team working on it, and they know exactly what to do. That's why we can build it so quickly. We have been bringing new and exciting experiences to our guests every year, so why not continue on that path?"[24] He said the Orlando ride was exactly the same, with the only differences being the building exterior and the preshow layout.

This **PLAN** *is* **FANTASTIC**

AFTER SIX YEARS OF FIGHTING with the neighbors, on September 25, 2012, Universal Studio Hollywood finally received unanimous approval from the Los Angeles Planning Commission for its $1.6 billion expansion plan. The plan was supposed to guide development for the next 5–10 years. The breakthrough came when Universal dropped plans for an office tower at the Red Line subway station and 3,000 residential units. Commission president William Roschen said, "This is a significant, important project. The vision of this plan is fantastic."[25]

One of the most critical components was a regulatory change. Universal City had been divided up between the county of Los Angeles and the city of Los Angeles. As part of the agreement, the county annexed all of the areas controlled by the city. This meant Comcast had to deal with only one jurisdiction, thereby creating a more-streamlined process of approvals. This type of regulatory control had been fundamental to the success of the Walt Disney World resort.

Comcast did not hesitate in implementing its plans. Construction on various components started immediately. The long-empty Wild West arena at the center of the park was torn down and replaced by the Universal Plaza in the summer of 2013. The poorly conceived 37,000-square-foot Art Deco–styled plaza is a multipurpose gathering space. The meant-to-be park icon is a 70-foot-tall tower.

Another big change was the removal of the Gibson Amphitheater. For 40 years, the best performers in the world came to the hilltop at Universal City. The amphitheater was the site for many historic performances by the likes of Bob Marley, Stevie Wonder, David Bowie, and Steve Martin. It was frequently the site for television shows, including the MTV Music Awards, NAACP Image Awards, and HBO's Comic Relief.

Although the concert hall was a success, it took up a lot of real estate, and the expansion plan meant the theater's days were numbered. On December 6, 2011, Universal announced the theater would present its last shows in September 2013. Demolition began within days.

The success of Harry Potter was having other effects on the Universal parks. In the past, rides and shows were placed behind the facades of a traditional back lot. Now Universal was fully committed to creating themed environments that could compete directly with Disney's recent efforts. Barry Upson said, "Disney understands and executes theming as well or better than anyone, yet I believe they would be the first to admit that the theme environment of California Adventure was mediocre at best and impacted attendance." The benefit of "effectively linking a film's elements to its name-sake attraction through images, dialogue, sound effects, musical score, and special effects is always desirable, because it grounds the guest more strongly in that specific entertainment experience," said Upson.[26]

A recent example of taking something that is very familiar to millions and bringing it to life in three dimensions is Springfield USA at Universal Studios Florida. The front facade of The Simpsons ride was redone as a carnival featuring midway games, such as Eye Carumba, Help Santa's Little Helper, and Sledge Homer. Other little details include a fake pay phone on the side of the Kwik-E-Mart, where guests who dare to answer hear taunts from Nelson Muntz, the neighborhood bully. Inside of Moe's Tavern is a telephone that allows guests to be taunted by a prank phone call by Bart Simpson. Taking after the popular static character statues at Knott's Berry Farm in Buena Park, Springfield has photo opportunities with many of the television show's most popular characters, including Milhouse Van Houten, Barney Gumble, and Bumblebee Man.

Along the waterfront are Bumblebee Man's Taco Truck, a statue of the town's founder Jebediah Springfield, and Duff Gardens, an outdoor dining and drinking spot. At Lard Lad's Donut Shop, guests can taste the fuel that powered Homer Simpson. Adding kinetic energy to Springfield USA is a new spinner ride called Kane & Kodos' Twirl 'n' Hurl. A comic take on the traditional Dumbo-like spinner, the aliens taunt guests to activate targets and to enjoy killing humans along the way.

The International Food Court was redressed to appear as the facades from Krusty Burger, the Android Dungeon Baseball Card Shop, Comic Book Guy's storefront, and Moe's. Inside, guests can experience familiar foods from the animated series, such as a Krusty Burger or a Clogger, or drink a Duff beer or a Flaming Moe. Springfield USA is filled with puns, as one would expect in an area based on *The Simpsons*. The new addition has been so popular that Hollywood got into the action with a much larger version to open in 2015.

Fox Television had the final say. Throughout the early testing period, a number of pieces were installed and then removed until everybody was happy. One example is Barney. The larger-than-life-size lovable drunk was placed inside of Moe's with a full mug of Duff beer. Some guests complained that it was not right to allow children to pose in front of such a rough figure. Barney was removed. Days later, he reappeared with a mug half-full of Duff beer. Universal was never about being subtle.

The first step in Hollywood's transformation was the importation of Despicable Me: Minion Mayhem from Florida. The Universal

Creative team crammed two theaters inside of the *Terminator 2: 3-D* building. At the exit to the ride is Super Silly Fun Land, a new mini-land directly targeting younger children. The Silly Swirly is a Dumbo-like spinner with flying exotic bugs. Kurzwell joked, "That is our first real kiddie ride."[27] A water play area and an elaborate play structure joined the ride.

Like The Simpsons, the old show building was lightly redressed with no major external elements changed. However, the queue was masked by a new facade featuring Cru's neighborhood. Universal promoted the facade "as a crucial turning point for the theme park, as the adventure represents its first foray into fully expansive themed environments aimed at immersing visitors from the moment they enter the space."[28] It was not noted that the path toward the ride was through the Streets of the World sets, which had been standing almost 25 years.

Easily the most anticipated new addition in 2014 was the expansion of Harry Potter in Universal Studios Florida. "Seriously, Hogsmeade had only been open a week when we first began talking with Warner Bros. about ways we could possibly expand the Wizarding World," said Thierry Coup. "I mean, we'd had such a great time working with Stuart Craig and the production team from the Harry Potter films. And there was so much more to the world that J. K. Rowling had created, which was worth exploring."[29] Stuart Craig, production designer for the Potter films, was brought back to guide the design of many of the elements. Construction began in June 2013 and took just over one year. By placing Potter in Universal Studios Florida instead of expanding the area in Islands of Adventure, Universal created the first centrally themed, multipark experience.

Facing the lagoon are facade facsimiles of King's Cross Station, Charing Cross Road, Wyndham's Theatre, and 12 Grimmauld Place. The tall buildings isolate Diagon Alley from the rest of the park. Familiar elements from the movies, including the Eros Fountain from Piccadilly Circus and a Knight Bus, are placed out front. Despite the level of architectural detail, the facade is still a movie set. Dale Mason proudly revealed, "There's not a real brick in this entire place. Everything you see in Diagon Alley is either modeled fiber glass, steel or carved concrete."[30]

Just like the tunnels under the railroad tracks at the Magic Kingdom and Disneyland, guests are forced to pass through the narrow space of the red-tiled arch of the Leicester Square Station to enter Diagon Alley. Another lesson learned from the Disney parks was to place something irresistible at the end of the street. What could be better than Gringotts Bank, with a fire-breathing dragon perched on top? Inside the bank building is the area's headliner attraction, Harry Potter and the Escape from Gringotts. The ride is a blend of a 3-D dark ride with a Premier Rides roller coaster track. Riders board twin

20-passenger Victorian-inspired open-air cars. Pushing ride technology forward, the vehicles have a motion-base component, making it a blend of the Revenge of the Mummy and Transformers. Inside, riders pass through Gringotts's vaults and encounter various baddies from the movies and books inside the vast caverns below the bank. With regard to the audio-animatronic figures, Universal was competing directly with Disney. Just like Forbidden Journey next door, the queue was an attraction in itself.

"J. K. Rowling actually gave us a lot of creative leeway when it came to Escape from Gringotts. You see, the story that we wanted to tell with this Universal Orlando attraction kind of ran concurrently with the events that occurred during *Deathly Hallows*," Thierry Coup explained. "Our guests just happen to be at Gringotts Wizarding Bank opening a new account on the exact same day that Harry, Ron and Hermione are trying to break into Bellatrix Lestrange's vault to retrieve a horcrux."[31]

A breakthrough ride is the park-to-park Hogwarts Express train. For the first time, two major theme parks in North America have been connected by a ride. Guests board the train through an optical illusion that makes it appear as though people ahead of you in line are actually passing through the wall of Platform 9¾. Although the train travels backstage, the guests never know it. Instead, they see the English countryside through specially designed projection windows with randomized experiences with more than 400 variations, including an attack by Dementors and Hagrid flying on his motorbike.

Knockturn Alley borrows from and expands on the Villains' Alley concept at Marvel Super Hero Island to create a space dedicated to the villains from the Potter novels. Within the alley is Borgin & Burkes, a store dedicated to the dark arts.

Heavily themed retail shops with exclusive merchandise are becoming a signature element for the Universal parks. This was something that had become a lost art at Disney, as its per capita spending continued to dwindle year after year. The very popular Ollivanders wand shop in Hogsmeade was added to Diagon Alley with an improved queue and much greater capacity. Weasleys' Wizard Wheezes joke shop is a three-story shop that is so complete, Universal closed Zonko's in Hogsmeade and expanded Honeydukes candy store. The shop features interactive elements inspired by a scene in *Harry Potter and the Half-Blood Prince*. Adding to the mix of retail is a clothing store called Madam Malkin's Robes for All Occasions, Quality Quidditch Supplies with brooms, bludger bats, and golden snitches for sale. Other shops include Magical Menagerie, Wiseacre's Wizarding Equipment, and Scribbulus. Food can be found at The Leaky Cauldron and Florean Fortescue's Ice-Cream Parlour.

The FUTURE

IF STEVE BURKE COULD JUMP INTO A DELOREAN time machine and go back into the past, no doubt he would have stopped at the point just before Vivendi sold off thousands of acres adjacent to their resort. As a sign of confidence in the parks, Comcast bought more than 52 acres in July 2013, including the land under and around the Wet 'n Wild water park.

Universal had been operating the water park for some time on leased land from the Southwest Land Company of Newport Beach, California. No more. They paid $30.9 million for the prime property along International Drive. Speculation was rampant as to what the company planned for the property. Steve Burke said, "We have 2,400 hotel rooms today; we probably should have 10,000." He added, "Hotel rooms are strategically important because if people stay in your hotels, they spend an extra day in your theme park."[32] Disney officials were silent on the move.

Then came Comcast's January 2014 announcement to stock analysts in Las Vegas. For theme park fans, it must have sounded like they hit the jackpot. "We're doubling down on theme parks," according to Comcast's Brian Roberts. Steve Burke said, "We think there is a lot of 'there' there in the theme-park business for many years to come and that we have a low market share—and only one way to go." Although many market analysts expected Comcast to shed the theme park division, Burke's experienced eye recognized that the business was an untapped growth engine. He knew that theme parks were one of the few areas of stable entertainment industry growth outside of cable television.

Burke referred to a recent feasibility study that showed that Universal could build an additional 10,000–15,000 hotel rooms on its property. Burke said, "We need to get those hotel rooms open and build out the resort."[33] One competitive advantage over Disney was the compact and non-auto-oriented pattern of development at the Universal resort. Disney was becoming more and more dependent on a costly bus network. Burke pledged to invest at least $500 million per year in new attractions and upgrades to the North American parks in perpetuity. The goal was to open a new attraction every year at both Universal parks. Universal was going full steam ahead. Theme park designer Phil Hettema said, "Comcast has a thirst for the business and enthusiasm and has been willing to ante up and say 'let's go for it.'"[34]

Universal Studios Hollywood is undergoing an unprecedented $1.6 billion expansion. By the time all of the construction is completed in 2016, virtually 70% of the park will have changed. The goal of the expansion is to appeal to younger children as well as reinforce Universal's lead over Disney in thrill rides. Larry Kurzwell, president of Universal Studios Hollywood said, "We're trying to significantly broaden our base. This isn't about adding rides. It's about a complete transformation."[35]

Universal City has always been limited by parking and access. The redevelopment plan includes thousands of new parking spaces in new structures built around the perimeter of the hilltop near Falls Lake. The E.T. parking structure has also been expanded. Comcast had to commit to more than $100 million in local transit improvements as part of its obligation to the city and county in exchange for the annexation.

Larry Kurzwell also announced in April 2014 a new addition to the tram tour called *Fast & Furious: Supercharged*. The *Fast & Furious* franchise has earned Universal more than $2 billion at the box office over six films. The show will be a hybrid movie and thrill ride as well as the new start of the tour. A 400-foot-long movie screen, touted as the world's longest and most expansive 360-degree screen, will surround the tram. Show producer Chick Russell said, "We're going to make it feel like those trams are being pulled through the streets at speeds over 100 miles per hour" using a dynamic hydraulic motion base and 3-D-HD imagery.[36] Eighteen projectors will provide the images through a first-of-its-kind front projection system.

Joining *Fast & Furious* will be Hollywood's expanded version of the popular Springfield USA. Like Florida, it will primarily serve as a food court and photo opportunity. Within the limited space of the Universal City hilltop, the facades of Springfield will hide the planned Harry Potter–themed area on the other side. Universal also announced a nighttime tram tour for 2015, complete with special lighting effects. The most anticipated part of the transformation will be the addition of The Wizarding World of Harry Potter, slated for 2016.

Brooks Barnes of *The New York Times* wrote, "To some degree, the remaking of Universal Studios Hollywood is less about stealing market share from Disney than catching up after years of underinvestment." He blamed that lack of reinvestment on General Electric, Vivendi, and Seagram.

Ron Meyer, vice president of NBC Universal said, "Our guests at this park used to start at about 11 years old and go up from there. We now have something for everybody, even very young children, with much more on the way."[37] Longer term, the *WaterWorld* and the *Special Effects Stage* were listed for the chopping block, providing additional land for future attractions. Beyond that, nobody is talking on the record.

1   Paul R. La Monica, "Comcast Bids for Disney," *CNN/Money,* 18 Feb. 2004.

2   Ibid.

3   Comcast Corporation, "Comcast Corporation Makes Proposal to Merge with The Walt Disney Company," press release, 11 Feb. 2004, tinyurl.com/comcastproposal (accessed 30 Apr. 2014).

4 "The Battle for the Magic Kingdom," *The Economist,* 12 Feb. 2004.

5 La Monica, "Comcast Bids for Disney."

6 "The Battle for the Magic Kingdom."

7 La Monica, "Comcast Bids for Disney."

8 James B. Stewart, *Disneywar* (New York: Simon & Schuster, 2005).

9 Bob Mervine, "Storming the Wrong Castle," *Orlando Business Journal,* 16 Feb. 2004.

10 Comcast Corporation, "Comcast Withdraws Its Proposal to Merge with Disney," press release, 28 Apr. 2004, 11 Feb. 2004, tinyurl.com/comcastwithdraws (accessed 30 Apr. 2014).

11 Ibid.

12 Noelene Clark, "Ringside Seats to Kong vs. Rex," *The Los Angeles Times,* 30 June 2010.

13 Hugo Martin, "Kong's 3-D Comeback," *The Los Angeles Times,* 27 Jan. 2010.

14 Clark, "Ringside Seats."

15 Ibid.

16 Ibid.

17 Jim Hill, "Why For Wouldn't J.K. Rowling Let Universal Studios Build a Harry Potter Stunt Show?," *Jim Hill Media,* 14 Aug. 2003, tinyurl.com/jimhillhpstunt (accessed 12 Feb. 2013).

18 Phil Hettema, interview with author, Pasadena, CA, 16 Jan. 2014.

19 Hettema, interview with author, 16 Jan. 2014.

20 John Robinett, "The Global Picture," *TEA/AECOM 2011 Theme Index: The Global Attractions Attendance Report* (Burbank, CA: Themed Entertainment Association, 2012), 7–8.

21 Meg James, "NBCUniversal to Fully Own Universal Orlando," *The Los Angeles Times,* 7 June 2011.

22 Arthur Levine, "Interview with Universal Creative's Thierry Coup about Transformers: The Ride-3D," About.com, 2013, tinyurl.com/tcoupinterview (accessed 13 Nov. 2013).

23 Ibid.

24 Ibid.

25 Dana Bartholomew, "Expansion Ok'd by Los Angeles Planning Commission," *Los Angeles Daily News,* 26 Sept. 2012.

26 Barry Upson, interview with author, Napa, CA, 10 Mar. 2014.

27 Ibid.

28 Universal Studios Hollywood, "Universal Studios Hollywood Makes Unprecedented Investment in Epic Theme Park Transformation," press release, 9 Apr. 2014, nbcumv.com/node/865776?network=33127 (accessed 30 Apr. 2014).

29 Jim Hill, "Diagon Alley Nears Completion at the Universal Orlando Resort," *Huffington Post,* 23 Jan. 2014, huffingtonpost.com/jim-hill/the-wizarding-world-of-ha_b_4651060.html (accessed 3 Feb. 2014).

30 Ibid.

31 Ibid.

32 Jason Garcia, "Universal Orlando Buys Wet 'n Wild Land," *Orlando Sentinel,* 27 June 2013.

33 Jason Garcia, "Universal Wants to Add Thousands of Hotel Rooms," *Orlando Sentinel,* 11 Sept. 2013.

34 Hettema, interview with author, 16 Jan. 2014.

35 Brooks Barnes, "A Makeover of Universal Studios Hollywood Aims to Catch Up to Disney," *The New York Times,,* 8 Apr. 2014.

36 Barnes, "Makeover of Universal Studios Hollywood."

37 Ibid.

INDEX

ABOUT
the AUTHOR

SAM GENNAWEY IS THE AUTHOR of *The Disnelyand Story: The Unofficial Guide to the Evolution of Walt Disney's Dream* and *Walt and the Promise of Progress City,* a contributor to *Planning Los Angeles* and other books, as well as a columnist for the popular MiceChat website. His unique point of view, built on his passion for history, his professional training as an urban planner, and his obsession with theme parks, has brought speaking invitations from Walt Disney Imagineering, the Walt Disney Family Museum, Disney Creative, the American Planning Association, the California Preservation Foundation, the California League of Cities, and many Disneyana clubs, libraries, and podcasts. He is currently a senior associate at the planning firm of Katherine Padilla and Associates.